THE EDUCATION OF AN AMERICAN

A RECENT PHOTOGRAPH OF MARK SULLIVAN

THE EDUCATION OF
AN AMERICAN

MARK SULLIVAN

DOUBLEDAY, DORAN & CO., INC.

New York   1938

PRINTED AT THE *Country Life Press*, GARDEN CITY, N. Y., U. S. A.

LC

PN
4874
S78
A3

ILLUSTRATIONS

THE EDUCATION OF AN AMERICAN

CHAPTER 1

On the tenth of September 1874 the President of the United States was Ulysses S. Grant. He, on that day, was occupied with despatches from Indian uprisings in the West; one from General Philip H. Sheridan, in charge of the Military Division of the Missouri, reported that the army had defeated five hundred Comanches in a five-hour engagement. *Leslie's Weekly* the following week printed a lurid woodcut drawing of "Comanche and Arapahoe Indians Holding a Council of War," and also one of "General Custer's Expedition to the Black Hills of Dakota."

Among matters making less call on official attention at Washington, but nevertheless engaging universal newspaper interest, the steamship Great Eastern had payed out 822 nautical miles of a new cable, the second, to Europe. . . . The former President of the Confederate States of America, Jefferson Davis, reproved violence practiced by Southern whites upon recently freed slaves. . . . The ample matrimonial experiences of the head of the Mormon Church, Brigham Young, then seventy-three years old, were a matter of public interest and (outside Utah) acute indignation—*Leslie's* reported that the latest addition to his wives was "said to be a good-looking Irish woman." . . . Phineas T. Barnum's "Roman Hippodrome" was touring the country's large cities. . . . A Philadelphia newspaper was printing a translation of a book of impossible fantasy which had recently made a sensation in France, *Around the World in Eighty Days*, by Jules Verne. . . . Transatlantic cable despatches reported the official activities of the prime minister of Great Britain, Benjamin Disraeli, and of the chancellor of the German Empire, Prince Otto Bismarck. . . . Victor Hugo was reported as saying, "My head is full of novels, but shall I ever have time to write them?"

[1]

II

These and other matters of high import were recorded in the newspapers of September 10, 1874, and near-by dates. But these affairs of public moment did not come to the attention of my father, for his Pennsylvania farm was not reached by any metropolitan periodical; the only paper he took regularly was a local weekly from the near-by county seat, the *Village Record*.

Besides, even had the great city newspapers come to my father's home, he would not have read them on that day, for he was busy with "raising" his new barn. During the summer and preceding winter, in intervals between farm work, he had gone to the woods, where he cut down great oaks, hewed them into beams and hauled them to where the barn was to be. There he mortised and tenoned the ends, and cut wooden pegs, which were to hold the beams together. With everything ready, he, in accordance with the genial custom of the day, invited his neighbors to the barn-raising.

While they were rearing the logs and putting the frame together, my father told them he must leave them for a half-hour; he must make a trip to the village to get a bar of castile soap. The unusual errand—obviously not related to barn-raising—excited curiosity, and my father explained that in the house a child, his tenth, was about to be born. One of the neighbors—his name was Mark Hughes—said to my father, "If it's a boy name him after me." My father replied, "That I will, Mark." Doubtless my father was glad of a suggestion, for he had already exhausted the more familiar of the saints' names that were practically a requirement in Irish Catholic families—he had used up Cornelius, Mary, John, Thomas, William, Joseph, Benjamin, Francis and Edward. Of the nine children, three had died in infancy. His tenth and last child, the youngest of the seven sons who grew up, he named Mark Sullivan.

III

My father was born in Ireland, on the night of Shrove Tuesday, 1820, on a little farm which, family legend said, had been occupied by his forebears, as tenants, for seven generations. The farm, in accord with Irish custom, had a name: it was called Red Gate; in Gaelic, by another name, Shon Brae, and it was in the townland of Kanturk, near the village of Banteer, in the northern part of County Cork, close by the border of Limerick. For some reason, and in some way I never learned— he was not talkative about his youth—he received an education better than was common in that time and place; one of his youthful recollections was of reading aloud the account of the coronation of Queen Victoria in 1838, to a gathering of neighbors who could not read. All his life he preserved a precision of pronunciation and phrasing which I, as I advanced in schooling, came to recognize as distinguished. As a child, when young folks were visiting our home, I used to be a little embarrassed to hear my father pronounce "boiled" as "biled," and "tea" as "tay." But as I began to read selections from English poetry in my schoolbooks, I observed the rhyming of "sea" with the final syllable of "survey" in Pope's

I am monarch of all I survey
From the center all round to the sea [say],

and was interested to recognize that my father's pronunciation of "ea" as "a" was eighteenth-century English, preserved in Ireland after it had changed elsewhere. I observed also that my father's way of saying "opposite," with the emphasis on the second syllable, "op-*pos*-ite," was a conformity to the cadence of Elizabethan verse.

During his early life he was a teacher, which meant, in his circumstances in rural Ireland of the 1830s and 1840s, that he lived with families to whose children he acted as tutor in the simpler elements of education, including instruction in playing the violin and in dancing. About his leaving Ireland, different legends grew up among his children. One said that he used to play the violin at "patterns"—Irish term for outdoor picnics— that someone told him he ought to charge a fee, and that once he did so—but came to feel so much shame at having taken money for contributing to a neighborhood pleasure that he left the country. Another legend ascribed his leaving to romance. The home in which he last taught was that of a widow, and this legend said, variously, that a tenderness for him grew up in either the widow or the widow's daughter. In either case, and more so if it were both, the situation was unsuitable, and he ended it by going to America. There was some substance, I think, in this story. Nearly a hundred years later, in the attic of the house in which I was born, I, with my daughter, looked through faded letters which suggested that he left a sentiment behind him in the hearts of both mother and daughter.

A quite different legend said that his family raised what must have been, for them, a considerable sum, twenty-five pounds, and paid it to a draper—dry-goods merchant—in the city of Cork, to take the young man into his business. But my father, dreading the prospect of an indoor, behind-the-counter job, left for America. In this story there may be some residuum of fact, for subsequently a half brother of my father was apprenticed to a draper in Cork and later became owner of the shop and a man of wealth. When I was a young man I visited his home on Sunday's Well Road, along the river Lee.

IV

My father came to America on a sailing vessel, the Saranac, early in the 1840s. Landing at Philadelphia, he went to work for a Quaker named Evans Harvey, on a farm about thirty miles west of Philadelphia, about five miles north of Wilmington and about the same distance from Delaware Bay. Although the Quaker was kind to him, as were all the Quakers with whom he came in contact, he was very homesick. Years later, in one of his few departures from reticence about his youth, he told of going at evening to the highest point on the farm, the bridgeway to the barn, looking in the direction of Ireland, which he knew was opposite to the setting sun, and weeping. Occasionally, to these sunset nostalgias, he would take his violin and, for his solitary ear, play and sing one of the most poignant tunes of lonesomeness ever heard:

[4]

Shool, shool, shool a grah,
I wish I were on yonder hill.
'Tis there I'd sit and cry my fill
Till every tear would turn a mill. . . .

Shool, shool, shool aroon,
I'll sell my rock, I'll sell my reel,
And I will sell my spinning wheel
To buy my love a sword of steel.

Shool, shool, shool a grah,
I'll dye my petticoats, I'll dye them red,
And round the world I'll beg my bread.

Presently, however, he made acquaintances among other young folks whom he met at the local Catholic Church, motherly focus of the life of all the Irish immigrants. Soon, at picnics and other gatherings, he was playing livelier tunes—music of jigs and reels, of which he had quite a repertoire, including "The Irish Washerwoman" and "The Connaught Man's Rambles," and "Rocky Road to Dublin" and "Miss McLeod's Reel" and "White Cockade" and "Haste to the Wedding." In the course of his party goings he met a young Irish girl named Julia Gleason, and fell in love with her. They were married at St Joseph's Church in Brandywine Hundred, Delaware, March 9, 1855.

V

My mother was born on a small farm in the parish of Toonadromun, not far from the village of Ballyvourney, a few miles west of Macroom, where the plain and mountains meet in the western part of County Cork. The farm had a lovely name, Shahn Valla Shahn—in English, John's Old Home. As a boy I used to think that if ever I had a country place I would call it John's Old Home, but by the time I could have a country place I had come to think that to have names for them is, in America, slightly pretentious, and I donate the glamorous phrase to anyone who shares my pleasure in the name without sharing my disrelish for the custom.

[5]

When I was a young man, in a vacation after graduating at Harvard, I took a walking trip in the country about my mother's birthplace, approaching it through the southwestern Irish mountains, by way of Bantry Bay and Killarney. I found some of my mother's relatives. One of them told me that a connection of my mother's, Aunt Joan, was still alive; she was ninety-six years old, she lived at his house, he was her nephew, and if I liked he would take me to see her. We found her standing before a peat fire, in her hand a long staff; she was erect and vigorous, her face fine-lined with age but ruddy as a winter apple, her blue eyes piercing and shrewd. The nephew explained to her—with the gusto of detail about family connections which the Irish cherish—just who I was: So-and-so had married So-and-so, they had had a son, the son had had a daughter, the daughter had gone to America, and I was the daughter's son. As the old lady took it in, her sharp eyes ranged up and down my American clothes from shoes to hat and she noted my perhaps conspicuously American manner. After she had heard the nephew's recitation of my genealogy and identity she nodded vigorously toward me. "I have ye now," she said. "Ye're one of the Haleys." Then, with abrupt and disapproving force, "There was a bad streak in thim Haleys." That I had no Haley connection, and that the Haleys were, so far as I knew, universally respectable, did not lessen her satisfaction in having subjected me to a familiar Irish social discipline; she had "taken down" a young upstart from America.

VI

That early visit to the scene of my mother's birth was my first contact with Irish ways on their native soil. I enjoyed it the more from having read, just before, some of the best accounts of Irish life ever written, the stories of Somerville and Ross, especially *All on the Irish Shore*. Those stories are authentic Ireland. They are good by any standard, and alluring to any reader, but especially to me, because their locale was near the region of my mother's birth, and they pictured the Irish life that my mother had described to me.

Years later, when I met the Irish journalist and long-time member of the English Parliament, T. P. O'Connor—always called "Tay Pay"—he confirmed my judgment about *All on the Irish Shore*. He was one of the best of critics of the literature of his own and all countries; our shared affection for Somerville and Ross and the Ireland they wrote about was a bond between us. We used to talk much about the Irish life that composed our common background, the Irish books that pictured it. As he felt the Somerville and Ross books were the best picture of recent Ireland, so did he think that the books of an almost unknown writer, W. E. Carlton, were the best picture of the Ireland of an earlier era, much more faithful to life than the generally accepted portrayals in *Rory O'More*, *Handy Andy* and other books of Samuel Lover and Charles Lever.

Tay Pay felt that the Somerville and Ross books, written mainly in the 1890s, were the last records of an Irish life that was centuries old, but which, soon after the books were written, ceased to exist. And he told me that my own youthful Irish journey, taken in 1903, was close to a last opportunity to see that Irish life in being. Twenty years later, in 1923, when, in London, I told him I was going to take the trip again, with my children, he advised me sadly not to go; he felt I would be disillusioned.

Tay Pay's theory was that the Irish humor, their charm, their disarming ingratiation, was in part a refuge which they had built up within themselves during seven centuries of alien domination, as a solace and defense against subjection, oppression and poverty. With economic subjection largely ended by the taking of the land from the landlords and the placing of it in the ownership of the tenants during the early 1900s; with political oppression ended by the Irish revolution in the 1920s, and poverty ameliorated, the Irish—this was Tay Pay's theory (which I do not fully share)—the Irish became commonplace. To him they had become hard-working farmers and obsequious shopkeepers like those in any other country. "They're"—Tay Pay took a pinch of snuff and wiped from his eye a tear that was

[7]

partly synthetic, partly natural—"They're just God damn Rotarians now."

My mother's coming to America was a direct result of the Irish famine of the 1840s, part of the flight from economic distress that took some four million Irish overseas. Her father had had some substance, and the family some slight station. When he lost everything—"broke up" was the Irish expression—he came to America, hoping to send for the family later, which ultimately he did. Of the family left behind, my mother, at about thirteen, was the oldest of six children. With her mother stunned by the tragedy and preoccupied with her young brood, responsibility descended upon the girl of thirteen. She it was who went forth and back to the depot of corn meal, which a generous American movement had sent to the stricken land. Until her father sent money to pay the cost of the family's passage to America she, with her mother and young brothers and sisters, suffered privation. The opportunity for education—she had a mind that could have profited by it greatly—was denied her. The effects of poverty descending suddenly during adolescence upon a high-strung girl remained with her to her death.

Never in her life could she bring herself to be sure that she, or hers, might not sometime want for food. Always she felt pathetically frustrated when she could not succeed in impressing on her children the prudence which she felt was the only security against penury, the humility which she felt was the only precaution against fall of pride. Years later, when she was an elderly woman, and her family prosperous, her sons would bring to her, on their visits home from Philadelphia and New York, presents of shawls, bonnets, pieces of dress goods. On subsequent visits they would reproach her for not wearing them. "Ah," she would say, "sure ye can't tell"—the phrase an Irish euphemism designed to convey that we might someday see poverty. When she died the bureau drawers in the house bulged with bolts of dress goods, sprinkled with tobacco and wrapped in camphor-strewn newspapers to keep moths away. The dress in which she died—suddenly, and alone at the farm except for a hired boy; her sons all grown and gone—the dress she wore was of calico, made with her own hands.

VIII

My father, just before he married, worked for a man who, in the adaptability of the American 1850s, was partly a farmer, partly a small contractor. His headquarters was near a tiny village called, variously, by the name of its ancient inn, the Hammer and Trowel, or by the name of an Indian clan that had once hunted in the near-by hills, Toughkennamon. From the Hammer and Trowel my father, with his employer, helped to build trestles for an early Pennsylvania railroad, the Baltimore Central. The work took him some fifty miles west of Philadelphia, and that was the longest distance from the place of his landing in America that he ever went until after he was sixty years of age.

After my father married, his employer loaned him money to help buy a small farm—a practical helpfulness which, in my father's experience, was an unfailing American trait. The little farm was close by a hamlet called Pottown, so named from a pottery once located there. It was an early settlement and center of community life. After the railroad came, and left Pottown a mile off the line, its reason for existence ceased. Today I sometimes drive past it, and the ruin of the blacksmith's house, relatively a manor in the early days, is all that is left to suggest it was once a busy little settlement.

The Pottown farm was very small, eighteen acres, and my parents were poor; their first dining table was the top of the trunk that brought most of their belongings. The farm bore a mortgage; payment of interest upon it was a rite having importance in proportion to anxiety about getting the money together each April 1, and in proportion to the satisfaction felt in security of possession for another year. Memories of the ceremonial of paying the interest remained for more than half a century with those who had seen it as children.

[9]

Once, years later—it was toward the end of the Great War—my oldest brother visited me in Washington. "Well," he said with the manner of a man sure of his knowledge, "the war will end now in about three weeks." His confidence arrested my attention, for he was an experienced businessman with good judgment. I had no such expectation, and I was at the time in a position in which I would be likely to know about any approach of peace in Europe rather earlier than most. I asked him the basis for his assurance. He replied that he had observed that the price of hogs had recently risen to twenty cents a pound, and—he spoke with the dogmatic certainty of one who knows whereof he speaks—"and wars always end a few weeks after hogs reach twenty cents a pound." I asked him what was his authority, or how he knew. "Well," he replied, "I can recall the end of the Civil War in 1865. I was eight years old. We were living on the first little farm we had, at Pottown. Father had to pay the interest on the mortgage on April 1. It was eighty dollars. Currency was scarce and he paid it with two hogs—I remember because I helped drive the hogs to Isaac Slack's place. The hogs weighed four hundred pounds and Isaac took them at twenty cents a pound. That was April 1, 1865, and the Civil War ended two weeks later."

After my parents had lived at Pottown some nine years, and children were growing up, my mother felt that the language they heard about the blacksmith shop, and from soldiers straggling back from the Civil War, was not good for young ears. She was one to drive determinedly for her purposes; she made my father sell the farm, though there was no other suitable home available and the Civil War inflation had made the purchase of another farm inexpedient. They lived for a year or two in what in that neighborhood was called a "tenant house"; it was a rude structure of primitive masonry and logs, situated near the edge of a low-lying woods; local usage called the spot—I presume from abundance of raccoons—Coony Hollow. My father worked in the only neighborhood industry there was, a flower and tree nursery, called locally "the greenhouses."

Later he got employment, at a stipend of two hundred and fifty dollars a year, carrying the mail, on what used to be called a "star route." The government contract stipulated that he should perform the duty "with celerity, certainty and security." Twice a week, on horseback or with a sulky, he followed a route about twenty miles long, from a point on the railroad, Stanton, Delaware, north into Pennsylvania, through a number of little hamlets, which, after the branch railroads came, shriveled, and today are mere crossroads, unrecognizable as ever having been centers; their names were charming: Corner Ketch, Pleasant Hill, Mount Cuba, Little Baltimore, Chesterville.

In 1867 my father, hungry for ownership of his own bit of land, bought an outlying piece of one of the large farms of the neighborhood, fifty-two acres that had barely been wrested from wilderness, containing a small house and a barn that was little more than a shed. On this, with little help other than his own hands and those of his growing sons, he cut the trees, grubbed the brush, ditched the bottoms, split the rails and made the fences, improved the house, built a new barn. Hardly a square inch of the land but was fertilized by his sweat. As his vitality went into the soil, he loved it. There his younger children were born, including myself, the last.

Sometimes when my mother, with a not seriously meant manner of petulance, would suggest selling the place, he would say: "I will never leave this farm till I go in my long box." And he never did. Always he admonished his sons, "Never sell this farm; no matter what happens to you in the cities, this will be a shelter to you." We never did. I write these words in the room in which I was born.

CHAPTER 2

THE HOUSE, and the farm on which it sits, is in a country of soft, gentle hills and little winding creeks, about fifteen miles from the Delaware River, where river widens into bay. The two small streams that flow through the farm, and one that rises on it, find their way into Delaware Bay. A few miles west of the farm is a rise in the land, a watershed, so slight as to be almost imperceptible, beyond which the streams flow into Chesapeake Bay and the Susquehanna River.

The village near by is called Avondale; some time before my father bought the farm it was called Stone Bridge. In those early days it was just a tavern and a blacksmith shop, an overnight stopping place for waggoners on the first turnpike in America, the one from Newport, Delaware, to Lancaster, Pennsylvania. When the railroad came it divided all the countryside hamlets into two classes, those which the railroad passed through—these became stations; and those which were left—phrase of doom—"off the railroad." Avondale was one of the fortunate former. It, like the railroad stations everywhere, drew into itself the little businesses and trades of the now isolated hamlets. Avondale became a village of some three or four hundred people; in eighty years it has not greatly expanded.

The country thereabouts is fertile, smiling, kind. A place name given to a township by the early settlers, expressive of their delight with the land, is New Garden. Other place names —Locust Grove, West Grove, Harmony Grove—recall the woodlands the early settlers found, of oak, hickory, beech and poplar, parts of which they preserved and which still stand as wood lots here and there among the open fields.

II

My earliest memory, that I can identify, is of a scent. It was late on a sunny September afternoon, "potato-digging time."

My father was plowing up the long furrows of fresh earth in the potato field, which sloped southward from the house. Following behind him, my mother gathered the potatoes into pails which, when full, she emptied into bags set at intervals along the rows. She rarely worked in the fields—with a family of growing boys she did not need to; but potato digging coincided with the opening of school. In order that the children should go the first day, and every day, she took on herself the potato picking. Because there was no one in the house to look after me she took me to the field with her. I was not more than two or three years old; I suppose I spent the afternoon playing in the fresh earth. Here and there among the uprooted potato vines grew two herbs, pennyroyal and St-John's-wort. Both were strong-scented and were prized in our neighborhood as having medicinal value. Some wisps of these my mother gathered into a small bundle which she laid aside. In the evening, walking back to the house, she carried me, the fragrant pennyroyal and St-John's-wort in her hand brushing my face.

There this memory ends. But other memories recall the herbs tied into bundles and hung from hooks in the kitchen ceiling, against the winter weather when the children would have colds, for which "pennyrile tea" was believed to be a remedy.

All the more vivid of my early memories are of smells, farm smells: the acrid scent of burning weeds in the fall, at the end of a day of clearing the field for planting wheat; the faint fragrance of blossoms wafted down from the orchard in May, followed in midsummer by the strong, mellow odor of ripening apples, and in fall by the cidery scent of apples pared and sliced and spread in wooden racks in the sun, to provide our winter store of dried apples; the harvest smell of mown grass and of threshed straw; the barn smell of dried hay; the dank scent of the woods after a rain; the odor of bloodroot, the first spring flower, and of sassafras as the sap began to run; the pervading smell of October, which settled for weeks upon the whole countryside, so heavy it seemed almost visible, almost like a mist, a potpourri of ripening walnuts, ripening wild grapes, leaves fallen and just beginning to decay. Each season, almost each day, each spot on the farm, had its special scent. All are still vivid to me. One bred on a farm knows that

Smells are surer than sounds or sights
To make your heart-strings crack.

Next to scents, my most vivid early memories are of sounds: the whir of the mowing machine in outlying fields in June; the two-note *clunk, clank* of the whetstone against the scythe, which we kept for mowing corners of the field and bits of hillside too steep for the mowing machine. Another two-note sound was of the ax cutting down a tree in the woods, a low-pitched *chug* from the level stroke that made the bottom of the incision, a higher-pitched note made by the downward chop—both followed, after a half-hour of chopping, by a moment of silence, having the effect of suspense, by which I knew my father had stepped hurriedly back, and then the swish of the falling tree against the twigs and limbs of its neighbors, the sound gathering volume and tempo until it became a roar, climaxing in a mighty crash as the tree struck the ground. The two-pitched whine of the crosscut saw, a high note as the faster of the two sawyers drew the blade toward him, a lower note made by the slower worker.

In the fields, as the sun told us noon was near, we listened for the dinner bells. On our farm we had none—we depended on my mother's voice. But on many of the neighboring farms was a huge bell, as big as a school or church bell—indeed, I think the makers of the bells did not differentiate in size between those designed to summon to spiritual refreshment Sunday mornings and those designed to announce the noonday meal of the flesh. The dinner bell hung from a tall post, with a chain attached to it. This the housewife pulled at a moment nicely chosen to enable the men to get back from the fields just as the dishes came hot from stove to table. The bells rang about the same time, their deep-toned voices a rude neighborhood carillon.

From the swamps and bottoms in early March came the chorus of the young frogs. They sounded hurried, breathless, as

THE FARMHOUSE, ABOUT 1890, WITH MARK SULLIVAN'S FATHER, MOTHER AND ONE OF HIS BROTHERS.

if passionately eager to bring the spring, of which they were the heralds. We called them "knee-deeps." For that name we had two explanations: one that the frogs were still knee-deep in the swamp, the other that their cry sounded like *knee-deep*—the first note low in pitch, the second high, almost a whistle. The knee-deep was not musical, much less so than the bobwhite or the dove; nor is the frog a glamorous creature, whether young or full-grown. Yet of all the sounds my childhood knew, the cry of the knee-deeps remained the most vivid, the most potent to evoke the past. During all the middle years of my life, wherever I was, in cities or in distant lands, I never saw March come on the calendar without thinking of the farm and wishing I could hear the knee-deeps.

One spring, while living in New York, my wife and I became troubled by the weedy pallor of the young children of the janitor who lived in the basement of our apartment house, shut off from the sunlight, and close to the street noises. We arranged that the children, with their mother, should go for some weeks into the country, a country not very remote, for it was on Staten Island, with the Manhattan skyscrapers in sight. Our satisfaction over our good deed was brief. After two days mother and children were back in the noisy, gloomy basement. The mother explained she did not like the country, she could not stand "the noise of those little frogs at night." The incident was fruitful of many reflections, including that which says that one person's music may be another person's noise, one person's pleasure another's intolerable annoyance.

III

The house, wooden, had four rooms downstairs, three above. Two of the rooms, one downstairs, one up, had been added by my father about the time I was born. The addition was the occasion of some confusion to me as a child, and one of my earliest intellectual illuminations was to become aware that the family's name for the southern part of the house was not one word, "newend," but two, "new end," and that the phrase was descriptive—I had supposed it to be the term for a part of every house, like "kitchen" and "shed." Building the new end strained the family finances; for several years the whole house stood unpainted. We could have whitewashed it, but my mother resisted; she, though never an optimist, felt the time might come when we could have it painted. By the law of her nature, in everything, she would have either the best or nothing. When the time did arrive when we could afford painting it, choice of a color consumed weeks of family discussion. A memento of that, a sheet of sample colors, little squares of stiff paper about an inch each way, differently colored, was one of the prized possessions of my childhood.

Within the house the seat of the lares and penates was the clock shelf. The clock was a familiar type that had been manufactured in Bristol, Connecticut, about 1835, and distributed by peddlers; they are now common at sales of antiques. Ours still keeps time. On the shelf alongside the clock rested the prayer book and on Christmas nights the blessed candle. From a nail hung the almanac. Behind the clock, between it and the wall, were kept important papers, bills, receipts and letters that came to the house, which during my childhood were not numerous. Inside the clock, between the pendulum and the bottom, was a space which served as the family safe. There was kept what cash we had, commonly not more than two or three one-dollar bills and some silver. As "interest day" approached the cash in the clock would increase; after it became large my father thought it prudent to take it upstairs with him at night and put it under his pillow.

Only three framed pictures were in the house. One was a print depicting the last hours of Andrew Jackson; he was lying in a huge bed with high posts supporting a frame from which hung heavy curtains; by his bedside were relatives in attitudes of extreme grief. Another was a colored poster of the presidential campaign of 1844 containing likenesses of the Democratic candidates, James K. Polk and George M. Dallas. Below them, ornately printed in an inverted arc, was the campaign slogan, expressed in rhyme, not perfectly achieved:

Polk the young hickory
Dallas and victory.

The last item of our art gallery was a large framed engraving issued at the time of the Philadelphia Centennial in 1876. In the center was a reproduction of the Declaration of Independence and the Great Seal of the United States—the eagle, in every detail of his outspread wings, his clutching talons, his curved beak and his piercing eyes, expressed extreme fierceness; to a small boy he was a little menacing. The border of the engraving was a circle made up of the seals of the states, at that time thirty-seven in number. The seal that impressed me most was that of Virginia—a female figure with a sword in her hand, her foot on the neck of a man lying prone. The legend, "Sic Semper Tyrannis," was not translatable by me or anyone else in the house, but I understood it was something very heroic, admirable and worthy to be emulated.

IV

In the neighborhood were tree nurseries. From one of them my father got four young evergreens, firs, which he planted in a row in front of the house, to the east. There was another evergreen, a cedar, called by the family "Johnny's tree," for some association it had with one of my brothers. After I grew up and went away the cedar was removed; when I returned on visits I missed it, poignantly. But the four tall firs are still there, landmarks to the country round.

One of my serenities in recent years has been to sit on the porch on late afternoons, with the descending sun behind me, and watch the tall shadows of the firs lengthen and swing toward the right, like a four-columned army deploying. The shadows march down the slope of the field in front of the house, cross the little stream and the road and, with increasing speed as the sun goes down, march up the other hill.

Once, watching the tips of the shadows advance through the

clover field an eighth of a mile away, I observed them give notice of nightfall to a hen. She had been, with the rest of the flock, catching grasshoppers in the clover. This hen was an individualist, she had enterprise and industry. After the rest of the flock had gone home she had remained busily pursuing the hoppers. She had resourcefulness, knew how to adapt herself to circumstance and make it serve her. In the pursuit of grasshoppers she had developed an individual technique. In the field was a horse, grazing. As he moved his nose forward in the grass, he stirred up hoppers. The hen placed herself a yard or so in front of the horse and facing him. As the horse stepped forward the hen stepped backward. As each forward move of the horse's munching mouth caused a barrage of grasshoppers to leap forward, the hen kept herself at the bottom of the arc where the barrage descended. Busily clutching and gulping, she neglected the passage of time until the tip of one of the tree shadows reached and covered her. As it shut off the sun she cocked her head alertly, looked toward the sun, observed it close to setting, and at once, without another peck at a hopper or a look behind, started down the hill toward home. She was startled but not disturbed. She did not run, but walked rapidly and directly in a straight line, with a continuity of intention, a settled purposefulness, that marked her off from the race of hens as a whole. Belated but safe, she arrived at the chicken house with her craw better filled than her less assiduous sisters'.

On three sides of the yard my father planted rows of young evergreens close together, as a hedge, partly for ornament, more for utilitarian shelter against the wind. But as the trees became so tall as to shut off the sun he cut them down. On the front the yard was enclosed by a fence of upright white palings, with a red gate. When I was a boy the palings were whitewashed— that was one of my spring tasks. By the time the first fence began to decay we were, in the phrase we used, "better fixed," and the successor fences were painted white, the gate green.

Along the lane my father planted a row of pines; they are there yet, excepting four that succumbed to various disasters and have been replaced. The first that was lost came to its end through my unintentional hands. Each summer, after harvest, with a scythe we cut the weeds along the edges of the field close to the fence. I raked some of the dried weeds into a pile and set fire to them. The wind, changing direction, blew the flames close to one of the pines, the tar in the needles took fire, and in one leaping blaze the tree was stripped and gaunt. It was a tragedy, to me and to the family, for we cherished the trees, had for them some of the same feeling we had for the farm animals.

Where the lane entered the road there was, when my father came to the place, a giant old oak. It was cut down while I was still a child. I remember it only as an immense stump, over four feet in diameter, the low flat top making an excellent place to arrange the broken bits of bright-colored china which for a time were my principal playthings. To replace the oak, my father planted two maples; they remained for half a century, tall sentinels at the gate.

Back of the house, a field away, standing alone, was a tall old poplar, always referred to, almost with a manner of ritual, as "the poplar tree," as if to distinguish its age and dignity and solitariness from the scores of other poplars that were in the woods. The poplar tree—we put the emphasis on the last word —was almost one of the farm's personalities. It was a place of family council. In the house we children would notice our parents grow serious, perhaps as the result of a letter, or of information brought from a neighbor by my mother, or from the village by my father. They would move toward the door and go out and walk slowly toward the poplar tree, talking earnestly, their heads bent. After a while they would return, walking more briskly, with the manner of decision arrived at.

Always, when my parents went to the poplar tree, I felt that something serious was afoot, though not necessarily ominous. Once, when they remained at the tree for what seemed a long while, I, a little disturbed, walked out toward the tree myself, simulating what I meant to be a manner of casualness. As I got near them I heard my mother conclude the conference, saying firmly, "We'll sell the Whitie cow," by which I knew the question whether my older brother could go to boarding school another term had been settled, the funds would be provided.

As the older children grew more mature they were admitted to the poplar tree councils. On Sundays it was a place of cheerful family gathering. After church, and dinner, and a period of replete repose, as the afternoon began to wane, we would all go out to the poplar tree—it was on the highest point on the farm—to enjoy pride in the view. There was stimulus to my imagination in looking at the horizon and speculating about what was beyond it.

Back of the house, on a northward slope, my father planted an orchard of apple trees. He had selected the varieties with an eye to graduated ripening; from the middle of July until late fall there were always two or three trees in bearing. When I was a boy they were in their prime; without any spraying or other care they produced prodigious yields. I used to gather wagonloads and take them to the village to peddle. Late in the season, when the more juicy varieties were ripe, I would gather cartloads and take them, with an empty barrel, to the near-by mill, where they were ground into cider, which we drank sweet, or relatively sweet, until about Thanksgiving Day, and then rather hard until near Christmas.

The trees had charming names. The earliest-ripening one, coming to fruit in the time of wheat harvest early in July, we called simply the "harvest apple." Overeager anticipation of its ripening led to intestinal disturbance which I understood the doctor to describe, much to my mystification, as "cholera marbles." About August came the Townsends, large, mellow, mealy apples; in September the Smokehouse, of firmer flesh and more cidery. Later came the Red Romanites, the Baldwins and the Rambos (originally, I suppose, Rambeau). The Rambo was the apple of my teacher's preference; each morning I would pick the largest to take to her. The Russets, called by us "rusty coats," were not good for eating until well after frost. One immense white apple, the largest in the orchard, we called by a name which I can only reproduce phonetically as "Follow-older." One apple tree was called by a name aptly descriptive, the "Maiden's Blush"; it was cream-white with a reddish-pink glow. This tree stood on the edge of the orchard that was most distant from the house, at the top of a steep bank overlooking a ravine and a long swale of swamp. September afternoons I used to lie on the ground beneath the tree and look out across the autumn fields to the western horizon where the sun was descending. The place and the scene always stirred me to vague ambition and adventure.

CHAPTER 3

INTRODUCTION to farm work took forms which presented it in the guise of a privilege. To ride on the back of a horse as he plodded in from the field in the evening was, to a four- or five-year-old boy, an eagerly sought elevation. To help remove the harness was an extension of the pleasure. Presently I was permitted to remove the harness without help, and to curry and comb the horses, the privilege being conferred as a responsibility carrying with it recognition of progress toward grown-up. Imperceptibly privilege became duty. By the time I was seven or eight I was not only harnessing and unharnessing the horses, I was driving them, whole days or parts of days, in the lighter farm operations, the harrowing and rolling by which clods were broken up and the soil made fine after plowing.

Work I always liked was driving the horse rake in haying time. As the long, curved iron fingers accumulated enough hay, I tripped with my foot a pedal which raised the rake and emptied it. I have an imperfect small toe whose defect came from descent of the pedal on a bare foot. When the hay tedder came, a mechanism of long, jointed iron rods with forks at the end, which picked the hay up and kicked it about to dry, I liked that, too, for it, even more than the rake, involved pedals and levers. My claiming the rake and the tedder as my function was due to a liking I had for the mechanical features of them and for the horse driving; it was not a stratagem to escape the drudgery of pitching the hay onto the pile that grew upon the wagon, or pitching it from the wagon to the barn mow. Before I was of age to handle those tasks I went away from the farm.

While much of the farm work was hard, my parents did not burden me beyond a boy's strength—against that my mother was vigilant. Instinctively she wished to preserve her feeling that I was a child, even to the time when it was an illusion. For twenty years she had always had a boy in the house, a

JULIA GLEASON SULLIVAN.

About 1890.

succession of boys; as one passed into adolescence he was succeeded by another. But I was her last; when I should cease to be
a boy she would have no more. To her my progress in adolescence was at once a pride and a pang. One time when, in a
boy's assiduous imitation of his elders, I climbed upon a chair
to be able to see into the looking glass, and lathered my face
and drew over my cheek my father's razor, which met nothing
to cut, I saw, through the glass, my mother furtively get rid
of a tear.

She took pride in the work I did, treated me as a valiant
Hercules. When I was very young I would come from the fields
at night saying, in our vernacular, and with pride, not com-
plaint, "I been a-workin' an' a-workin' an' a-workin all day."
My mother would quote that to visitors with beaming pleasure
—inspiring comment from my brothers which, when she was
present, took the form of skeptic looks, but in her absence expressed itself in acid remarks about "mother's pet." Occasionally she would say in the morning that she needed me that day
to follow a turkey hen into the distant fields to find where she
had hidden her nest, and I sometimes observed that her need
of me for turkey stalking coincided with days when the farm
work, for which I otherwise might have been commandeered,
was especially hard. I fear I took advantage of her consideration.
I was able to milk, but never did; my mother continued to help
with the milking after I was old enough to relieve her. My
immunity, I think, I may have achieved through precocious
exercise of the wisdom described in a story the colored folks of
our neighborhood used to tell; it must have come down from
slave times. The colored folks, so the tale went, held that the
mistake which had brought upon them the curse of toil was
their failure to practice the acumen of the monkeys. Monkeys,
so they said, could talk just as well as colored people, but the
monkeys had had the shrewdness to realize that if they let it be
known they could talk they would be put to work.

Yet work I did. From the time I was six until I was sixteen,
every weekday of every summer (the period when I was not at

school) I did farm work. And during the school months I did chores before leaving in the morning, and quite serious tasks after I returned in the afternoon. I did it as a matter of course; we knew no other way. Excepting Sundays and Christmas, there was no holiday, except, one Saturday afternoon each summer, the picnic at the Catholic Church. Fourth of July and Washington's Birthday meant no cessation of toil; Labor Day had not been invented. An afternoon in my thirteenth year when my older brother took me to see a baseball game some four miles away was long remembered. A few days of picking wild blackberries in August, a journey to buy a load of peaches from a distant neighbor, a trip to the mill or the village or the black-smith shop—these counted as prized diversions.

Some work that I did for long days at a time was sheer toil, not mitigated by mechanical gadget or collaboration of a horse. Planting corn gave me many a tired back. My father, walking ahead with the hoe, would scrape a little depression, into which I would drop five grains of corn. He, with a stroke or two of the hoe, would cover the corn with a little mound—we used to speak of the tiny mounds as "hills of corn." After the corn was a few inches high, I had to hoe it, stir the soil gently and draw fresh soil toward the hill, and pull up the shorter plants, leaving only two. When the corn was a foot or so high it was necessary to pull from each stalk the parasitic "suckers" that sometimes grew from the base.

All that was boy's work. So was weeding the potatoes. Through long, hot July days, straddling the row, with back bent, I would finger among the vines for the ragweeds and smartweeds. It was sheer toil, which no exercise of imagination could turn into anything else; the only satisfaction was in seeing the number of cleaned rows increase, the unweeded ones di-minish. Picking potato bugs could be relieved by thinking of the bugs as enemies to be destroyed. Holding a shallow tin pan in one hand, I would edge it under a leaf of the vine, and with the other hand shake the bugs into the pan. Poisoning the potato bugs, going along the row with a watering can from which the poison was sprayed upon the leaves, had even more the spirit of making war on an enemy. The bugs, when young, were ugly—moist, pulpy slugs; I hated to touch them. When grown, with a hard shell striped black and yellow, they might have been seen as pretty had they not been associated with disagreeable work.

The planting of the potatoes in the spring was disagreeable too. It began in March, in the cellar, where we spent many days cutting the potatoes for seed. The planting, setting each piece in the furrow carefully, with the eye upward, so that the sprout could ascend, took place in early April, while the ground was still cold to the hands, and, in my case often, cold to bare feet—though my going barefoot so early in the spring was my own choice, achieved against the protest of my mother, who would have postponed the rite until warmer weather. One phase of the potato growing was a pleasure. In October, after the potatoes were picked, on a dry night when the hunters' moon was high, the denuded vines and the weeds were raked into large heaps and set afire. The burning weeds and vines had an agreeable acrid smell; an occasional potato that had escaped our picking and was now roasted tasted better than potatoes orthodoxly cooked.

One task I disliked, definitely and always. I resented being called by my father from my sleep in the early morning to bring in the cows from the meadow for milking. In the fall the meadow was cold. As I roused the reluctant cows one by one from the spots on which they had lain during the night, I would stand awhile on each spot to warm my bare feet.

If I had not had a lifetime of continuous good health, and if I did not believe that some of this was due to my farm boyhood, I would say that to call a boy from bed before his sleep is completed is a detriment and a cruelty. For some of my life, at boarding school and occasionally elsewhere, I was called from sleep by bells. For other parts of my life I have been under the necessity of being at an office at a fixed hour, sometimes of punching a time clock. I never liked it; even though I enjoyed my work I resented the decreed punctuality. One of the motives that led me to work and save was the wish to achieve an independence that would enable me to choose my own hours for work, including the hour of beginning in the morning. After I had achieved that status I sometimes began at four or five, other times at nine or ten or twelve, and continued, often, for ten or twelve hours or more. But my permanent conviction about the proper hour for rising is like Lincoln's answer to his own conundrum about how long a man's legs should be. They should be, Lincoln said, long enough to reach the ground. And my notion is that the time to get up in the morning is the time when you have finished sleeping.

One aspect of our changing world that I have liked little has been the increasing dictatorship of bells and signals and lights and time clocks. For each person there is a natural tempo and rhythm; for human nature as a whole an average tempo. And this tempo is in many situations less rapid than the pace which modern life demands and modern machinery dictates. The larger justification for reducing hours of factory labor from sixty a week to fifty-four and later to forty-eight and forty is the rescuing of men from prolonged subjection to a pace that is too rapid for them. A farmer, and persons in some other occupations where the worker can set his own pace, can work long hours and is often happier and better off when working than when doing some of the things he does when not working. The justification for shorter hours in repetitive factory work is to increase the period during which the worker is released from the tyranny of machinery, of bells and signals and time clocks.

One farm chore that I liked, though it is not commonly regarded as agreeable, was cleaning the stables. For this, when I was going to school, I had to hurry home promptly when school closed. I liked pitching the manure out the stable doors into the barnyard, and then scraping the stalls with a shovel. Although the stable smell is not usually listed among agreeable aromas, I liked the sharp ammoniac scent that made my nostrils tingle. After the stalls were cleaned I would climb the barn

MARK SULLIVAN, ABOUT SIX.

From a tintype.

stairs and throw straw down from one of the mows for fresh bedding. From the haymow I would fork hay into the mangers. In a small box at the end of each feed trough I would put corn or bran. Then I would open the stable doors, letting the eager animals in to eat and be milked. I liked to hear them munching and the sharp *ping-g* as the first squirts of milk struck the bottom of the pail.

After the milking was over, and after we had gone to the house and had our own supper, my father would return to the barn to see that everything was in order for the night. I liked to go with him. On a winter night it was nice to open the stable door and feel the impact of the warmth of the animals and the smell of them. With the opening of the door they would stop the rhythmic chewing of their cuds and turn their heads to gaze at the visitor. Reassured, they would contentedly resume their chewing. One of the most pleasurable satisfactions a farmer can have is to know that as winter approaches he has closed all the crevices of the barn against the weather, has packed sheaves of fodder along the place where the wooden frame of the barn meets the stone foundation, and has his mows filled with hay, his bins with grain; and then, on a winter night, to close the stable door, knowing that the animals dependent on him are well fed and warm.

For our farm animals we had names. We thought of the cows as individuals, not as a herd; possibly the good reason was that we never had enough to be a herd—from seven to nine was the number when I was a boy. Each had a name and in some cases the name was hereditary; there was Old Rosy and Young Rosy. That the horses should have names was universal on all farms, but we used the names in an unusual way. Addressing the horses, we would follow the ordinary custom, saying, "Get ep, Harry!" "Whoa, Charley!" But talking about them among ourselves, we would always say "the Charley horse," or "the Harry horse." I think this manner of speaking may have come from Ireland, and may have denoted intimacy; the horses were personalities, part of the farm circle. It reflected affection for the horses, consideration for them. When my father and mother were first married, and had but one horse, they would, on Sundays during seasons of heavy weekday work on the farm, walk the six miles to the church, saying, "The poor horse needs the rest." One of the most awing experiences of my boyhood was coming home from school and finding my mother with her apron over her head, weeping. To avoid infecting me with her emotion she stopped. But to me as to her there was tragedy in what she told me: "The Harry horse is dead."

To ride horseback—in my case it was muleback at first—was a progress toward maturity, ardently desired and eagerly sought. All the young men on the neighboring farms rode horseback on trips to the village. We knew the gait of each horse; at night, hearing hoofs strike the wooden bridge on the road below the house, we would say, "That's Will Dantz," or "That's Charlie Burnite."

The mule we had, a small one, was named Dinah—we did not give her the distinction of calling her "the Dinah mule." When my father, yielding to urgent importunity, said I could ride Dinah to the village, he put me under a strict injunction—I must let her walk all the way. The injunction I obeyed as far along the road as I could be seen from the house. At the precise point—it was marked by an old willow tree—where the road passed behind a hill out of sight of the house, I dug my bare heels into Dinah's sides, achieving a mild similitude of cowboy on mustang. On three or four subsequent rides I did the same. Then one day my father drove Dinah to the village in the shafts of a wagon. As she reached the old willow she suddenly dashed into a gallop, in the manner of a runaway. My father was almost thrown from the wagon. Dinah's action seemed to him astounding and wanton. He was as indignant as surprised. It happened several times at the same place. My father grew to watch for it, and was never disappointed. He was puzzled. Speaking of it at home, he said, "Dang me if I can understand it." I did not enlighten him. Dinah's mentality had to cope with what must have been, to her mulish intelligence, an unsolvable eccentricity of human beings: the old willow tree was a place where, when somebody was astride her back, she was suddenly prodded into a gallop, but where, when she was between the shafts of a wagon, the lines were suddenly drawn tight to prevent her from galloping.

CHAPTER 4

IN OUR IRISH FAMILY we did not, as children, hear the nursery tales which, in most families, are standard juvenile entertainment. I did not become acquainted with Simple Simon or Jack the Giant Killer until after I had gone to school and could read.

But we had a form of entertainment which was not available to American children less fortunately born. We heard Irish stories. Stories about fairies, leprechauns, ghosts, the devil, the banshee. We were not limited to getting our fairy stories through the inert medium of print, of so-called "children's books"; we had the stories firsthand, from the very persons who, so they assured us, had seen the events and themselves participated in them. And such is the convincing vividness of the Irish in telling stories that we were enabled to believe, and thereby acquire an authenticity of thrill not possible to children who could get this form of entertainment only through the cold pictures and type of nursery books.

My father told few, and told them with a manner designed faintly to suggest that of course they were just stories. Almost the only one of his that I can remember now was about a warning he had received from his dead mother. This story he told, as much with an intention of conveying a moral as of expecting us to believe it. One evening, as a youth in Ireland, he had departed for a dance without completing certain chores his father had told him to do. On his way he came to a stream which he must cross by a log bridge. As he was about to step on the log his mother appeared to him, saying: "Connie, don't cross that log." He turned back and, in the mood put upon him by a supernatural visitation, completed his chores with a conscientious fidelity that was sharpened by contrition. Next day he learned that fate had intended to punish his neglect of his chores in a manner all the more dire for being indirect. For on that night a murderer had been waiting at the opposite end of the bridge to kill an enemy who, the murderer had supposed, would be the only traveler that way on that night.

My mother told many stories of fairies, fairies who danced along the tops of the hedges or mischievously chased the sheep in the fields. I observed, as I grew a little older and the spirit of inquiry unhappily descended upon me, that my mother's stories of fairies were secondhand—it was her cousin who had seen them, or a neighbor, never herself. I never could tell to what extent she believed, or to what extent she was consciously providing entertainment, entertainment made more engaging by asserted authenticity.

About my mother's banshee stories, however, there was no secondhand nor other indirection, nor doubt. She had heard the banshee herself, heard it again and again, heard it presage the death of every relative or close friend who had died while she lived in Ireland. In the Ireland of her girlhood experience the banshee was as certain an incident preceding death as the wake that followed. And, indeed, it was easy for an imaginative race to persuade themselves that a strange sound heard in the night was the omen of death, and easy for a mystical and generous race to assume that the supernatural would not permit death to come without warning. I observed that, while my mother expected me to believe the banshee stories that had happened in Ireland, she never claimed that any death in America had been foretold by an authentic banshee.

We had one Irish neighbor who, in the tales he told us, happily felt no parental obligation not to frighten the children, nor any responsibility to minimize fiction by omitting to insist it was fact. On one occasion that I remember well he had been to the village and was returning late on a summer Saturday afternoon. A short cut across fields to his home brought him past our house. I think he may have drunk a drop or two at the village tavern. If he had I am grateful for whatever was the liquor that, on this particular night, gave his natural talent for storytelling an especial vividness.

He said that once in his youth in the old country he had dis-

[*31*]

obeyed his parents. They had always told him never to enter a shebeen and never to play cards, especially never to play with a stranger. But he had grown to that age at which boys feel they must show some independence of parental guidance. One evening he had gone into a shebeen and taken a drink. Some cardplayers in the room invited him to join the game, and he boldly did. Presently he dropped a card. Reaching to the floor to retrieve it, he could see under the table the feet of the player opposite him. They were not feet at all! "I saw[1] the hoofs; I knew it was the divil and I ran for my life."

At this exciting denouement my father said, "Ah, you ought not to be telling such stories before the children." Whereupon the author, raising his right arm toward heaven, solemnly averred, "As God is my judge, Con Sullivan, I saw it with my own eyes."

Many of the stories told by and about the Irish arose from a condition that was ephemeral, the presence in America of recent Irish immigrants in large numbers, the contact of the "green-horn" with a country that was new to him, and ways that were very strange. Since the condition has long passed away, I suppose the stories have gone too; I doubt if these stories have been told since Irish immigration waned; I doubt, too, if the stories were ever in print; they are primitive folklore of the limited group about whom and by whom they were told. Today they exist only in the memories of the persons, now not great in number, whom once they hilariously pleased.

One was about the recently arrived immigrant who, passing a woods in the night, heard the cry of an owl, *whoo, whoo, whoo.* The greenhorn, unfamiliar with the bird or its cry, supposing the call to be an interrogation of some sort, and eager to conform punctiliously to whatever was required by the customs of the new

---

[1]The flavor of Irish stories lies in part in the Irish way of pronouncing many words. Many a story which, when told by an Irish person, is a delight, falls flat when told by another. "Saw" is "sàh"—I do not think the "aw" sound exists in Ireland. "John" is "Jon," with a very short o—never "Jawn." "God" is always pronounced with the *o* very short—"Gawd" is so barbarian as to seem almost impious. Even "ought" is "aht."

country, answered, "I'm Patrick Moriarity." Upon repetition of the *whoo, whoo, whoo,* the greenhorn was further explicit, "Patrick Moriarity, Mike's son, from Ballymagool; I have a character from Father Walsh." (A "character," pronounced with accent on the middle syllable, "char-*ak*-ter," was a written recommendation from a priest or former employer.) A fourth cry of *whoo,* however, brought an end to Irish patience. The greenhorn exclaimed, "Ah, the divil take ye, thin, find out for yerself."

That phrase, "The divil take ye"—it was the mild Celtic equivalent of the Anglo-Saxon "To hell with you!"—was the ending of many of the Irish stories, especially those which reflected irritation or bafflement. And irritated bafflement was the frequent mood of the endings of the stories, especially those which dealt with the greenhorn's first acquaintance with a fauna he had not known in Ireland. A hundred yarns, pungent in more than one sense, dealt with the greenhorn's first encounters with the skunk, called in our neighborhood a polecat.

A story frequently told was about a bullfrog and a greenhorn. The greenhorn one night was carrying home a jug of rum. Crossing a bridge, he heard from beneath a voice which, while deeply bass, seemed to him plaintive and appealing; it was uttering sounds which he interpreted as *more rum, more rum.* The greenhorn supposed it to be someone who had had a few drinks but wished more. Stirred by fellow feeling for that condition, he, with the openhandedness of the Irish, took the corncob stopper from his jug, tipped the jug gently over the edge of the bridge and let a little rum gurgle out. But the voice repeated, *more rum, more rum.* That desire for yet more touched his sympathetic understanding, and he tipped his jug again. The importunity was repeated. An equal number of times the generosity was repeated, until the story ended with the greenhorn dashing his empty jug at the voice, and the usual conclusion, "The divil take ye!"

A story dealing with a fauna not new to the immigrant but which, in America, had habits unfamiliar and amazingly advanced, pictured two greenhorns asleep. One, awaking, saw a lightning bug in the room. Startled, he woke his bedfellow. "My gorry, Mike, look at that: the bedbugs in America carry lanterns." Similar misinterpretation of phenomena familiar in America but strange to the greenhorn was the basis of a story about two other sleepers. These were in a room on a city street. When some fire engines, of a type now extinct, dashed by belching fire and steam, Mike rushed to the window. Making an inference based on incomplete data, he called to his sleeping friend, "Come quick, Pat, and look; they're movin' hell; two loads of it have gone by already."

Unfamiliarity with the American vernacular accounted for the deep perturbation of a recently arrived Irish girl working as a servant, who was told to "serve the tomatoes without dressing." When she came from the pantry in attire diminished by absence of waist and overskirt, she misinterpreted the startled dismay of the family for disapproval, and truculently declared, "I won't take off another stitch if I lose my job."

That one was rather daring; it would not ordinarily be told in the presence of the womenfolks. But while, in the jokes the neighborhood boys told, we were scrupulous about sex, we did not extend the taboo "coarse" as far as a later generation might, to jokes about other bodily functions.

After my brothers went to the city they used to bring back from the minstrel shows the "latest jokes," a latest which today is half a century old. Yet those quips of the 1880s were not ephemeral except in their application to what was then current. Essentially they were as old as the race, and they have never lost their vigor. As I listen to the gags of some radio comedians in 1938, the pleasure I get is less that of humor than of nostalgia. The Mae West jokes of the 1930s were the Lillian Russell jokes of the 1890s, adapted—one could not say that any Mae West joke was streamlined; perhaps "revamped" is the appropriate word. The automobile jokes that went in a wave over the country about 1915 were the trolley-car jokes of 1885, brought up to date. The trolley-car jokes of 1885, no doubt, were in turn the lineal descendants of the railroad jokes of the 1830s; and those,

THE EDUCATION OF AN AMERICAN

I suspect, went back to the jokes that primitive man made when he first saw a horse hitched to a wagon.

There was one railroad quip that was still alive in our community; it was about a local road, the Pomeroy Branch, and it dealt with the leisurely ease with which the road was run, its amiable consideration for the convenience of its patrons. Indeed, I think this jest had some relation to the familiar railroad phrase, "accommodation train." According to this story, when the train stopped at New Garden Station a farmer's wife hurried up to the conductor, explained that she wished to take a dozen eggs to Wilmington, that she had eleven of the eggs, that the speckled hen was on the nest, and that she had reason to believe she could patronize the train if the conductor would hold it twenty minutes.

In the lack of much reading, and with no access to the stage at all—until I was fifteen I never saw but one professional entertainment, and that without fee, a Kickapoo Indian medicine show—we made drama of events within our farm circle. We recited them over and over, perfected the telling of them, added here and there a touch which dramatic construction called for but which ungracious fact had neglected to provide.

In this repertoire of family comedy was an experience of my brother and myself. One hot summer night we slept on the porch. In the clover field beyond the lane we heard a hen squawk. We knew a hen was setting in a clump of weeds near the fence. We assumed she had got off her nest and we went out to find her and put her back. Circling about in the knee-high clover, my brother called to me, "All right, Mark, I've found her," and stooped down. Then, in explosive dismay, "Great gosh, Mark, it's a skunk!"

One afternoon my brother was trimming the hedge along the road with a pair of long-handled shears. Tiring, he stuck his shears in the top of the hedge and lay down in the grass to nap. Waking, still half asleep, he groped for his shears—but grasped a snake, the size of which, in the family telling, was made as large as a good story required.

Once my brother went to the village to spend the evening. While he was away a tramp arrived at the farm. Tramps were familiar to us. My father had a formula for them and for the favor they always asked. He would give them supper, ask them if they had any matches, make them give him the matches until morning and then let them sleep in the barn. That night my brother, returning from the village late and putting the horse in the stable, heard from the haymow sounds which he could interpret as either murder being done or the eerie wailing of a ghost. He dashed to the house, up the stairs and into the bed-- room which he shared with me—he preferred to come to me rather than to our parents because, though terribly scared, he was calm enough to remember that waking our parents would reveal the lateness of his return from the village. I listened to his excited story and at once surmised the explanation, but did not reveal it to him until I had relished the little drama. Afterward I went with him to the barn to complete the stabling of the horse and wake the tramp from his nightmare.

Many of our stories we located in a place on the farm which we called, and which is still called, the "Glory Hole"—from what that esoteric name derived I cannot say. Today it is difficult to invest the spot with mystery. I have not been able to make it seem sinister to my own children, for it has been ditched and cleared and most of it is now close-cropped by the cows. But when I was a boy, the sides were covered with large trees, the bottom with dense bushes and high rank weeds. The Glory Hole we made the scene of ancient gory crimes, the hiding place of marauders, the home of giant snakes, the habitat of ghosts. About the only story that had any degree of authenticity—and it was halfway between legend and invention—was to the effect that long ago, before our occupancy of the farm, the ravine had been the hideaway of a horse thief.

In the woods on a neighbor's farm there was a small mound, about six feet long and three wide. Passing through the woods on expeditions for honeysuckle and sassafras, as well as 'possums and coons, I often speculated upon what could have been the origin of the mound, and asked my father and brothers without getting light from either my own speculations or my elders' information. Then one day, reading the *Youth's Companion*, I came, for the first time, across an account of Indian mounds in the Middle West. Thereupon, without question, the mound in our neighbor's woods became an Indian grave and in it tomahawks, arrowheads, pottery, wampum—everything that my reading led me to believe Indian graves should contain. So complete was my conviction that I was able to communicate it to two of my brothers, although they were older than I by six and ten years, and were by nature less imaginative.

The mound must be opened at once. But there was an impediment. My parents would be sure to forbid us either to open the mound without permission, or to ask the owner of the woods for leave. Since prohibition was certain, we avoided encountering it. For several nights, after the family had gone to bed, and after my parents' bedroom, either by the cessation of talk or the beginning of snoring, conveyed assurance that they were asleep, the three of us slipped out our bedroom window and down a shed roof to the ground. Getting shovels and a pick, we went silently across the fields to the woods and dug, with an earnestness which I am confident must have surprised the shovels and pick, for they had never encountered it in their daytime and normal acquaintance with us. We went six feet deep. We found nothing except a few traces of white chalky material which, it pleased us to assume, though without too great confidence, were the remains of bones.

The adventure soon passed from our minds; in the procession of the day's work and diversions other concerns occupied us. Then, late one afternoon, about the time night was beginning to fall, I was with my father planting corn on a hilly elevation in one of our fields. Presently I saw coming out of the woods an old Negro who lived in a tenant house on the neighboring farm. He came across the field with a straight directness quite different from his ordinary ambling way, and with a speed which his elderly limbs did not often practice. It was clear he had something to say to my father, something urgent, and my father leaned on his hoe and waited until Jossy came breathless to the top of the hill. "Mr Sullivan," he said, "they's somebody goin' to be murdered; they's dug his grave."

My father, startled and slightly stern, said, "What do you mean, Jossy Gibbs?" Jossy said that he had been in the woods getting poles for his lima beans, that he had seen a pile of fresh earth, that he had approached it, and that there before his eyes he found a new-dug grave. My father, silent and concerned, walked with Jossy down the hill to the woods. I felt it prudent to go along, lest failure to be interested should seem suspicious. But as I went I shrank farther and farther into inconspicuousness. In the woods my father said nothing to Jossy, but I knew he was disturbed. So was I.

That evening while my father recounted the incident to my mother, I, in a quite different spirit, gave a more illuminating account to my conspirator brothers. We concluded that, as often, silence would be golden.

Within a day the neighborhood was electric. The ominence natural to the circumstances was increased by a fairly recent neighborhood memory. A few years before there had occurred a few miles away one of the classic murders of America—the story is included in one of Edmund L. Pearson's murder books. Two men in Baltimore had entered into a conspiracy to defraud an insurance company by pretending that one of them was dead. The one simulating death had come to a village not far from our home to remain in seclusion. By and by impatience with rural life led him to tell his partner in Baltimore that he wanted to come back. Thereupon the partner had come up to the country, taken his friend on a buggy ride, murdered him and buried him a grave in the woods. Eventually there had been discovery. The ensuing murder trial, ending with the execution of the murderer, had been for years a principal topic of interest throughout the whole county. When, now, a fresh-made grave in the woods was discovered, everybody thought of the Udderzook-Goss murder, and assumed that something like it was about to take place.

Within a day or two the colored woman living in a tenant house near the woods was able to recall having been wakened after midnight a few nights before, having looked out the window and seen through the dark something which she now supposed to have been two white horses hitched to the fence along the road near where the grave was found. Another neighbor, generously contributing to the community's avid interest, said that late at night he had heard a team galloping along the road drawing a heavy wagon which he could hear pounding from rut to rut.

As the interest spread, other volunteers contributed to it. The community seethed. The following Sunday our meadow was crowded with sight-seers. They came by wagon and on horseback from everywhere near by, and by train from West Chester and Wilmington and Philadelphia. Agents of law and dispensers of justice came; their presence deepened the apprehension into which I and my brothers had by this time descended. Yet I recall that when a local justice of the peace, Squire Dougherty, who was very fat, bent stertorously over to measure the grave with a tapeline, I was able, in spite of my very serious perturbation, to whisper to my brother, "What the devil difference could it make whether the grave was thirty-six inches wide, or only thirty-five?"

But that flash of defiant insouciance was short-lived. The tension of the community, the deepening concern of my parents, was too much for me. I told my mother. I can still see her hurrying from the house to carry calm to the excited neighborhood.

Soon, as I moved about the roads, I could observe, on the faces of elders passing, looks of an intentness with which they had not previously honored me. The intentness was in some cases accompanied by a manner of disapproval; I was made to feel that some of the neighborhood elders considered that I would come to a bad end. The neighbor who had heard the galloping horses and the rumbling wagon seemed to entertain this notion with especial strength. The incident, I think, accounted for a dubious speculation about me that lasted for some years. After I had left the community, when stories began to come back about my doing well, the stories encountered skepticism.

That passed away in time, and in due course I became the beneficiary of that generous trait of human nature which attributes to the successful greater worthiness than they themselves claim. Legends arose about my goodness, my seriousness, about my precocity and resourcefulness, legends based on specific incidents which I was not myself able to recall.

One story still told in that community after I had grown children—indeed, told to my children as proof of their father's high quality—was concerned with the death of the dog we had when I was a child. I remember him well. His name was Tare. And I remember his death, administered to him in kindness when age made him miserable. I can still see the zigzag wound made by a load of shot, the deep red blood and the slightly less red flesh—the spectacle was one of the searing experiences of my childhood.

Nothing more than that can I remember. But the legend says I determined Tare must have a funeral. The consignment of a dog to his eternal resting place could be simple enough. I needed only to load his dead body onto my little wagon and pull him halfway across the field to the brow of a hill where it was our custom to bury the animals that died on the farm. But, so I am assured, I felt that an interment so simple would not be adequate to the virtues of the deceased dog. There must be mourners, a funeral procession. This I achieved by putting some corn into my funeral wagon, and strewing it as I went, thus insuring a retinue of chickens and ducks who, so far as they were concerned, were intent only on corn, but to me were a cortege of mourners.

My brothers and I knew every nut tree for miles about, and in the autumn stripped not only the trees on our own farm but every other one that was not pre-empted by other boys. Farmers who did not have boys of their own were willing to let us take the nuts; on farms where we were forbidden, we entered anyhow, as marauders, the expedition the more alluring for that. To gather a bushel or so of chestnuts in an afternoon was easy. We culled the ones that might have worms—we knew how to recognize them—and stored the good ones in the attic, where they dried out, the meat shrinking inward from the hull and becoming sweet. Today there is not a chestnut tree in all that countryside: a blight destroyed them.

Whether the boys in the neighborhood today know what they have missed, I cannot tell. Perhaps they do not care. I observe they do not gather the walnuts, which are still abundant. When I was a boy not a walnut escaped us, except such few as the squirrels reached before we did; and the squirrels must have found our competition severe. From the trees on our own farm we would bring the walnuts home in bags. To strip the trees along the roads some distance away we would go in a wagon. The pile we accumulated behind the woodshed was sometimes three feet high. Smashing the green, pulpy outside hull, I enjoyed the acrid scent and did not object to—on the contrary, regarded with pride—the stain that for several weeks gave greenish-black palms to the hands of every boy in the neighborhood. The nuts, cleaned down to the hard inner shell, we spread on the sloping roof of a shed, until the sun should dry them. Afterwards we stored them in the attic, in receptacles safeguarded against mice. Winter nights, or snowy Sunday afternoons, we cracked them, usually with a stone or hammer; I once encountered serious disapproval for using my mother's flatiron, sometimes called, to my mystification, a sad iron.

With trap, gun and stalking dog—and without any hunting license, for none was then required on a farmer's own land, and indeed without great regard for legally limited seasons—we pursued every living wild thing in the countryside. Much of our marksmanship with the gun we learned at the expense of ground hogs which had their holes in the clover field, the more wary ones in the edge of the woods where they were safer from being dug out, and from which they could make forays into the clover. A dog we had, a Newfoundland named Frank, was famous for his skill in creeping between a feeding ground hog and his hole. I could do that myself; I would grab my game by a hind leg or by the tail. The quail and the gray squirrels we pursued so constantly that for a few years they were exterminated.

In two rocky clumps on a neighbor's farm were dens of foxes, who did not conform to the legend which says a fox is too intelligent to steal chickens in his home neighborhood. Against them we pursued constant warfare, but never succeeded in driving them away. Weasels, equally destructive to chickens, lived in crevices of the rocky side of the Glory Hole. Raccoons inhabited hollow tree trunks in our woods and in the woods of a neighbor; one old tree has been the home of successive generations of 'coons for more than fifty years, to my knowledge—I see the tracks of the latest generation frequently. Opossums I frequently caught in traps, without reward except the fun of it, for their hides were valueless and we would not eat their flesh, though many said it was palatable. Trapping skunks was more remunerative; some of my spending money came from that source; a hide almost all black was more valuable than a black and white one.

After the sons had left the farm, when I used to come home on visits, I could measure the effect of our absence, and of my father's increasing years, by the greater daring of the wild life. Year by year the rabbits chewed the bark off the apple trees nearer and nearer to the house. Once, coming home, I noticed that a squirrel had built a nest in the eaves of the woodshed, and reflected, with some feeling, that he would not have dared do that when the house teemed with boys. On a later visit, when my parents were getting quite old, I saw a fox run leisurely across the field beyond the lane. At a point not more than two hundred yards away he stood and stared for some minutes at the house as if he speculated on whether it meant much danger to him. I felt unreasoning anger. The sight caused in me at once resentment and poignance. I had been reflecting on my parents' increasing age, their gradual drawing inward, my father letting more and more of the fields lie uncultivated, weeds and bushes growing unmolested which once he would have grubbed relentlessly. To the somber mood I was in the impudence of that fox was the final touch; it turned my mood to angry resentment against something I could not prevent.

We almost never had parties in the sense of people coming to the house in numbers. The only people I can recall as coming in the evenings were two or three neighbors who infrequently came to play cards. The game was called "forty-five"; it was the only card game I ever saw until I went away from home. How it was played I do not remember. All I recall is that from time to time there was an exciting climax, perhaps the winning of a game or a trick, marked by one player banging his card and his fist down on the table and shouting triumphantly, "Fahrty-five."

For parties in the sense of dancing and playing the fiddle there were enough of ourselves, with one or two neighbors, the whole group male except my mother. After supper we would raise the lid of the table upright on its hinges and push it and the chairs back to the wall. My father would get out the fiddle and run his bow across a lump of resin, and tune the strings; it was he who always began the fiddling, though during the evening two or three of my brothers would spell him.

In intervals in the fiddling one of my brothers would play the accordion—he could make it sound like a bagpipe playing "The Campbells Are Coming"; or a mouth organ—there were always one or two in the house; or a jew's-harp—one of my brothers was extraordinarily skillful at that. The dancing was mainly solo, jigs, and reels in which all took part, infrequently a waltz by two of my brothers. But both the dancing and the fiddling were incidental, the whole spirit of the evening was just fun.

Always the tunes my father played were the same, principally the eight or ten he had brought with him from Ireland; I have named some of them on another page. The only ones he learned after he came to America were "Old Dan Tucker," "The Virginia Reel," "Old Folks at Home," "Pop Goes the Weasel," "Money Musk," "Auld Lang Syne." By the time he had been in America four or five years he had completed his repertoire and he never added to it. He did not want to and we did not wish him to. What we liked was familiarity, not novelty. When my brothers occasionally made halfhearted efforts to introduce into our family parties tunes they had heard on visits to the city, it was an annoyance. Had they persisted we would have resented it.

Occasionally there was singing, but not often, and only a few tunes. The two songs my father had were not in key with the fiddling and dancing, which were gay. "Shool, Shool, Shool A Grah" was very mournful, and my father's other song, "Bonaparte Crossing the Alps"—it had another and less well-known name, "The Green Linnet"—while not so sad, was sober, majestic. It was a ballad written, I imagine, after the time the French sent a fleet and made other gestures toward helping the Irish in an uprising for independence in 1798, or perhaps it was written after Bonaparte's death—the song was in a spirit of heroic devotion to him, yet had a mood either of regret for the failure of his gesture toward Ireland, or of mourning for him. The refrain, after each stanza, was

Are you gone—will I never see you any more?

The song, in celebrating Bonaparte's feats, knowing its business was to be musical, quite properly refused to be inconvenienced by awkwardnesses of history or of spelling of place names:

The cold, lofty Alps you freely went over,
  Which nature had placed in your way,
That Marengo Saloney around you did hover,
  And Paris did rejoice the next day.
It grieves me the hardships you did undergo,
  Over mountains you traveled all covered with snow,
The balance of power your courage laid low,
  Are you gone—will I never see you more?

[44]

The crowned heads of Europe, when you were in splendor,
Fain would they have you submit.
But the Goddess of Freedom soon bid them surrender,
And lowered the standard to your wit;
Old Frederick's colors to France you did bring,
Yet his offspring found shelter under your wing.

One verse contained a phrase which I did not understand but which, by the mere sound of it, thrilled me greatly. I never knew what "the Mamelukes on the Nile" were, but I felt they were very sinister, something to be feared and resisted; and that Bonaparte's enemies were wicked to have joined them:

That numbers of men are eager to slay you,
Their malice you viewed with a smile.
Their gold through all Europe they sowed to betray you,
And they joined the Mamelukes on the. Nile.

My mother's song was less serious, indeed was lively. It was American, and old. I imagine she had learned it as a young girl about the time she came to America, in the 1840s:

It's every Sunday morning,
When I am by your side,
We'll jump into the wagon
And we'll all take a ride.

Wait for the wagon,
Wait for the wagon,
Wait for the wagon,
And we'll all take a ride.

The popular songs that sprang up in the cities during the period of my boyhood passed over our heads; hardly did we hear of them. As I look back I can recall only a few, and only fragments of those; they had been picked up, I presume, by my brothers in the city at minstrel shows or elsewhere. I recall one of my brothers singing a few lines from the *Mikado*, new in the early 1880s, and also "My Bonnie Lies Over the Ocean," and also

White wings that never grow weary
They carry me over the sea.

[45]

I remember another of my brothers humming "Climbing up Dem Golden Stairs," and a ditty of which two lines were

> *Is this Mr Riley*
> *That's thought of so highly?*

and a frivolous love song

> *Over the garden wall,*
> *The prettiest girl of all.*

But usually these modern ditties did not please us, either as to words or as to music. None was ever incorporated into our standard repertoire for family gatherings. For these, as for any airs that did not appeal to us, we had a phrase of derogation, derived from what source I know not, "the tune the old cow died on."

In the neighborhood years before, or perhaps where one of my parents had lived in Ireland, there had been a man who was very proud of his wife's dancing and singing. Her name was Narry, and when she was about to dance her husband would cry, "Make way for Narry!" If she was about to sing, he would command, "Silence for Narry!" or "Hark to Narry!" These sayings we adapted for ourselves. During the evening there would be cries of "Make way for Tommy!" or "Silence for Willie!" The one thus introduced would go upon the floor with much grandiosity; he would circle the room in a kind of solo grand march and, still with an air of mocking, proceed to the center and—in a phrase we did not know but could have made use of—"do his stuff." Endless repetition of the quip, throughout the whole period when the boys were living at home, never diminished our zest in it; custom did not stale but rather increased the never-ending fun we found in repeating it.

Best by far in the dancing was my father; when he took the floor the rest of us formed a circle and looked on at him as at a master. The whole neighborhood felt the same about him. For nearly fifty years his dancing was the feature of the annual Catholic picnic, and occasionally of other neighborhood gatherings. He kept it up until he was well past seventy;

CORNELIUS SULLIVAN.

About 1890.

strangers would come to picnics, wait until Con Sullivan had danced and then drive away.

Our family parties at home would last until ten o'clock or so, which seemed quite late. Their termination, however, was not fixed by the clock, but by nature, by the pleasurable fatigue that came with lively dancing. The jollity and laughing would subside to a lower pitch, the dancing would be abandoned. My father would sing "Bonaparte Crossing the Alps." Toward the end of the evening he, or my mother, would sing, 'Shool, Shool, Shool A Grah." By that time we would all be in a quiet mood. But always there was a last upflare of the gayer mood. Always, as my mother suggested bedtime, some one of us would repeat the old rhyme; it must have been recited thousands of times in that house, but always it brought back high spirits:

> *Come to bed,*
> *Says Sleepy-head.*
> *Wait a while, says Slow.*
> *Put on the pot,*
> *Says Greedy-gut,*
> *And have a sup*
> *Before we go.*

Always the argument was won by Greedy-gut. My mother would go to the cupboard and bring out two or three pies; we boys would gorge, while my father moved about his bedtime ritual—going out on the porch to look at the sky and see what the weather next day was likely to be, seeing that the doors were fastened and the windows down. Finally he would begin the closing rite, the winding of the clock, and we boys would clamber up the stairs.

CHAPTER 5

W<small>E HAD</small> little money. I doubt if as much as seven hundred dollars ever passed through my father's hands in one year—to support a family which, when we were all young, was nine, and even after the sons began to leave averaged five. But a family that owns a little land and lives on it—if the land is fertile and not overburdened with taxes—is never poor, need never know want. Fear of poverty never entered the minds of us children. Of food we raised more than abundance. About all we needed to buy was sugar and molasses, salt, coffee and tea, a little soda for my mother's bread-making. We bought more than that, but that was about all that was indispensable.

For what we bought we paid mainly with eggs. To "go to the store" usually meant to take a basket filled with three or four days accumulation of eggs, and with it two empty vessels to be filled at the store, the molasses jug and the coal-oil can. Cloth had to be bought for the clothes my mother made for us, but always she bought strong materials, durable enough not only to last the child for whom they were made but to serve as hand-me-downs for the next younger. Always a boy's pants were a man's trousers cut short. The treatment which my next older brother accorded to his clothes was observed by me with the jealous and sometimes resentful interest of an heir to a hereditary estate.

My recollection about food is all of teeming abundance. The loaves of bread my mother made were of the shape of huge round mounds with flattened tops; a slice cut from the largest diameter, spread thick with butter, and on top of the butter molasses spread out in patterns we liked to make as we let it trickle from the jug—one such slice would have been a meal for a city boy. There were heaping piles of potatoes boiled or mashed, great bowls of toasted bread sopping in hot milk, immense dishes of corn-meal mush. Stirring the mush while it cooked was a long task—it was frequently mine.

From the kitchen ceiling hung a quarter or two of dried beef, flitches of bacon, hams. The latter were the fruit of hog killing, which occupied a busy day of late November. My father, usually with the help of a neighbor or two, would build an outdoor fire of logs, into which he threw several large stones. The stones, when hot, were placed in a barrel of water. This preparation and some other parts of the hog-killing ritual were fascinating; but the killing itself was a dreadful sight, from which I turned my eyes. The hog, caught by his hind legs, was turned upon his back, his squeals quickly ended by the long blade of a sharpened corn cutter thrust into his throat. He was hung by his hind legs from the limb of an orchard tree until the blood drained from him, after which he was dipped into the barrel of hot water, to soften his bristles. Once more the corn cutter was availed of, this time as a razor or scraper. With the animal cleaned and dressed, there followed a busy afternoon of carving and putting the smaller bits of meat into a grinder, from which issued coils of sausage. One by-product of the slaughter was a recognized trove of the small boy. The bladder, dried and filled with air, its orifice closed with a tightly knotted string, made a dearly prized toy balloon.

Autumn butchering was the only time we had fresh meat; I was not familiar with steaks or chops until after I had gone away from the farm. Freshly killed chickens we of course had often. From the garden we had fresh vegetables throughout the summer; in the fall cabbages and turnips were preserved in pits dug deep enough to escape frost and covered with earth. Potatoes, large piles of them, were stored in the cellar. In the cupboard were usually a big pan of rice pudding, and pies—apple, raisin, currant, blackberry in season, custard—of a size which later became obsolete, certainly in the circles in which I spent my maturity.

In the springhouse, set on flat stones in the water to keep them cool—the only refrigeration we knew—were pans of fresh milk with the yellowish cream at the top, other pans of skimmed milk and buttermilk, yet others of "bonny clabber," which was skimmed milk after it had stood for some days and turned into thick gobs of curds at the top with watery whey beneath. At any time, except perhaps the day after the weekly churning had emptied the pails of fresh milk, a troop of hungry men could make an ample meal without leaving the springhouse.

The springhouse was one of our principal sources of income. Every day my mother would skim the milk from the preceding day, lifting the cream that had come to the top by means of a "skimmer," a shallow circular rimless vessel of thin metal with holes in the bottom through which the watery part of the cream would drop back into the pail. Once a week the accumulated cream was churned. The churn we used was a barrel-shaped vessel, smaller than a barrel but larger than a keg. Churning was a plodding chore; the task was frequently mine. It did not lend itself to any exercise of the imagination except, after an hour or so, speculation about whether the butter had yet "come," to determine which there was increasingly frequent stopping of the churn, opening of the little door in the side and peering at the contents.

After the butter had come, my mother would take it out and knead it in a mass until the last trace of liquid was squeezed out. Then she would take in her left hand the butter mold, a circular wooden disk about three inches in diameter, upon the top of which was a pattern deeply engraved in the wood—the pattern on ours was a large strawberry. Using this as a base, she would build upon it short, large-bottomed cones, weighing a pound each.

The following day my father would take the butter "to town" with a few other farm products, dressed chickens, in season dressed turkeys, frequently a few bushels of potatoes. "Going to town" meant going to Wilmington, fifteen miles away. The trip, with one horse pulling a Dearborn wagon over dirt roads, consumed four or five hours. I make it now by automobile in thirty minutes. He would start not long after midnight so as to be at the market by the time customers arrived in the morning. If it were the dark of the moon, or if the weather made the road difficult for night driving, he would go the afternoon before, and sleep in his wagon, covered by a horse blanket, until market opened. His return I watched for eagerly. He would bring me a stick or two of candy or a few ginger cakes, in season an orange or banana.

Those trips to town accounted for perhaps half the farm income. Most of the rest came from sale of the heavier crops, wheat, corn, hay, straw. To supplement this my father occasionally worked on the roads. The custom of the community was that each farmer "worked out" his road tax, which meant, as a rule, that he kept up such roads as passed through his farm or abutted on it. To maintain such roads as were not thus cared for, and also the roads in the villages, the township supervisor employed such help as wanted the work. The pay was $1.25 a day; my father, being a kind of foreman, got $1.50. A boy got fifty or seventy-five cents, depending on his age. In an old account book my father kept I find an entry reading, "boy and mule, $\frac{1}{2}$ day, $62\frac{1}{2}$ cents." The boy was I. My task was picking stones, tossing them into the cart drawn by the mule and dumping them at a spot where the road passed through a swampy place.

Occasionally the near-by nursery sent us work to do nights at home. It was spoken of as "wiring labels." The labels were little flat pieces of wood, with a small nick on each side, by which a wire could be attached, so as later to tie the label to the plant. The labels were brought to our house in barrels, together with the wires, cut to right length. Our work was to attach a wire to each label, by a little twist; it was easily accomplished. The whole family sat down to it after supper, in the kitchen, and talked happily as we worked. The pay was twelve cents for a thousand labels. An old letter shows we received fifty thousand labels on a Monday and had finished them by Saturday.

One other source of income there was. After the sons began to go to the city each would send back fifty or a hundred dollars from his year's savings. Sometimes this was to aid toward the interest on the mortgage. Other times it was to help pay for the schooling of the younger boys; each son, as he went out, felt responsible for seeing that the next younger one got an education. I, being the youngest, had the benefit of this system without the burden. Nevertheless, for several years after I became an earner I sent back something each year. By this time the money meant less, for all the sons were mature and beginning to prosper. My contributions could be used for small comforts for my parents, by this time aging.

Sometimes what we regarded as comforts for our parents were by them regarded as fantastic and unnecessary modernities. What we regarded as desirable ornaments they looked upon as wanton extravagances. When my brother wanted a window cut in the barn, for the sake of better architectural balance, he avoided sending for the carpenter until a day when he knew my mother would be away. On her return there was a scene. For years my brothers, concerned about my parents alone on the farm, wanted to put in a telephone so that we could call them up and talk with them. The innovation was resisted successfully until within a few years of my father's death, and was accomplished then only by some intimidation. The brothers came in force, with the telephone materials and workmen ready.

Once I took the high hand with them. I was annoyed by finding that nice dress goods and good carpets we sent my mother were put away in bureaus and closets, while the floors remained bare or covered with ancient carpets home-made of rag, and she continued to wear dresses that continued to grow older. New furniture we sent to the farm was carefully wrapped and stowed away—coming back, we would find the old chairs and tables and bedsteads and bedspreads still in fond use. I was especially annoyed by the recalcitrance of my father about a cushion and blanket. It was his custom, as he grew older, to take long naps on a settee by the stove. The cushion on the settee was a patched relic; the blanket my father preferred and clung to was a rough horse blanket.

One day, returning for a visit, I deliberately prepared myself to act as if I were angry. The moment I greeted them, while they were still in the gentle mood of welcoming me, I pretended to erupt at sight of the horse blanket. Storming, I tore it and the old cushion from the settee and carried them out into the orchard. Then I carried out a broken-legged table and two decrepit chairs, together with some old clothing from the closets. After replacing them with new things we had brought on previous visits, I made my revolution secure by going out and making a bonfire of the discarded articles. Returning to the house, I overheard my father saying to my mother plaintively, "That Markie is a destructionate bye." The manner of both of them was one of pathetic helplessness. The net of the experience was sadness for me, which increased as I grew older; I felt I had triumphed only because age was weakening their wills. I do not like to dwell on that memory.

CHAPTER 6

SUCH PART of culture—points of view, codes of conduct, traditions and the like—as came to me from within the family, was, of course, purely Irish, though an Irish already modified in the direction of English by residence of the two races side by side in Ireland for seven centuries. Both my parents knew Gaelic well; they fell into it whenever they wished to discuss anything which they preferred to keep from the children. Possibly it was for that protective reason that they never taught it to us. I never knew more than half-a-dozen words—one was *alannah*, by which my mother would address me in tenderness, or in commiseration for a childish sorrow; it meant "my dear" or "my child." Stray copies of a periodical devoted to Irish immigrants, the Boston *Pilot*, came to the house occasionally, but I saw this less frequently than any of a dozen American periodicals. In myself I can recognize many qualities that are Irish by blood, few that are Irish by communication from without.

Such part of culture as came to me from the community, from the public schools or other neighborhood contacts, was in derivation completely English. The early settlement had been English exclusively, and the stock remained exclusively English for more than a century and a half. I have a map of the county dated 1860; on it the only farm marked with an owner's name other than English was my father's, though the Irish were already present in some numbers as immigrant laborers and artisans. By the 1880s the Irish became farm owners in considerable numbers.

The background of the community, its origins and its traditions and ways of life, was as English as England itself. Nearly all the place names were British. When I was a boy we used to describe ourselves as living in "Londongrove Township, Chester County, Pennsylvania." Two other townships within a few miles contain the name "London"—one the early settlers named, ambitiously, New London; the other the settlers designated with two tokens of ancestral affection, London Britain. Of the fifty-odd townships in Chester County, almost every one shows by its name a tie to some community in England: East and West Nottingham, East and West Marlborough, Upper Oxford and Lower Oxford, Kennett Township and Kennett Square, East and West Fallowfield. A few townships, villages and creeks have Indian names: Wawaset, Hockessin, Toughkennamon, Octorara. One is named for an animal that once roamed there, Elk. That spot must have been the farthermost eastern point of the elks' range.

The early settlers were Quakers; within a few miles of the farm are ten old Quaker meetinghouses—I doubt if anywhere else are so many within so small an area. They are about equally divided between "Orthodox," which was the old sect, and "Hicksite," the name taken by a dissenting group in the early part of the last century. Some of the old meetinghouses are still in use. But some open their doors only once a year or so, when some venerable Friend is carried to rest beside his forebears. When I was a boy the "plain" dress of the Quakers was a common sight—on any day in the village you would see a dozen. Now it is extremely uncommon. I doubt if I have seen a Quaker hat or bonnet in thirty years. The locution "thee" survives but is rare.

Just to the west of us was a section in which the early settlers were Scotch and Scotch-Irish Presbyterians. Some twenty miles to the north and east was a tract settled by Welsh Baptists, marked by the township names of Uwchlan and Tredyffrin. About thirty miles to the north are the tracts that William Penn gave to various German sects, the Mennonites, Amish, Dunkards, Lutherans. All the German settlers came to be called, locally, "Pennsylvania Dutch." To this day they keep many of their ancient ways, preserve their forms of worship, speak a modification of their early tongue, wear austere black clothing.

In the immediate neighborhood of the farm most of the early ways of life came from the Quakers, some from the Presby-

[55]

terians. Both groups conformed, quite as much as Emerson's New England, to the ideal of plain living and high thinking. The plain living—perhaps because the land was so fertile— did not, as in New England, express itself in parsimony or excessive frugality, but rather in hard work, thrift and the amassing of substance. There are farmhouses still standing, built nearly a hundred years ago, of brick or masonry, some of them three stories high, which in any city would rank as mansions. Along the streams, even the tiny ones, every mile or so were mills, saw or grist, occasionally a primitive mill for making cloth. Because the land was level, water races had to be dug half a mile long to get a few feet of drop for the power. Within two miles of our farm were eight mills; today only one is still in use, two are in ruins, five have so completely disappeared that hardly millsite, dam or race is identifiable.

The high thinking expressed itself in zeal for education, concern about public affairs, devotion to good causes. The country thereabout was dotted with ancient academies, the seats of learning before state-supported public schools came; at one academy near by, New London, three members of the first Constitutional Convention were educated. Two little hamlets, so small you could drive through without noticing them, were the publication places of pre-Civil War newspapers.

Strong antislavery sentiment was universal. Not merely sentiment but works; half-a-dozen houses near by were stations on the "underground railroad" along which the abolitionist Quakers secretly transferred runaway slaves toward Canada. Some fifteen miles away occurred one of the important episodes of pre-Civil War history, the Christiana riot, caused by the attempt of a Southern slaveowner and a posse to take back a runaway.

Everywhere there were neighborhood "literary societies," their meetings prized diversions of the winter months. A principal feature of the program was a debate. In old letters of my brothers I find mention of having taken part in debates on "Resolved that Women Should Vote"; "Resolved that the Indians Should be Made Citizens"; "Resolved that Education

Has More Influence than Wealth"—in that community the affirmative of that proposition would always win.

Because the Quakers were the old settlers, while the Irish were recent immigrants, the former had the larger farms, the Irish the smaller ones. Neither that economic distinction, nor the sectarian one, nor anything else, made for anything but liking between the two. The Quakers, by a tenet of their faith as well as by their character as individuals, lived up, in that small community, to the spirit of neighborly obligation. The responsibility which Quakers, by a rule of their sect, accepted for the well-being of their own they extended to their neighbors belonging to other churches. The sick cow of a small farmer who had but five or six would bring a visit from the owner of thirty or forty, with advice about treatment, or more practical help if that were needed. The owner of one horse could get the loan of another for farm operations in which two were essential. If a farmer fell sick during a period when seasonal activity was essential, his neighbors would plant his crop for him or harvest it. The Quakers took pleasure in seeing their neighbors of another sect and race grow in prosperity, and facilitated it. If a man who had not yet attained a farm of his own wished to buy, a well-to-do Quaker would loan him the money; on mortgage to be sure, and with interest, of which the rate, in those post-Civil War days, was high—I observe from old records that my father, during a few years of the 1870s, paid eight per cent. But if payment was difficult when interest day came around, the lender was patient and helpful. I have seen a Quaker lender accept an interest payment of two hundred dollars, and then make the payer a present of a mule worth nearly a third the amount.

The regard between the two sects was not modified by any faintest self-consciousness about difference of religion, though the Irish, with unfailing insight and humor, had their occasional laugh at the Quaker capacity for observing punctiliously the requirements of their religion without letting it interfere with their worldly practicality. This ingenuity in achieving difficult consistency was illustrated by a story which we greatly enjoyed telling and hearing—in all unsophisticated communities a story, if it is good and well told, is valued less for the novelty than for its familiarity. A Quaker, driving a cow in the road, encountered provoking frustration when the cow, through some inherited bovine caution, refused to cross a bridge. The Quaker, when all his gentler arts of coaxing had failed, was obliged to consider forms of urging which to most farmers were commonplace but which to Quakers were made dubious by the rules of their faith. "Well," he addressed the cow, "I cannot swear at thee, for that is against my religion; and I cannot strike thee, for that is against my religion, too, but"—with a spiritual release of energy brought by decision arrived at under difficulty—"I can, and I will, twist thy tail the damnedest."

CHAPTER 7

Wʜᴇɴ ᴛʜᴇ sᴛᴀᴛᴇ of Pennsylvania, in the 1830s, decreed free public schools, the first one for our neighborhood was built on a lot adjoining a corner of our farm. Made of timbers from the neighboring woods, it did service as a school for some forty years. Afterwards it became a tenant house, occupied by a colored family. The boy of the family, about my age, was my frequent playmate; each spring, when the plow went over what was now the colored family's garden but had been the schoolyard, we used to search the upturned furrows for coins or other relics that a former generation of boys might have lost. We never found any.

The building has long been torn down; the land on which it stood is now part of a field. Only one who remembered it would be able to tell where the schoolhouse stood. In the road that gave access to it, now long abandoned, are trees as big as a man's trunk. Though that old school gave education to forty years of that community, there is no trace of it left, unless it be in the minds of those to whom it gave learning—or, rather, as an intangible legacy in the minds of their children, for I think there is no person now alive who went to the old log school.

The successor to the old timber schoolhouse, the one I attended, was on a lot adjoining another corner of our farm, on the edge of a woods which gave the school its official name, East Grove. The community, which prized education, gave care to building it. It was of brick, solid and substantial, with a stone porch and pillars supporting an overhanging roof. It still stands. During the 1920s the spirit of progress relegated it to disuse; it and the half-dozen other one-room schoolhouses of the township were supplanted by a "consolidated school" to which the children are carried in buses.

The change, I think, may have been accompanied by, or led

[59]

to, a change in point of view. There is a difference between going to school and being taken to it; between the old way of my boyhood, when we trudged to school through all kinds of weather, or were taken in the family wagon by our parents when the weather was too bad, and the new way, in which children are picked up by a tax-paid bus at their front doors or at the point in the road nearest their homes. True, in both the old way and the new, the state provided the education, but the introduction of buses makes a difference in the amount of effort required of pupils and parents, a diminution of self-help, an increase in dependence upon the state; an increase in disposition to look upon the state as a giver.

After the buses and the consolidated school made the East Grove school obsolete it stood for some years vacant and forlorn. Lately the local branch of the Izaak Walton League of America, taking advantage of the solidly built walls, made it into a rural clubhouse. Within, where once hung a hallowed inspiration to industry and thrift, a picture of the venerable countenance of Benjamin Franklin, now hangs a symbol of the building's altered function, a stuffed sailfish that I caught in Florida.

My starting to school was late: I was eight years old. On a day in early September—the year was 1882—as the school bell clanged the opening of the term, my older brother took me on his back, carried me across the field and down the hill. That my brother took me suggests that I must have been shy, although I was a year or two beyond the age at which most of the children of the neighborhood made their debut at school, without benefit of elders and on their own small legs.

When my brother and I reached the school he set me down in the porch, took me by the hand and led me through the door. I could see at the farther end a platform the whole width of the room, raised about six inches, in the middle of it the teacher's desk. On the rear wall, and covering almost the whole of it, were two immense blackboards, at their bottoms narrow ledges on which were chalk crayons. In the middle of the room was a huge stove. On each side were two rows of desks and seats for the pupils, the left side for boys, the right for girls. From the ceiling dangled a rope, its lower end high enough from the floor to be reachable only by the teacher; it rang the bell that was in a tiny turret above the roof. On the walls of the room were a few prints and chromos, accompanied by forceful admonition to correct behavior. The one I most vividly remember—though after I was some thirty years of age I ventured to disobey its behest—was a picture I never saw at any other place; it was of a young man with a strikingly vacant countenance, smoking a cigar, and a legend reading: "A cigar is a weed with fire at one end and a fool at the other."

The teacher was a young woman of the neighborhood. During the four years I attended there were three in succession. I adored all three, and doubtless would have adored any other young woman having the relation of teacher to me. I recall discussing gravely with another Catholic boy whether the teacher—she bore the prim name of Amanda Goodwin—was equal in beauty and goodness to the Virgin Mary, whether it would be a sin to revere her as much as the Virgin.

Our progress in the school was measured by gradation from First Reader to Fifth. We described ourselves as "in the Second Reader" or "in the Third Reader." The "readers" were the backbone of education, in East Grove and throughout the nation; they were to the America of the 1880s what the "New England Primer" had been to the America of the preceding century.

The series of readers used at East Grove was Barnes'. They were an imitation of but inferior to McGuffey's, which were the standard readers throughout most of America. But of this inferiority I was gloriously unaware. Quite a few of my circumstances were less than best, but at the time I did not know it, and by the time I was aware of it, it did not matter.

Barnes' readers in our community (as McGuffey's elsewhere in America) were, to all the children, the introduction to good reading, to literature—to many of the pupils the readers were practically all the literature they ever knew. While writing this volume I procured from the Congressional Library a copy of Barnes' Fifth Reader, to see what residuum of it remained in my memory. More of it, of course, remains than I was able to identify, for no amount of probing into the depths of any mind can tell certainly how much of its contents came from any one source.

Of the selections in Barnes' Fifth Reader the ones I could identify as having first come into my mind from that source included the familiar ones that were common to most readers: Poe's "Raven," Whittier's "Snowbound," Drake's "American Flag," O'Hara's "Bivouac of the Dead." The last was very familiar at a time when the Civil War was only twenty years past, when the members of the Grand Army of the Republic were the most glamorous figures in every community, their annual parade on Decoration Day standing rather above Fourth of July and equal to Christmas as a national holiday:

> The muffled drum's sad roll has beat
> The soldier's last tattoo. . . .
> On Fame's eternal camping ground
> Their silent tents are spread,
> And Glory guards with solemn round
> The bivouac of the dead.

There were, of course, Gray's "Elegy" and "Curfew Shall Not Ring Tonight." While I do not find "The Wreck of the Hesperus" in Barnes' Fifth Reader, it must have been in the Fourth or the Third, for I recall declaiming it on a painful Friday afternoon, with an inadequacy of gesture which was disappointing to the teacher, for she believed that superiority of performance on "recitation day" was an index of all-round excellence.

One bit of verse, not widely known, that found long lodgment in my memory was "An Order for a Picture," by a minor poetess, Alice Cary:

> Oh, good painter, tell me true,
> Has your hand the cunning to draw,
> Shapes of things that you never saw?
> Ay? Well, here is an order for you.

EAST GROVE SCHOOL IN 1891.

The figure on the steps is Mark Sullivan's brother, then teacher of the school.

The picture which the painter was thus besought to depict was of

> *Woods and corn fields a little brown . . .*
> *These and the house where I was born,*
> *Low and little and black and old*
> *With children as many as it can hold. . . .*

We were taught simple arithmetic, spelling, geography and some elementary American history. The only suggestion of science was some teaching of physiology, for the inclusion of which, in the curriculum prescribed by the state, we were indebted to the zeal of temperance leaders. The teaching consisted largely of vivid emphasis upon the effect of "drink" on the body, conveyed by means of terrifyingly colored pictures of the internal organs in progressive stages of alcoholic degeneration. In most of the common schools of that place and period there were branches of the L.T.L., Loyal Temperance Legion. I remember being taught and reciting a "piece," tragic in nature, which began:

> *On a rich man's table, rim to rim,*
> *There stood two glasses, filled to the brim. . . .*

The rest I have forgotten, but I am confident research would reveal that one of the glasses was filled with water, the other with wine; that one young man drank the water and lived a happy life, while another drank the wine and went to destruction.

In the part of the grove that had been partially cleared as the schoolyard the trees left standing were happily so situated with relation to each other that by adding a little imagination to geometry we could consider that three of the trees marked the lines of a baseball diamond. First base was a beech tree, second a black oak, and third the stump of a chestnut. This improvisation made the distance between first base and second quite short; it was accomplished by almost any runner, and getting to first meant, practically, getting to second. But the distance between second and third was terrifying. Many a runner met a fate he did not deserve through the whim of nature that had caused a chestnut tree to grow a greater distance from an oak than was provided by the rules of baseball.

We did not know our game as baseball but merely as "ball," and in other respects we failed to conform to the orthodox formula. Our ball was just a sphere of solid black rubber, about an inch and a half in diameter. Putting a runner out was accomplished not by touching him with the ball but by throwing the ball across his course, between him and the base toward which he was running. Sometimes running boy and flying ball reached the same spot at the same time, and the encounter could be painful. But we were accustomed to such impacts, for with the same ball we engaged in a diversion which we called "sockey up." I do not know the derivation of the name, and I never heard of it nor read of it anywhere else. The game consisted merely of one boy trying to "sock" another with the ball, and the other trying to dodge. The one who submitted his body to the role of target stood close to the schoolhouse wall, so that the ball, if it missed him, would bounce back to the boy who had the more fortunate role. Another game, equally simple, was called—I spell it phonetically for I have never seen it in print—"tickily high over." It consisted of a boy on one side of the schoolhouse throwing the ball over the roof. The only element of game, or chance, lay in the fact that the boy on the other side, who was to catch it, could not know which part of the roof the ball would come over.

I remained at East Grove four years. East Grove corresponded to what would be called, in a system more elaborately organized, a primary, or elementary school. I think I did well in the simple studies, though the only evidence I have is some cards, brightly ornamented with pictures of flowers and birds, bearing the inscription "Reward of Merit" and authoritatively signed by the teacher.

When I was twelve I went to a slightly more advanced school, at a near-by village, West Grove; it would be called now a high school. In good weather I walked the two miles forth and back; for a few weeks in the depth of winter I boarded from Monday to Friday with a family in the village.

That was my first experience of being away from home overnight. It did not disturb me. For I was adventurous, had always a zest for reaching out into widening circles of my little world. I liked to go fishing and follow the stream farther and farther away from home. If going to the mill were up, I liked to go to one as far away as practicable, or one that had not become familiar. I liked to be, in the phrase we had, "on the go." But always I liked coming home, always felt pleasure as I neared the house. Monday mornings, setting out for West Grove, I would go joyously, skipping all the way. But Friday afternoons I liked to return, taking a way that led across fields through the snow. Coming that way brought me to the house from the west, with the sinking sun gleaming against the windowpanes. Hurrying on, as I came nearer I would see through the window the glow of the fire in the stove—it had a girdle of isinglass around it—and my mother lighting the coal-oil lamp. As I entered the house I would feel the rush of warmth and the scent of rusks, baked for my welcome.

CHAPTER 8

IN THE NEIGHBORHOOD a "sale" was a social event. Like a wedding or a funeral, it had an appreciation additional to that which attended its primary purpose. In that day, when motion pictures did not exist, when professional entertainments of any sort were rare, long before the radio was dreamed of or the telephone familiar—in that day any occasion that would eke out the church as the principal place for coming together was prized as an opportunity for neighborly gathering. Happily conforming to this purpose, the sales usually came in early March, in anticipation of April 1, which was "moving day" for such families as had sold their farms or were for any reason moving from one home to another. The season was propitious, for in early March farm work was not pressing, and the members of every family were eager for release from the home-staying that had been enforced by snow and roads deep in mud or frost-made ruts.

At the sales my father would occasionally bid on a cow or a wagon or any secondhand farm tool of which he felt in need. My mother would follow the offering of furniture and dishware. Toward the end of the sale the auctioneer would put up odds and ends in lots, often dumped together in a barrel or in one of the "bushel baskets" which on every farm were used for measuring potatoes and corn. Often such books as the house contained were dumped into a bushel basket and offered for bids that began with one cent and rarely went above ten; whatever the price, the buyer paid it more for the container than for the contents. In this part of a sale my mother was occasionally the highest bidder, justifying the strain on her instinct for economy by the thought that a bushel basket was always useful—but thinking, in the back of her head, that the books might include something that would facilitate the education of the children, one of the very few purposes that to her were more compelling than economy.

When she brought her treasure trove home I would dig eagerly into the literary omnium gatherum, usually finding, to my disappointment, that most of the books were collections of the sermons of George Fox or old biographies of William Penn; or the life, travels and religious labors of Quaker missionaries; or other exegeses of Quaker dogma, not appetizing to a young boy. Occasionally, however, there would be a more satisfying nugget. From such a source came the first novel I ever read, a copy of *Uncle Tom's Cabin*, with, tragically, the last ten or twenty pages missing. I can recall devouring it in the house, until time for a chore in the barn, to which I carried the book concealed beneath my coat, and there digging myself into the hay to keep warm while I shuddered at the cruelty of Simon Legree and cried over Little Eva.

That incomplete copy of *Uncle Tom's Cabin* was, during the early part of my youth, the only novel in the house and almost the only book of any kind, excepting the prayer book and the schoolbooks of the children. The only pamphlet permanently in the house was the almanac, a yellow-backed annual presented each New Year's Day by the keeper of the village store. Its contents, in addition to the calendar and the accompanying table of phases of the moon and the weather predictions, consisted of testimonials and other laudations of Hood's Sarsaparilla (some years it was Ayer's Cherry Pectoral) together with anecdotes, jokes and brief paragraphs of uplifting moral admonition. No periodical came to the house regularly, and no newspaper regularly except one, a local weekly. At first it was the county-seat paper, the West Chester *Village Record;* later that was displaced by a weekly started in a town nearer our neighborhood, the Kennett *Advance*. There came irregularly, however, occasional copies of Philadelphia and New York papers, and chance copies of magazines.

The Kennett *Advance* provided my first periodical reading. I knew when the weekly issue would arrive at the post office, and used to walk to the village to get it. Sometimes I would put the folded copy to my nose to enjoy the smell of fresh ink. On my way home I would read as I walked. To me, for a brief period of my youth, the Kennett *Advance* was not merely a weekly paper, it was the whole world of reading, of print. The editor was a man of unusual cultivation; his writing had personality, style, which I am quite sure influenced me; I owe him a debt. He is long dead, the paper has long ceased publication.

Acquaintance with the Kennett *Advance,* and the pleasure I got from it, led me to look about for other papers. I could hardly have been ten when I conceived and began to carry out a project which I never heard of any other boy attempting. I undertook to collect issues of every newspaper in the world; it was a youthful zest for collecting, more intense, I think, than other boys' preoccupation with stamps. I got from the store in the village a pine dry-goods box, in which I began my amassing with copies of the local weeklies. As chance Philadelphia and New York papers came to the house I added one of each. When in my reading I saw quotations to which were appended the names of newspapers in other towns and cities, I sought ways of getting them. One device that consumed many of my pennies consisted of sending a postal card asking for a sample copy, in the slightly devious hope that the publisher would look upon me as a potential subscriber. I can only condone the deviousness upon the plea that collectors in every field have an ethics flexible only as to collecting, and otherwise not peccable. When, in school, I learned about the cities of Europe and Asia, I assumed they had newspapers, and tried to find what the names of the papers were, and how I might get copies. I recall being thrilled by seeing mention of a paper called the Bombay *Gazette,* and wondering by what device I could get a copy, since a United States postal card would not reach Asia, nor a Bombay publisher think it worth while to venture a sample copy upon the possibility of getting a subscriber on a farm in Pennsylvania, especially since—so I assumed in my speculation upon this enterprise—the Bombay *Gazette* must be printed in a language other than English.

Hardly ever, I think, was any boy's zest for reading obliged to find satisfaction in material so fragmentary, diverse and altogether heterodox as that which drifted to our Pennsylvania farm. As my memory digs down through many strata of remembered reading I find the lowest to consist of strange and unrelated shards. The earliest reading, which in persons of normal experience consists of accepted children's classics, is in my case made up of fantastic scraps of unknown origin and dubious standing. I suppose that a child's early reading is important; the rhymes and story plots and characters he first comes in contact with are remembered longer than his later reading; his earliest reading becomes an especiallly permanent part of his mental furniture. In most respects, I think, I had a better youth than my children; almost the only times when I have envied them have been on the occasions when I came home from work in the evening, opened the door, heard upstairs the hum of my wife's lovely voice, went up and attended the family ritual for bedtime—my wife reading aloud, out of Scott or Dickens or Stevenson, while the children plashed abstractedly in the bathtub or gave a slow and divided attention to putting on their nightclothes.

The foundation stones of my house of reading are unique in their unorthodoxy. The earliest bit of verse I can recall—it has remained while poetry more worthy has escaped—was four lines which I think were in a school reader of one of my older brothers, read to me and memorized by me before I myself went to school:

> I hear a sound below me,
> A twitter of delight;
> It is my friend the swallow,
> Come Northward overnight.

The earliest thing I ever read that could be called a story was a bit of fiction in the *Village Record*. At that time local weeklies had not yet become exclusively devoted to neighborhood news. They were still close enough to the pre-telegraph and pre-railroad era to think of their function as in part the printing of accounts of world events and general literature, of a sort.

The *Village Record* story, which remains with me while a thousand subsequent novels are forgot, was about an ancient house, occupied by an old family. House and family were associated with a venerable tree that stood by the door. Through the generations there had been a legend, expressed in two lines of verse, which I can reproduce, though I have not seen or heard it since I was eight years old:

> *The house, the tree and the family—*
> *When one goes, then go all three.*

The story ended in a blasting devastation which began one night with the fall of the tree before a great wind, and the accompanying fulfillment of tragedy that the omen foretold.

Much of my earliest reading was just the flotsam of print that happened to drift to the farm—old newspapers that came as the wrappings of packages, periodicals left by visiting neighbors or picked up in the village by my older brothers; occasional copies of periodicals for boys loaned by a neighbor's son. I remember a copy of the Philadelphia *Sunday Press* containing an account of the death of Ulysses S. Grant; a *Harper's Weekly* containing a picture of General John A. Logan, then a candidate for vice-president on the ticket with James G. Blaine—Logan's immense mustache fascinated me; I decided I would have a mustache just as soon as nature would permit, and did not doubt that nature would give me one as long as Logan's. I recall, too, a copy of *Leslie's Weekly* containing a full-page woodcut of the death of the son of the Empress Eugénie, killed with an assagai while fighting the Zulus in Africa. Possibly it was the words "assagai" and "Zulu" that so strongly impressed me—I can remember the place I sat and the time of day when I gazed big-eyed at that lurid picture.

I cannot fathom what circumstance it was, of my youth, or of that Chester County community, that deprived me when grown of the nostalgic pleasure my American generation found in recalling the dime novels they had read as boys. I regret the deprivation, for it restricts my appreciation of Irvin Cobb's essay about his early reading of *Old Cap Collier*—I can appreciate Cobb's classic only for its literary quality; I wish I could appreciate it also as an experience shared. But I can remember reading only one dime novel. The circumstances conformed to tradition; it was in the haymow on a rainy afternoon. I do not think this was an enforced furtiveness; in the miscellaneousness of the jetsam of print that came to our house, my parents would hardly have singled out a dime novel for proscription.

I read the equivalent of dime novels, and parts of some dime novels themselves, in serial form, in a type of periodical of which chance copies came to our house. One was called the *Family Story Paper*, another bore the sentimental title *Golden Days;* another, *Fireside Companion;* another, *Hearth and Home*. One that was especially widely circulated was the New York *Ledger*, which described itself as "devoted to choice literature, romance, the news and commerce," though in fact its contents were almost exclusively romance, choice or otherwise. Since these periodicals came to us only by chance, and very irregularly, the serials in them could be read only as widely separated installments with gaps of many weeks between.

In the *Fireside Companion* were printed several detective stories by an author who was better known for his connection with the world of the theater, Tony Pastor. Pastor wrote "Old Sleuth, the Detective," and "The Lightning Detective," "The Gypsy Detective" and "The Irish Detective"; and one mastodonic opus in which all four co-operated, "Old Sleuth in Harness Again, or Four Noted Detectives Unveiling a Mystery."

A practice universal in the *Family Story Paper* and *Golden Days* was to generously enrich the reader's anticipation with a double title: "Cassie Lauderdale's Diamond, or An Entailed Curse"; "A Tangled Web, or A Fight for a Fortune"; "Chris the Car Conductor, or A Brave Man's Fight with Fate"; "Lillian's Bitter Ordeal, or Hearts Rent Asunder"; "A Mad Mistake, or the Honor of the Hansboroughs"; "Hard to Kill, or the Mystery of Bradhurst."

Such melodramas, and their melodramatic phraseology, provided, to subsequent generations, material for satire. But satire could not be more lurid than the original. An illustration to a story in the *Fireside Companion* bore the caption, "There was a swift plunge, a cry of mingled rage and horror, and then the black waters closed over their victim and the lonely mountain torrent rushed on as before."

It may be that this sort of reading was, for a child, either worse or better than the "comics" that came to be a feature of nearly every newspaper by the time I had young children of my own. It may be—indeed, I suppose it should be conceded —that "A Tangled Web" or "A Mad Mistake" was not as improving to a boy as better selected standard novels would be. I merely know I read this lurid fiction at a time when a boy's mind is susceptible to stimulation, and that I was stimulated. I recall, one winter night, reading until the family bedtime. Perforce I went to bed when the others did. After I knew they were asleep I crept back to my *Golden Days*, read by the dying kitchen fire while the house grew bitter cold, finished in the early morning, and then, to satisfy some impulse the story had awakened, went out into the dark, dashed across the snow-covered field, ran through the woods until my impulse wore itself out.

It was strong meat, yet I wonder if it was not as good for boys as the rather tepid *Youth's Companion*, though I adored that, too, and read every line of the occasional copies that came to me as the gift of a neighbor's boy. The *Youth's Companion* was carefully edited, by persons who thought boys should be properly brought up. Published in Boston, edited and mainly written by persons having some literary status, the *Youth's Companion* reflected the still continuing Puritan tradition that fiction was slightly wicked, entertainment for entertainment's sake slightly sinful. Its stories and articles aimed to suffuse the entertainment with useful instruction. The publishers' aim was more to get parents to subscribe than to get young folks to read. "The *Youth's Companion*," said the flag on its editorial masthead, " . . . exemplifies and exalts all that is best in living, without sacrificing the interest and vitality of the stories and articles it publishes; its pages are dignified and enriched by the contributions of the most illustrious living authors."

A periodical so pedantically edited could give only pallid pleasure to a boy who had eaten stronger meat. To me the *Companion's* best stories were those about wild animals and hunting; the editors did not feel any need to inject moral uplift or useful instruction into the writhings of a tiger or the saurian threshings that William T. Hornaday described in "A Croco-dile Hunt in Florida." But I suspect the *Companion's* strongest appeal to boys was its system of getting circulation. For getting so many new subscribers, two or five or what not, a boy would receive a Waterbury watch, a Barlow knife, a magic lantern, a stereopticon set, a velocipede or a "stylographic pen."

A farm paper came to us irregularly. It was called the *Farm Journal;* it appealed to me because of a print it carried on its first page, part of the permanent heading, an idealized picture of farm life. There was a noble farmhouse, with a great tree in front, the lawn enclosed with what we used to dis-tinguish as a "board fence," in differentiation from the less recherché paling fence or rail fence. In the lane in front of the house a boy was driving a yoke of oxen. In one corner of the picture a farmer was driving a harrow drawn by three horses— three meant a rich farmer. In another corner a mother and two daughters were making pies; elsewhere in the picture two little girls were finding a nest of eggs in the bushes, another little girl was picking flowers. A mare was suckling its colt, and bending her head toward the colt maternally. That old wood-cut, judged by an artistic standard, was, I suppose, crude and absurdly crowded. But to me it was lovely. I welcomed it each time I saw it. To have a farm like that was, for a few hours after each time I saw the *Farm Journal*, my ambition for my manhood.

Of the contents of the *Farm Journal* not much could be alluring to me. Yet, in the sparsity of printed matter, I suppose I read the expositions of best methods of fattening cattle and fertilizing clover. But a feature that I awaited eagerly and read with lively interest was one which from week to week recounted the habits and traits, and especially the failings, of a character called Peter Tumbledown.

Old Peter Tumbledown leaves his entry door open at nights and his feed chest lid up. This is not so bad, however, as there is no feed in the chest.

You just ought to see the edge of Peter's axe—the one his wife has to chop the kindling wood with! But that you could not do, for it lost its edge a full year ago.

Old Peter Tumbledown is growing in grace, for he has been seen to pump fresh water three times in one day for his horses. He never used to do it more than once a day.

Peter was shiftless, ne'er-do-well. Reading what Peter did, and thereby learning what prudent and frugal persons should not do, was my equivalent for reading Benjamin Franklin's *Poor Richard*, which I never read at all.

The sparsity of my access to books during the early part of my youth was ameliorated, after I had been in school two or three years, by the sympathetic understanding of a teacher, who loaned me *Cudjo's Cave* and some other books for boys by John T. Trowbridge. And I was introduced to a very heaven of books when some public-spirited persons in the village started a small library. The librarian, a middle-aged Quaker lady, liked me, which was fortunate; but she had no knowledge of books, and perhaps that, too, was fortunate. Totally unguided, I bored through the shelves with as little aim or direction as a mole in a meadow. I read the standard boys' books of Henty, Oliver Optic and Captain Marryat. Later, still by self-direction, I found the novels of Cooper and Scott and Dickens.

The lack of books in my home, the limited range of those in the village library, and the unguided self-selection by which my reading was chosen, left strange gaps. Many books, standard for children whose reading was directed by their parents, were unknown to me; I never read *Alice in Wonderland* or *Grimm's Fairy Tales*.

If these lacunae were unfortunate, there were compensations. My reading of *Uncle Remus* did not take place until I was a mature man, thirty-five years old. I was in Atlanta, Georgia, on a writing errand. I had finished my work and had an afternoon to kill before taking my train. In a bookstore I bought *Uncle Remus*, got on a streetcar, went out to a park and sat down to read—with results that brought upon me the attention of a kindly but puzzled policeman. He, professionally accustomed to regard alcohol as the only cause for unconventional behavior, could not understand that a grown man with a book in his hand, rolling in laughter on the grass, had been brought to that condition by any agency other than liquor. When I told him I had been reading a story about a rabbit who got his paws stickily smeared through hitting a "tar baby" made by a fox, he was skeptical. When I offered to read him the story he rejected my proposal, with a manner suggesting that it would impair his dignity. He strolled away, but kept an eye on me. I felt that my further enjoyment of Uncle Remus had best take place within four walls, or with persons equipped to understand my delight.

CHAPTER 9

Summer evenings, after supper, with the chores all done, we, with the youths from four or five neighboring farms, would gather at the bridge by the crossroads. Too tired for any kind of play, infected by the mood of the descending dusk, we would sit, some on the railings of the bridge, some on the fence, observing who was "going the road," and quietly talking. The talk was of girls and sex; of murders described in papers that came to us from the cities, and of the one ancient murder in our own neighborhood—it provided conversation for a decade (we Irish knew that merit lies not so much in a new tale as in an old tale well told); of local minor crimes; of the tricks of thieves, the one who reversed the shoes on a stolen horse so that pursuers tracking him would think he was going in the opposite direction. Some talk there was of baseball, though the irregularity of our access to daily papers kept us unfamiliar with the scores of professional games. One time or another most of us had seen a game between two locally celebrated teams, the respective prides of two larger towns near by, the Mohicans of Kennett Square and the Brandywines of West Chester. Very much talk there was of prize fights—the one in which John L. Sullivan won the championship from Jake Kilrain was to us a much more vital event than the victory of Cleveland over Harrison. We Sullivan boys, bearing the new champion's name, had by that fortuitous fact an elevation above our fellows.

So far as our crossroads evenings dealt with our ambitions, most of our talk was of "the West"; in that time and place "going West" was the most alluring of anticipations, at once an adventure and a career. Of the dozen farm youths who used to sit by that roadside bridge, half went West. One slipped away without telling his parents, and they never heard from him; two others also disappeared into death or silence—years later, after I had gone into the world and returned for visits, the parents of the lost sons would ask me had I, in my travels, heard anything of Johnny, or Gene, or Will. One youth of the neighborhood, older than I, who had gone West some years before, used to come back once a year, bringing with him a carload of Western horses to sell to the farmers. His little cavalcade, moving up the country road, was a stimulant to our ambitions. One youth who had gone West some years before was a cowboy on a ranch along the Little Missouri River, owned by a dude from New York. Years later, when the cowboy had returned to live a quiet life in the neighborhood that was his old home and mine, and when the dude ranch owner had become President Theodore Roosevelt, I helped to bring it about that Roosevelt should make his former cowboy postmaster of one of our neighborhood villages.

II

The contour of the land about my home could be compared to a shallow saucer, a mile or two in diameter. On the little rise in the middle of the saucer stood our house; from there the land sloped down very gently to a belt of meadows, in which quiet little streams meandered. Beyond the meadows the land sloped gently upward again, to the rim of the saucer, which was the horizon of my boyhood. That a boy should wonder what went on beyond that rise of land was a natural result of that kind of environment. That he should contemplate someday crossing the rise to see the scenes beyond was the most boyish of traits.

The condition was accentuated by the relation of the railroads to our home. There was no railroad in sight of the house, but just over the horizon were two branch lines, both so near that the passing of the train was always heard. The sounds of the engine bell and the rumble of the cars were a perpetual allurement. On one of the railroads the train, though out of sight on the other side of the horizon, passed at one point so close that by going to one of the upstairs windows I could almost, yet not quite, see the top of the locomotive stack. I was able to see the upward surging of the smoke as it came from the stack, in winter curling crisply.

One railroad, somewhat farther off, had a definite psychological effect on me. The main line of the Baltimore & Ohio was about nine miles away. Ordinarily the whistle of its locomotive could not be heard; but on frosty winter nights it came faint yet plain through the cold, clear air. The B. & O. trains, unlike those on the branch railroads nearer home, were expresses. They went with a thundering dash, and the whistle of them, heard across the hills as I stood on our porch on winter evenings, had a kind of rushing impetuousness, a headlong imperativeness, a summons to adventure; a call to Carcassonne —they were going to distant places, and sometime I must go too.

All of us, as we reached adolescence or a little later, left the farm; first to boarding school and then to jobs in the city. We never came back. The passage of the seven sons down that farm lane was as inexorable as an operation of nature. Our parents put no impediment in the way; on the contrary, the going to boarding school was encouraged, would have been insisted upon had insistence been necessary. They had come to know that the packing of the trunk for school was a ceremonial of permanent parting; after finishing school we would be off to the cities, and we would not return except for visits. They did not repine; or if ever they did, they did not let us know; they put no plea of sentiment in the way. My father occasionally, when one of us was looking forward to the city, would say that farming was a good life, that no city occupation could be better, but he said it in the spirit of what he thought was best for us. If in his mind there was ever any wish to keep us with him, any concern about being alone when he should come to old age and the farm work would be too much for him, he never let us see it. I, the youngest, was the last to go. I was not yet fourteen. As my father drove me to the station, my trunk in the back of the wagon, he gave me parental advice, with emphasis that I should "take care of my soul." He knew that he was launching the last of his brood from the nest, and forever. Excepting summer vacations from boarding school, and occasionally for a few weeks or months between jobs, none of us came back to live.

Our visits home were frequent; all but one of us were within one to three hours distance; one or the other of us would be back, perhaps one Sunday out of four; and on Fourth of July and Christmas all of us together. The gathering on Christmas Eve, the table heaped by my mother with turkey, oysters, vegetables and pies, was a true festival, a spontaneous jollity. There comes to my mind a jest that I had not thought of for many a year. My mother had two or three kinds of pie, among which each son had his liking. The preference of one of my brothers was mince. When my mother, happy and hurried, cut into the crust and found it was raisin, the incident was occasion for laughter and teasing. My brother had a quip for the occasion: my mother, when she baked, ought to put distinguishing marks on the pie crust while it was yet soft—on the mince "T.M." for "'tis mince"; on the others "T.M." for "'tain't mince." After dinner there was playing of the fiddle and dancing, my mother the only woman, and later, talking, long talking until after midnight, and finally the Rosary, all kneeling, my father leading, the rest of the family responding.

The following day, late in the afternoon, all would leave, usually walking to the station. I can remember them, on occasions when I was young and remained behind, going down the porch steps, crossing the yard, laughing as they raced with each other, and in their young vitality leaping the fence of the field they crossed. I lived to see them on visits years later, very willing to open the gate and walk with the staidness of men beginning to age.

That my father and mother were lonely when we were gone I knew very well. Age crept upon them. Coming back, I would find my father spending longer and longer afternoon hours on the settee near the warm kitchen stove. I knew they wished we would come oftener, though they never said so. Usually

I did not tell them to expect me, but would appear, as a rule on Sunday morning, coming afoot by the path that led from the village across the fields. The path arrived at the farm at a point between the barn and the corncrib, so that the buildings concealed my approach until I was within a few score yards of the house. Once as I rounded the corner of the barn I saw, through the kitchen window, my mother. She was leaning, her hands resting on the window sill, peering out over her spectacles toward the opening between the barn and corncrib. She knew when the one Sunday morning train was due at the village, could hear it arrive and could calculate the time it would take for one of her sons, if he came, to reach the point at which she could see him. I reflected that many a Sunday morning she had leaned and peered without seeing any of her sons, and turned and sighed and resigned herself to another week of waiting, hoping nothing was wrong with her boys.

On another occasion I had ridden my bicycle to visit my brother, who at the time lived in a village some four or five miles from the farm. I counted on staying with my brother until Sunday afternoon, when I would ride my bicycle to the farm, visit my parents for an hour or so, and then take the train back to my work. But after I set out from my brother's this day something went wrong with my bicycle, requiring about an hour to fix before I could go on. The road by which I came approached the farm in such a way that I could see the house when I came within half a mile of it. As I rounded a turn and looked at the house I could see my father sitting on the porch. He had placed his chair far out on the end, where he could see farthest down the road upon which any of his sons, if they came, might arrive. On his lap he had his little fox terrier, which he was stroking. He looked lonely and old. I realized it all; but I had lost the hour I intended to spend with him, and if I was to catch the train back to my work I must hurry on to the station, keeping to the road, which at its nearest point to the house was a field away. I thought that merely to call out to him without going on up to see him would mystify and disturb him. At the crossroads at the corner of the farm I took the turn to the railroad station. I have had my share of experiences I would rather not have had, and memories I would prefer to forget; of them, that Sunday afternoon when I chose work and duty above pleasure to a lonely old man is the most poignant.

CHAPTER 10

WHEN I WAS a few days less than fourteen I took my first railroad journey. In distance it was short, fifteen miles, but in experience many a league. For the destination was boarding school. The school was at the county seat, West Chester; it was called the West Chester State Normal School, colloquially "the Normal." The students spoke of themselves as "Normalites."

The institution, designed for the training of schoolteachers, was supported largely by the state, hence the charge to students was small. Five dollars a week paid for everything—tuition, room, board, books, laundry. The bill, a little over two hundred dollars each year, was sent to my father. He paid it as he could, sometimes sending as little as twenty dollars on account, and always receiving patience and consideration from the principal of the school.

Aside from the annual bill, the only other expense was a few cents now and then for stationery. This, and an occasional purchase in the town, candy or what not, was met by small amounts sent me from home. In the attic at the farm are upward of a hundred letters to me, each beginning, "I enclose $1," or "I enclose $2"—never more. The letters from my father had a similar uniformity of conclusion; always he ended: "We are all well here, thank God, hoping you are the same."

Sometimes it was one of my brothers who sent me a dollar or two. One letter from him I quote because it pictures the simplicity and affection that characterized the family life— my brother was at the time living at home and teaching the local one-room school:

I am sending you $1, that is all I have to spare just now. About Thanksgiving—I don't believe if I were you I would come home that day since it is so near Christmas. Well, all the work around home is done up. Corn crib is full of corn and we sold 100 bushels besides. Fodder is all hauled and stacked. I have been having some good times at Will's lately, there were some girls there from the city. As I write, mother is churning some butter in the old churn. Enoch Moore died last week, and father and I went to the funeral last Thursday.

Your brother,
B. J. Sullivan

A letter of my own, written to my brother, is, to the sophistication of maturity, utterly artless; appalling in the candor of its avowal at the beginning, charming in the humorous Irish indirectness of the request at its conclusion:

Normal School, Jan. 27, 1889.

Dear Bro:

This is a dull day and as I was tired of everything I thought I would write to you.

We had oranges for dessert today. Tonight we will have oyster soup. They treat us pretty decently up here after all.

Sunday always is a dull day up here and especially a rainy Sunday. I have read and read until I am tired of it. If it were dry I could go up to Evans [who, or what, Evans was I cannot now recall] or some other place, but I can't. I would prefer a busy week-day to a dull Sunday.

We have had our first two lectures of the lecture course and they were very good. Bob Burdette's especially. Bob said that "were all Gaul divided into three parts, the boy would have three of them."

The day before Belva Lockwood lectured here, Prof. Phillips [principal of the school] said: "I won't tell you how old she is but I'll just tell you she was born in 1820." I suppose he thought he was getting off a great joke.

My shoes need mending and I will need a new pair soon, so if you would send up some money I wouldn't send it back.

Yours truly,
Mark

II

It is not easy for an adult to know accurately what, as a boy, he was like. He himself cannot fully recall, and the recollections of those who shared his boyhood are as a rule no more dependable than his own. Especially, if they regard him as having risen in the world, do they remember virtues, talents, feats and good deeds which the beneficiary of this generous attribution cannot himself recall, and which, I fear, would not be confirmed by contemporary records, even if ample records existed. In the jumble of the attic at the farm are a few fragments of evidence. One of them is a letter I wrote home soon after I was at the Normal School:

Normal School, 9/27/88

DEAR BRO:

I thought I would write you and tell you my school life. . . . When I first came here I was a regular ignoramus. I could not find the class rooms or anything. But now I am well acquainted with everything about the school and about West Chester. And I am on speaking terms with every boy here.

I think this is what might be called a perfect school. Everything goes so smoothly and I could not get along nicer in my studies.

That seems to suggest cockiness. But I find other letters, from my family to me, which reproach me for letting them hear from others the news of small triumphs I had; for not having told them myself that the teacher of grammar had given me a higher mark than he had ever given anyone else, or that the teacher of literature put me in charge of the class when he was obliged to be absent, or that I had been very funny in the role of an animated phonograph at a school entertainment, or that I had achieved prowess in the gymnasium.

There is testimony of a contemporary in the form of a satiric presentation made me by a member of my class at a school gathering. To each member was given a token, supposed to have some aptness to his career in the school, and the presentation was accompanied by a pointedly personal address having the barbed candor that young folks sometimes practice with each other. The address to me was:

Mark, you are a very important man about the Normal, at least you think so, and really I don't know what will be done without you next year. I tremble for its future success. What will become of the Moore Literary Society, athletics, baseball and the young ladies?

I don't suppose *you* know, either. You are noted in everything for your originality and faculty of trying to be first. Why, if you were allowed you would run the class, the school, the faculty, nay, the managers and everything else. Now you are the very cream of perfection. Such phenomenal success as you have is apt to make you vain. . . . In order that you may see yourself in somewhat humbler surroundings more suitable to you, take this mirror.

For the acidity of that presentation there was a special and passing reason which robs the expression of some of its weight as a permanent judgment. The presentation was made by one of the young ladies of the class, and at the moment I was out of favor with them. We had just been through an election for class president. It had developed into a war between the sexes. While both candidates were male, the girls supported one, the boys another. I was the candidate of the male part of the class. Since they were only 9 to the girls' 22, I lost. I felt a bitterness beyond that which would accompany ordinary defeat; vaguely I felt that to be overpowered by girls was more humiliating than to be beaten by an ordinary bisexual majority. I made acrid post-mortem remarks, about the youth for whom the girls had shown favor, and about the girls for favoring him. The girls, annoyed with me, took revenge in the satiric presentation to me.

In a not too flagrant way, and never very offensively, I was disposed toward what is now called impishness but which at that time authority forthrightly called "devilment," which meant, mainly, that I was a skeptic of convention and of convention's forms, as embodied in the school rules. I was not a rebel against authority so much as a sly scoffer at it, an ingenious deviser of ways to make rules seem absurd. Rarely did I defy authority to authority's face, and only when I felt some deep sense of personal outrage, on which occasion my defiance was usually accompanied by angry tears. But even when authority did not inconvenience me at all, I felt a kind of moral compulsion to deny dignity to it. The forms and rules, the minutiae of system by which the school made round holes for the

[*85*]

pupils to fit into, found me often a square peg. I would squeeze myself into the allotted hole far enough to avoid outright disobedience, yet remain far enough outside to satisfy my self-respect as a nonconformist, usually managing my carefully gauged approximation to obedience in such a way as to cause a laugh and advertise the rule as slightly ridiculous. Fabrication for personal advantage I saw as odious, to be ashamed of. But a fiction or a conspiracy ingenuously devised and elaborated for the purpose of baffling authority and making convention laughable—that I regarded as a legitimate, useful and enjoyable exercise of ingenuity. Rule for the sake of rule had little compulsion upon me, and was often evaded, without any wound to conscience. A school rule said that no pupil might go home without permission. I liked to ride my bicycle home Saturday morning and return Sunday night. I knew that permission could be had for the asking, but I never asked. This dereliction the principal condoned, never spoke of it to me, and only in casual conversation mentioned it to my brother, who was a member of the faculty, saying to him: "That young brother of yours likes to go his own way."

I have one memory which tells me that I may have been, on occasion, a somewhat offensively forthcoming youth. There was a baseball game between the Normalites and a visiting school. I was a fan for the home team; indeed, I gather I must have been, by self-election, the leading fan, at least the most conspicuous one. While I was in a spasm of ululant vociferation over a hit made by the home team—it must have been a three-bagger at the very least—I noticed that two young men, disinterested spectators from the town, were gazing at me with something like mild awe. One of them said to the other, "Will you look at that mouth!" In the remark there was no malice, just wonder. I was at the age when a boy has strong susceptibility to the opinions held about him by youths a few years farther progressed in adultage. The incident had more effect upon me than a hundred admonitions by elders, or a thousand texts about genteel behavior. It was borne in on me that my zeal for achieving the maximum of noise might diminish my favor in the sight of observers. In that moment I consciously added to my personality an ingredient of subduedness, which for a lifetime wholesomely diluted my impulses toward unreined enthusiasm.

CHAPTER 11

O<small>F THE MANY VALUES</small> I got from the Normal School, one arose from the quality of the student body. They came from families who prized education, who were willing to make sacrifices to get it for their children, but whose means did not reach the cost of college. Such families, rather more than any other group, fit the description and justify the phrase "back-bone of American life." Boys and girls coming from that background compose a fine association. I am glad I had it from before I was fourteen until I was approaching eighteen. It was a good experience for understanding America, sharing the common touch.

The faculty were mainly from the same background as the students. The occasional teacher who came to us from New England was slightly an oddity—such a one received respect for his merit, liking for his personality, on the same basis as his fellow teachers, yet had faintly the standing of an out-lander. Most of the teachers, like most of the pupils, were rooted in our Pennsylvania soil. It was an excellent faculty. The outstanding characteristic of them was thoroughness.

Every teacher, I suppose, entertains among his longings the wish that his pupils should remember him with affection. For attaining that satisfaction there is no way more sure than to teach thoroughly. At the Normal School, as at public school and later at college, the teachers I remember with most regard are those who saw to it that I learned. That is a teacher's job. If he does that, nothing else matters much; if he does not do that, nothing else that he does will compensate. Of the scores of teachers I have had, the only one I remember now with any conscious lack of appreciation was one who through kindly easygoingness failed to make me learn Latin. My regret is the greater since I feel that to a writer understanding of Latin is important.

I never learned Greek, either, and that I also regret. But that is not the fault of any teacher, for I never had one. When I went to college I had to make up a condition in elementary Greek. I learned it, as much as I did learn, by getting a Greek grammar and copies of the *Anabasis* and the *Odyssey*, and puzzling the text out alone in my room. Not more than three Greek words remain with me, of which two belong together, *enteuthen exelaunei*, the army of Cyrus marched out, and *parasang*, the measure of the distance they marched. As at this moment I reflect on my experience studying Greek, the most vivid memory that comes back to me is not of any hexameter, but of a mouse that used to come from behind the wall of the room, approach me guardedly, satisfy himself of my harmlessness, climb on the instep of my shoe, stand on his hind legs and peer up at me.

If lack of Greek and Latin was a gap in my education, there was compensation in the thoroughness of my training in mathematics. Drill in mathematics is valuable to one who is to become a writer, for it leads to accuracy of thinking, and accuracy of thinking is, for some kinds of writing, the foundation of everything. Given accuracy of thinking, clarity of expression can ordinarily be attained.

For my thoroughness in mathematics I am indebted mainly to three teachers at the Normal School. They made their pupils learn. They were as exacting as the science they taught. By long experience with their subject, or by the personal qualities that led them into that science, they had common traits. A mistake was a cosmic calamity and a spiritual sin. Failure of a student to do well was to them a personal grief, a reproach as if they blamed themselves. Good performance by the pupil was a pleasure which warmed their hearts and which, when I conferred it, gave me a glow too.

One of the three taught algebra, one taught what we called "written arithmetic" to distinguish it from "mental arithmetic," which was the speciality of the third. Mental arithmetic consisted of standing up at the call of the teacher and answering, orally, questions of which the subject matter was familiar but which called for intricate calculation: "If eggs are worth 18 cents a dozen and sugar costs 6 cents a pound, how many pounds of sugar can be bought with 30 eggs?" I am told that mental arithmetic is not highly regarded in modern schools; it is supposed to belong with the horse-and-wagon era of education. If so, modern students are denied a valuable discipline. To stand up before others, to think on your feet, to drive through to the answer, is good training for situations that call for quick thinking; and such situations life frequently presents.

A subject in which I did well was grammar. The subject is thought of as far distant from mathematics, yet the quality that enabled me to do well in it was, I think, the same that enabled me to do well in arithmetic and algebra. Either that, or the trait that grammar developed in me was the same that mathematics developed. In either case the quality was precision of thought. The teacher used to require us to "diagram" sentences; we divided the sentence into parts and plotted it. The method enabled us to see the relation of clauses to each other, and therefore the relation of the thoughts which the clauses expressed.

I do not think highly of education that consists of mere imparting of information. I find, among the notebooks I filled at the Normal School, a large one packed with descriptions of cities. I assume I was led to believe this was as important as any other part of the schoolwork; a young boy would not be able to discriminate. The descriptions are written out conscientiously. I suppose I did not let the work bore me. But it ought to have bored me, certainly it does now. The only gleam of interest I find in those pages of notes is one that the passing of time has given them: most of those facts are now antiques. The description of Detroit says, "Detroit is the largest center in the world for the manufacture of railroad cars, stoves, pharmaceutical supplies and emery wheels." I suppose I cannot blame a teacher for not knowing in 1889 what Detroit would be known for in 1938. But all the hours consumed by teachers in teaching me facts about cities, and all the time consumed by me in learning them, could have been condensed to one minute and one sentence: Descriptions of cities can be found in encyclopedias.

Lists are, with some exceptions, an educational abomination; the memorizing of lists is not education at all. So far as education needs to do this sort of thing, it needs to do no more than teach the pupil where the lists can be found, and perhaps how to assemble information. There are in my old notebook lists, which we were required to memorize, of the highest mountains; of the largest cities, with their population; of the reigning rulers of the world; of the cabinet of President Harrison, then contemporary.

There is a list of the sixty-seven counties of Pennsylvania, with the county seat of each. Either by direction of the teacher or by my own interest, I took great pains with it, using black ink for the names of the counties, red for the names of the county seats. I have been able to live a long, satisfactory and reasonably useful life without once having need of knowing that the county seat of Wyoming County, Pennsylvania, is Tunkhannock (though I think there is value in inculcating interest and affection for local communities). There is another list of the names of the states, together with what are described as the "familiar names" of them. From it, I learn anew, and do not feel greatly edified by relearning, that Delaware is the Diamond State or the Blue Hen's Chickens State; Arkansas the Bear State; Nebraska the Blackwater State. Another list enumerates the popular names of cities. Does anyone now speak of Brooklyn as the "City of Churches," or of Baltimore as the "City of Monuments," or of Cincinnati as the "Queen City" or "Porkopolis"?

Some of my old notebooks are a veritable magpie's nest of unrelated facts, as heterogeneous as they are unimportant. I think my education would have been quite satisfactory without my being made to learn that "the first grammarian was Liebitz"; that Webster's Dictionary was completed in 1828, Wooster's in 1846; that "James Hamway was the first man to commonly

[*91*]

carry an umbrella in London (1750)"; that "Alfred Lord Tennyson's title is 'Baron Tennyson D'Eyncourte of Addiworth' "; that "there are 1326 locomotives on the Pennsylvania Railroad"; that "the highest chimney in the United States is 333 feet in height and is at Clark's Thread Works, Newark, N.J."; that "the highest body of water on the American continent is in Colorado, 11,500 feet above sea level, and containing trout."

From my old notebooks it is clear I was given much moral admonition and that I took some of it seriously—though not all remains with me. I wrote down that "Bob Ingersoll would not have his terrible power for evil if he had not such a fine command of speech; neither would Beecher have the power for good." I suppose that dictum was given us primarily as an incident of teaching us public speaking; the piety is incidental. I wrote down a list of the last words of famous persons, including those of Jefferson Davis, which were, "Pray excuse me." Virtuously, or smugly, in the spirit of a time when the Civil War was only twenty-five years past, I was told, or added on my own account, "They were certainly fitting words for a misled man to end an unsuccessful career with; he is a man of whom it might be said his life was not a success, he might better have never been born."

A detached adage that I wrote down said that "God has given us two eyes, two ears, and one tongue—hence he intended us to hear and see twice as much as we talk." That I may have recorded because the admonition to caution appealed to me. I wrote down and memorized and often repeated and still remember a bit of verse conveying the same moral:

> *Boys flying kites haul in their white-winged birds,*
> *But you can't do that when you're flying words.*
> *Thoughts unexpressed may sometimes fall back dead,*
> *But God himself can't kill them when they're said.*

From a line in a letter to my brother I infer that I was skeptical about some of the moral guidance that was thrust upon me. Writing about one of the women teachers, I said, "She has been trying to reform me in many ways, principally about reading Sunday papers." I am confident I did not cease reading Sunday papers, nor regard their effect as evil.

One injunction of warning, however, I accepted fully. It is difficult for the present generation to understand the odium which, in my generation, was attached to cigarettes. It is still more difficult to understand the distinction that was made between cigarettes and other forms of tobacco. The cigarette was supposed to be insidious, wicked, malign, ruinous alike to body, mind and morals. I find in my notebooks a doggerel entitled "A Theory of Evolution," which to the pipe conceded harmlessness, even affirmative virtue, but upon the cigarette visited the odium of biological perversion:

> Way back in those days when time for man got ripe,
> A tailless ape sat on a tree and smoked a penny pipe.
> And as he smoked, lo, thought began. He knew that he enjoyed.
> (Be not surprised at this. You see, that ape was anthropoid.)
> Thus thought began, and thought is all that makes a man a man.
> So be it known that thus in smoke the human race began.
> But mark how in a circle move all sublunary things.
> Events, like smoke, resolve themselves into expanding rings;
> And as the monkey's pipe made thought, and thought created man,
> The cigarette shall take him back to just where he began.

At the Normal School much was made of debate; I was supposed to be good at it. The only evidence of my prowess that remains in my attic papers is my argument for the negative— I liked to be on the negative, it savored of defiance against authority—on the question, "Resolved That Men of Thought Are More Valuable Than Men of Action." My gallant defense of the inferentially contemned seems to me now, alas, a little specious in spots:

The superiority of action over thought is shown in the fact that we judge a man's character by his actions, not by his thoughts. Actions, not thoughts, go to make up the record of our lives. Had Columbus stayed in Spain and thought about his great voyage, what is now termed the American people would be in a pretty fix today. But luckily, he was a man of action, and his actions have done more for us than any man of thought whose name is on the pages of history.

Was it men of thought who won our freedom in the Revolutionary War? No, it was men of action. The men of thought were the ones that stayed at home and wished the affair were well over. Were our Puritan forefathers men of thought? Were the sturdy colonists who settled America, men of thought? No! The men of thought were the ones that kept up a continual growling and wished they were well back in England. Upon a little reflection, it will appear evident to all, that the men who are of most benefit to mankind are the men who act, not the men who spend their lives in idle thinking.

For my closing and convincing point I devised an illustration which I believed to be unanswerable—as I read it now it comes back to me; I recall how pleased I was with it, and with myself. In advance of the debate I showed it to my friends; I regarded it as, in the slang we used, a "sockdolager," a "solar plexus":

Let us bring the question right home. Suppose there were a fire in the building tonight. Which would be of most benefit to us, the fellow who would sit in his room and think what an awful thing a fire is anyhow, or the fellow who would grasp the hose and do his best to extinguish the fire?

II

Each spring the county superintendent of education—he was an honored figure in that community, second only to the judge and rather more esteemed than the congressman—held examinations for persons seeking certificates to teach school. For convenience, in those horse-and-buggy days, they were held at various points throughout the county. I learned that one was to be held at a schoolhouse some two miles down the Wilmington Pike from the Normal School. With a sense of adventure compounded of the May morning and my own youth —I was fifteen—and my consciousness of making a venture into the world, I walked down the pike and took the examination. Afterwards I wrote home:

DEAR FATHER:
I enclose the certificate. . . . I hope you will be able to get me some school around there, though if you can't I know I can get lots of schools throughout the county.

[94]

My brother wrote back that "the chances are against you here for getting a school on account of you being so young, and people here know your age." He advised that I had better try elsewhere, and suggested that I might, within technical truth, "sign your age 16—that would be your nearest birthday anyhow." But shortly after, I wrote home:

I had a long talk with Professor Phillips about the matter and he says it is very desirable for me to let teaching alone next year and come back to the Normal. At the end of next year I will be fully prepared to teach both as regards age and scholarship. I might get some hard school if I apply this year and might fail completely, which failure would interfere with any future success I might have in Chester County.

When I wrote that I was fifteen years old, an age which, I gather, is in the 1930s regarded as much too young for work.

CHAPTER 12

My time in the Normal School, 1888 to 1892, was still within the heyday of the lyceum and the lecture course. It had passed its glorious noon—Emerson, who was the sun of lecturing when it was at its zenith, had been dead for several years. But there were many other lecturers, of varying stature, and the system was still highly thought of. Each winter there was a course in the Normal School auditorium, and another in the town, to which we were free to go, indeed, urged to go, for the cultural value of lectures was rated high.

I went assiduously, and of some of the lectures took notes, which I find preserved in the attic. My notes begin with a description of the lecturer:

Mr Jehu DeWitt Miller is a stout man although as tall as the average man. He looks like a man who has spent most of his younger days on a farm for he has an immense chest and strong high shoulders. He wears a lay-down collar, for it would be almost an impossibility for him to wear a high collar, so short is his neck. His lectures are full of satire and he talks in short disconnected sentences, bringing out a fact every time.

The Hon. Roswell G. Horr's subject was phrased as a question and an answer: "Has it been proven that the Baboon is our Cousin? No, sir." Of Horr I have no notes, and all that remains in my memory is a gesture, detached from whatever thought it was designed to enforce, the right fist raised high and then brought heavily down on the left palm, the resultant smack designed to emphasize the assertion, uttered in a high voice rising to shrill falsetto, "It won't work." The Rev. Sam Small's subject was "From Barroom to Pulpit." James Whitcomb Riley recited "Little Orphant Annie" and "When the Frost Is on the Punkin" and "Out to Old Aunt Mary's." Henry Watterson had a lecture on "Money and Morals." The Hon. George R. Wendling talked on "Saul of Tarsus"; his phrases were rounded, his voice sonorous. Bob Burdette was a humorist of some fame in the early 1890s; the title under which he assembled many jokes was "The Rise and Fall of the Mustache." Paul du Chaillu described "The Land of the Midnight Sun." George Kennan lectured on his experiences among exiled nihilists in Siberia; for an hour in the warm lecture hall he wore the furs that had defended him against frost in his Arctic travels. One lecturer was concretely useful to me. His talk was about health, "How to Get Strong"; it coincided with the completion of a new gymnasium at the Normal School, and stimulated me to make use of it.

Records would show, I think, that the lecturer who, with a single subject, was popular over the longest period of time, was Russell Conwell. Years after I heard him at the Normal School, when I was myself lecturing on the same courses with him, the bureau manager told me that Conwell, during a period of fifty years, had taken in over a million dollars for his lecture on "Acres of Diamonds." The theme was that it is not necessary to go far away to find opportunity, that opportunities, "acres of diamonds," lie all about our feet. Strangely, I do not recall the details of Conwell's parable about diamonds, though I do remember perfectly, and vividly, his other parable in which he made the same point:

A sailing vessel in the South Atlantic, becalmed far out from land, was out of drinking water. She signaled to a passing steamer. The steamer signaled back, "Dip down your bucket where you are." The sailing vessel thought the steamer could not have understood and repeated the plea for water. The steamer repeated its message, "Dip down your bucket where you are." The people on the sailing vessel thought those on the steamer were heartless, were jeering at them. Presently, however, one man on the sailing vessel, a person with a rare mind, suggested that they try what the steamer had directed. They dipped down their bucket—and brought it up filled with fresh water. The vessel, though far out of sight of land, was opposite the point where the Amazon discharges into the Atlantic a volume of fresh water so great that it makes the ocean fresh hundreds of miles out to sea.

Conwell's lecture, its message of self-help and resourcefulness, was kin to the America of that day; he and his message were greatly esteemed. It was an America in which every youth felt it his business to seek opportunity and make use of it, to "get ahead in the world." I am not sure but that a later America looked upon that phrase as passé; not only passé, but sinister. To "get ahead" came to be looked upon in a way described by another phrase, which we did not know—it became "antisocial."

Most of the money Conwell received for his lecture, and much that he collected in other ways, he used to found Temple University in Philadelphia. One of my brothers, when he died, left, among other legacies, some two hundred and fifty thousand dollars for a library at Temple.

II

In the lecture courses at the Normal School, interspersed among the serious discourses, were occasional entertainments more vivacious in appeal. Impersonators who gave recitals from Dickens or Mark Twain, the impersonator eliciting admiration by the facility with which, merely by turning his face away from the audience for a few seconds, he passed from one role to another, from Micawber to David Copperfield to Uriah Heep to Miss Betsy Trotwood. Theatrical companies which performed dramas of carefully guarded chasteness; concert artists who sang classics from the operas—classics not too esoteric, such as "I Dreamt I Dwelt in Marble Halls," and also popular airs sanctified by time, such as "Twickenham Ferry."

Among these lighter entertainments there came to us, one December night in 1891, the glee club of Princeton University. It was the first glee club I had ever seen from any college; indeed, it was my first sight of college men as a group. Their mere presence, their poise, their evening clothes—this was probably the first time I saw a dress suit—was glamorous to any adolescent a little less than them in age. To me the young men on the stage were like demigods; I watched them with fascination. All were, to my young eyes, extremely attractive; one among them stood out, for what reason I cannot explain. He was a second bass, a basso profundo, and he sang a solo called "Peter Gray":

> *Once on a time, there was a man,*
> *His name was Peter Gray;*
> *He lived way down in that there town*
> *Called Pennsyl-va-ni-a. . . .*

accompanied by a most entrancing chorus by the whole club:

> *Blow ye winds of morning,*
> *Blow ye winds high-o. . . .*

About the young man who sang that song all I knew was what I saw as he stood on the stage and I sat in the audience. I did not meet him—the glee club came and went with the hurried casualness of any other entertainment troupe on tour. It was not the song that made the impression on me, it was the singer. And it was not his voice, it was his personality—I imagine I would have remembered him had he not sung at all. Why it should be that one individual is salient, another not, let any explain who think they understand the mystery of personality. I remembered his appearance long after the others had passed out of mind. Indeed, I recalled it forty-five years later, when I was writing this book. He was rather tall, dark in complexion, with brown hair.

Yet I did not recall his appearance accurately. I thought he had black hair and a white spot the size of a silver dollar in it, and so wrote in the first draft of this manuscript. But it occurred to me to verify this point, and I wrote him a letter—many years after that boyhood sight of him at the Normal School I came to know him. His name on the Princeton Glee Club program of 1891 had been N. B. Tarkington; later, when he was a member of the Indiana Legislature, officially expanded to Newton Booth Tarkington; and later still, when he was an author and

[*99*]

playwright, condensed to Booth Tarkington. He replied on
August 5, 1937:

Interesting twist of memory, your remembering my black hair
with the white spot in it. Shows beautifully how that faculty of ours
plays with the pictures that get stored in our heads. You're right
about my having been a basso-profundo, and one of the solos I sang,
as you miraculously remember, was the jocularly lugubrious ballad,
"Peter Gray", and I was thin and tallish—about five feet ten and
three-quarters. Only my hair was brown. The boy with the black
hair and the white spot in it, just over the forehead, a striking face,
too, that caught everybody's eye, stood near me—a "first bass", John
Harding, '95, of Chicago. Your memory has just moved that hair
and the white spot about eighteen inches to your left as you sat
facing us.

The Princeton Glee Club and their singing, including "Old
Nassau" and "The Orange and the Black," would have caused
any youth to wish he might go to Princeton; indeed, I think that
impregnation with such wish mingles as a worldly motive among
the purposes all college authorities have who send their glee
clubs on annual tours.

In my case the wish created by hearing the Princeton Glee
Club was a wish merely. What turned wish into acute longing,
detonated it into emotional compulsion, was an incident as
casual as many of the merely fortuitous episodes with which
fate lays out the pattern of individual destinies.

Accompanying the visit of the glee club came some bits of
printed matter, one of which in some way came into my hands—
its descent upon me was as casual as the fluttering of a falling
leaf upon a boy's shoulder. I cannot remember just what the
printed thing was; it may have been a circular announcing the
glee club, or a program of its performance, or a copy of some
Princeton periodical. The one thing I remember, that bit into
my mind and remains there with deep-etched vividness, was a
drawing. I remember it was at the head of a page. It was a
drawing of a college room, and of a scene looking out from the
room. There was a long, low window seat. It was covered with
a cushion, and on the cushion, books lay carelessly tossed.
Above the seat was the window, quite wide, much wider than

high, suggesting that the room had the snugness of a low ceiling. Through the window one saw, against a background of setting sun, the towers and turrets of the college buildings.

The instant my eye took it in, as quickly as optic nerve could flash signal to brain, arose impulse imperative. I must go to college, Princeton or another. I must take the quickest way to bring it about. Everything I was to do from now on must be a step toward it. Not to go, from any cause, would be an intolerable deprivation. I must be about it at once.

Such seizures of emotional compulsion, descending upon me from detonations as slight as a picture, or a scene, or a phrase of music or a song, or a printed word, or a spoken one, have determined much more of my course than has been directed by calculated planning. The seizures have not been frequent, hardly more than a score in a lifetime, but their power has been in proportion to their infrequency. After some experience I learned that for me they were on the whole good. I have not had permanent regret for any of the courses they took me into. Always, if the means for action were at hand, I submitted at once to the compulsion.

In the present case action could not be immediate. By no means could I go to college without two or three years of preparation. With time the sense of immediate urgency subsided, but never did the sense of permanent compulsion disappear. In due course it had its fulfillment. I have no doubt at all that the sequence of events which, several years later, led me to Harvard included obscurely that surging of emotion which arose from sight of a picture of a college window.

Even before the visit of the Princeton Glee Club, I had made fitful yet earnest gropings toward getting a better education than the Normal School afforded. I knew that the Normal School, being designed merely to train teachers for public schools, did not equip us to pass college entrance examinations; while the Normal School was thorough in mathematics, it taught no modern language and only a faint beginning of Latin. From former Normal School students who had gone to college

I learned that the transition was awkward. So I sent for catalogues and made other inquiry about Andover, Exeter, Lawrenceville and other preparatory schools. These catalogues I searched, not to examine the curriculum—all that, I knew, would take care of itself—but to find the cost of attendance, and especially to learn what ways there were of reducing the cost, of working one's way through. The only gesture in this direction that went as far as negotiation was with Hill School at Pottstown, Pennsylvania; somewhere in the office files of that institution, in the time of its Meigs dynasty, are letters from a boy who asked if he could pay his way by working in the office, and responses which gave him kindly encouragement. The enterprise came to nothing, however. I remained at the Normal School because there was no other school as inexpensive and convenient to my circumstances. Besides, I liked the Normal School and felt I could make shift to overcome the maladjustment between the end of the Normal School curriculum and the beginning of a college one.

CHAPTER 13

For a time my desire for more education seemed to find promise of fulfillment in a chance to go to West Point. The opportunity and the urging that I try it came largely from my oldest brother, Cornelius. Himself the most bookish of my brothers, he understood and shared, and constantly stimulated, my wish for education—his desire for me a groping toward vicarious fulfillment of the wish he had been unable to carry out for himself; his schooling had ended with a brief period in the type of school that was then called a "private academy."

Cornelius learned that the congressman from our district would shortly have a vacancy at West Point to fill; and that the congressman, combining virtue with self-protection against importunity, had announced he would not consider personal applications, he would select the appointee by competitive examination. I took the examination and was one of the two who were fortunate, the other youth as appointee, myself as alternate.

The next step was to take the examination for admission to West Point. It was held, for geographical convenience, I assume, at Fort McHenry, Maryland. With fare supplied by Cornelius, I set out on a drizzling morning in March 1892, on what was up to that time the longest journey I had ever taken, sixty miles. The length of the journey gave me as much sense of adventure as the academic test that was the destination of it. From the Normal School I rode in a horse-drawn stagecoach five miles to a station on a small railroad, boarded an accommodation train for Wilmington, Delaware, and there changed to the Baltimore & Ohio, which had express trains. At Baltimore I went from the station by streetcar to Fort McHenry.

From Fort McHenry, two or three days later, I returned with a document which stated that my mental examination was satisfactory, but my physical one not. West Point would have none of me because I had—the term was most alarming to my family—a "systolic murmur at the apex." The apex, it turned out when I went to see the school doctor, was cardiac—I had heart trouble. The elevation this gave me among my fellow pupils would have been diminished had I added—which I did not for a while, because I enjoyed my distinction—that the doctor said the affliction in my case was impermanent, was probably an incident of adolescence, and could be overcome by attention to diet and other simple measures.

With this assurance from the doctor I asked the congressman to appoint me again, and he did. The second entrance examination, three months after the first, was to be held at West Point. Again my brother supplied railroad fare and saw me on the train at Philadelphia. At New York I transferred to a Hudson River steamer, the Mary Powell. She dropped me at six o'clock of a June evening at a little box of a station on the riverbank marked "West Point."

I took the only path in sight; it led up a steep ascent. At the top my eyes and ears took in the pomp and romance of the national nursery of war. Front of me lay the broad parade ground, green and smooth, bordered on the farther side by trees; beyond the trees the sun was sinking, throwing Titan shadows across the parade ground. On the right flowed the Hudson, beyond it the wooded heights of old Crow Nest. To the left lay the gray stone buildings of the Academy, oddly cloistral-looking, considering their function. From out of sight beyond the buildings came the rolling notes of "The Girl I Left Behind Me"; presently the fifers and drummers emerged and after them the winding column of two hundred young Americans in white duck and gold-braided gray. I was very thrilled.

In the adjutant's office a clerkly martinet looked at my appointment papers and turned me over to an orderly, who led me to a door on the first floor of the cadet barracks. I knocked, was bidden, and entered the presence of three youths in the uniform of the Academy, with the chevrons of corporals and sergeants on their sleeves. These were cadet officers, not army officers but members of the second-year class, who had charge of the incoming "plebes" or "beasts."

"Well, sir, what is your name?" asked one.

"My name is Sullivan."

"What!"

Had I provoked the wrath of heaven? They jumped to their feet; they crowded around me in angry excitement. "Mister-r-r Sullivan, sir-r-r," they shouted, with an emphasis on the first and last words which made me understand my breach. They ordered me furiously, each in his own way, and in chorus, and all at great length, not to "dar-r-re" to answer a cadet's question without saying "sir" at the end of my answer, and not to "dar-r-re" to call myself anything but "Mister" Sullivan.

When they had exhausted their vocabulary of emphasis they asked me if I understood, and I replied, as they well knew I would in my agitation, without the much enjoined "sir."

They jumped and stamped and gesticulated and shouted in frenzy. I was no gentleman, I was not fit to be a soldier, I never would be one, I was a stupid fool. I did not know what honor was. I did not know what truth was. I was everything in the world that a gentleman and a soldier was not.

At the end of it all they asked me again, and I managed to frame my answer correctly. A few more questions I got past without again rousing them, and I was told to follow the orderly to my quarters. With much relief, you may be sure, I answered, "All right, sir."

They were frantic anew. They jumped and stamped and shouted it into my head that at West Point one never says "all right," but always "very well." Finally I was permitted to go.

The next morning the plebes lined up in front of the barracks for inspection. We were a limp, desolate, woebegone lot. For many it had been their first night away from home. At that first roll call we were in part spared the wrath destined for our several shoulders. It was concentrated on one, an unlucky wight who was late and came rushing out of the barracks after the line had formed. The whole body of cadet officers left their places and gathered around him. I never realized before that a man could be mobbed and maltreated without the use of physical violence. Epithets were the weapons, and sarcasm, heavy scorn, scorn spelled with a rolling *r*, sarcasm of the kind that longshoremen use after cobblestones cease to be effective, sarcasm which comes through the nose, out of a screwed-up face, to convey the extremest abusiveness of inflection, the ultimate cutting edge of insult.

The cadet officers would lie in wait for us as we turned corners. They would lay traps for us. They would say something of the kind which fawning courtiers smile at. If we didn't smile they would upbraid us for refraining out of recalcitrant malice; if we did smile they would break out with, "Wipe that smile off your face, sir," and deliver a long lecture to the effect that the prerogative of smiling is reserved to upperclassmen.

One hawk-faced cadet officer, who was so small that his revilings were like the stings of a wasp which one dare not raise a hand to smash, picked me out—at least I thought at the time he did—for his especial prey. As we were marching to the mess hall he dropped into a lockstep behind me so that his mouth was within a few inches of my ear, and in a sort of hissing, intensely ire-raising voice he kept up a monologue of revilement. His theme embraced my personal appearance, my stupidity, the "swelled head" which the cadets impute to every "beast," and the disgust and contempt which I inspired in him. His terms of opprobrium were not the general epithets which one street ruffian hurls at another; he seemed to have a diabolic capacity for searching out and saying things that cut to the soul. I felt as if he had taken me bodily on the tip of his tongue, as an elephant might take one in his trunk, and was threshing me around in the mud and rocks. As soon as his tirade had distracted my attention from my marching and I fell into some violation of the drill, he would drop back and cry out shrilly, "Pull in that chin, sir, pull it in, I say, sir!" Then as my attention, diverted to that part of my anatomy, wandered from another, he would shout, "Hold those hands still, sir! Are you trying to swim?" And, as I now focused my attention on my hands, to the neglect of other bodily members and protuberances, he cried, "Suck in that stomach, sir, suck it in!"

What retaliation I might have wished to visit upon the wasp was supplied me vicariously by another. There was among the plebes a red-haired, insouciant youth, conspicuously Irish. On an occasion when the other plebes were drawn up for inspection the Irish boy, belated, came strolling out of the barracks with a rolling gait and a lazy swing as if he were miles from a military post. As leisurely, as unconcernedly as if he were coming down to breakfast at home, he was buttoning his coat. The sight fairly maddened the young officers. The wasp dashed forward: "Button up that coat, sir, button it up, I say, sir!"

The plebe stopped, threw back his head and embraced the fuming officer in a long look of contemptuous scorn. "Aw, go on, you," he said in a drawl that added much to the insolence of the words, "you go button up your mouth." Then he sauntered over to the end of the line and assumed "Attention!" The officers were horror-struck. Their experience offered them no precedent for such a thing. Their vocabulary failed them. They said nothing. West Point had suffered Waterloo.

Yet through it all the young cadet officers took pains to show kindliness. When the plebe who shared my room became discouraged and wanted to resign, a dark-eyed Southern cadet came around and was as tender as a woman in explaining that the faults which called forth so much abuse would soon disappear, that the officers meant nothing but to make soldiers of us in the shortest possible time. In the evenings the officers would hunt up any of the plebes who could play the banjo or sing, and would organize impromptu musicales on the veranda of the barracks. Then they would tell us stories of the Academy, indoctrinate us with its traditions, and point out the standards which cadets are expected to reach. And they would ask us whether we expected to "bone corp," which was vernacular for paying special attention to drill in order to be appointed a cadet corporal; or to "bone math," which was obvious; and they would advise us under no circumstances to "bone fem," which meant that it was not good for the yearling green to make love to the West Point girl.

At some point in the ten days or so I was at West Point I must have had a moment of dismay and I must have written to my brother in a mood of either discouragement or disgust, for I have a letter from him which is dotted with exclamation points, following such phrases as "Stick!" "Fight it out!" "Don't flinch!" "Never retreat under fire!":

The very test you are enduring is the very test, the very discipline that makes generals, that makes commanders of men. The experiences you are facing have been faced by Grant, by Sherman and Sheridan; suppose they had flinched and given up in disgust. Just face it, remembering that in enduring every grievance you are stooping to conquer. If you find it intolerable you can resign in a year. . . . Your action now will show how much and what kind of grit there is in your character.

The question was settled for me by the outcome of my physical examination. Once again I was rejected, this time on two counts, "heart trouble and defective vision."

Probably it was just as well. I am not sure about all my knowledge of myself, but I am confident I was not made for Mars. And I suspect that my family and my intimates would say that of all the persons in the world I would be the last to conform to regimentation. If I felt any pique against the army for not wanting me, I could, forty-five years later, reflect upon the reasons they gave, and retort that my eyes turned out to be able to see a good deal; and as for my heart, what trouble it has given me has not been physical.

CHAPTER 14

IN THE REFLECTION, the groping back into the past of my own mind that accompanied the writing of this book, one of my purposes has been to identify just how I happened to become a newspaperman, just what within me, and what circumstances outside me, accounted for it. I have said that as a small boy I read with great avidness such newspapers as came to the farm. But that may have been merely because I liked reading, and read newspapers only because books were not at hand. And I have said that as a lad I set out to make a collection of copies of different newspapers; but that may have been merely the collecting instinct, like collecting stamps or birds' eggs.

While at the Normal School I took a turn which seems to point toward the career I was destined for. It was suggested by a sentence in the letter home that I wrote within three weeks after I was at the school, "I am on speaking terms with every boy here." That was a true reflection of an authentic trait. I made acquaintances readily. I was interested in all the boys, and those that happened to be close within my circle I almost always liked. That trait, that liking for people, had, I think, something to do with my becoming a journalist, especially the particular kind of journalist I became.

The boys to whom I came close by some circumstance, rooming on the same floor or sitting close to them in classes, became my comrades. I wanted to keep touch with them when we were separated. During the vacation on the farm after my first year in school I was lonesome for them. I devised a kind of circulating letter which would give us news of each other. I wrote a letter in which I told about myself, and sent it to one of my friends, suggesting that he, after he had read it, should write a letter of his own, insert it with mine in an envelope, and send the two to another friend. This friend should add a letter from himself and so on, through a list of some fifteen of us. When the aggregate letter got around to me I would take out my first letter, write another and keep the chain going round.

That enterprise, though its cumbersomeness caused it to break down, and though the letters were wholly of intimate friendship—we addressed each other as "dear chum," sometimes, alas, spelled "dear chumb"—that enterprise was essentially a newspaper. The animating heart of it was interest in people, liking for them; eagerness to know what was happening to them; the mechanism of it was an expression of ingenuity. The project is, I think, identifiable as the first budding of a germ of journalism that was within me.

The next development was natural. There was in the school a publication, an annual, organ of the literary society to which I belonged, the *Moore Gazette*. It was heavy on the side of literary essays, moral disquisitions, articles on pedagogical theory. When I came to contribute to it I enlarged and lightened it on the side of personal interest, school notes, school athletics, news of the graduates, an occasional quip about the passing scene at the school.

But for that sort of news and timely allusion an annual was much too infrequent. So I, with some others, founded a monthly, which still endures after more than forty years. The name we gave it, the *Amulet*, was chosen, not because it was the word for a gem, but because of a significance suggested in a couplet from Emerson:

> *Give me an amulet*
> *That keeps intelligence with you.*

It was to "keeping intelligence," that is, printing news, that I mainly dedicated the *Amulet*. In Vol. I, No. 1 (February 1892)—I have a copy before me—we deferred to the literary tradition to the extent of including a poem by Edwin Arnold (reprinted), a description of "A Sunset Glimpse of Casco Bay," a pedagogical tract on the importance of psychology in the schools and a page of "Mosaics of Thought," elevating quotations from classic verse and prose. But my interest was in that part of the paper which recorded the news of students, alumni, faculty. To assemble this, I took much pleasurable pains; I wrote, by longhand of course, scores of letters to former students, asking them to tell what they were doing and to send news of other former Normalites in their communities. We had accounts of school meetings, of activities of student organizations, class banquets, plans for new school buildings.

This record of news was enlivened by some lightness. There was a jocular report of satirical presentations made to members of the faculty at a "Santa Claus party." One item in that first *Amulet* is a bit of local topical verse entitled "A Normalite's Wail." I may have devised this myself (I did that sort of thing sometimes), though I hasten to make clear that this specimen may have reflected not my authorship but only my eclectic quality as editor:

> *Latin and Geometry*
> *Tax my patience terribly.*
> *Philosophy,*
> *Psychology!*
> *It seems to me*
> *They ought to be*
> *Where Pluto rules his monarchy.*

In claiming association with that, I hope my memory is not warped by a plagiaristic motive. Perhaps my subconscious is moved obscurely by a preference to have my talent for rhyme associated with that rather than with the one authentic verse which is indubitably chargeable to me. If my responsibility for authorship of the "class ode" depended on memory, memory, I suspect, might evade recalling it; it reflects a lugubriousness which, I assert emphatically, was not usual with me. But parentage of this I must accept; it is there in cold print, signed by me in the role of class poet. But perhaps the man ought not to smile at the poetry of the boy—the sentiment was sincere and characteristic of adolescence:

> *The ties of our friendship are breaking—*
> *Farewell to each other we say;*

For the pathway that each one is taking
From the others leads surely away. . . .
The thought to each one is trying,
That our days as students are o'er;
But the joys that sweetly are dying,
Will in memory live evermore.

II

My next step in journalism flowed naturally from my work on the school paper; I began to report school news for the town newspapers. I worked at it assiduously and I liked it. Since there was no money remuneration and since I could have dropped it any day for any other use of my spare time, whether work or diversion, it must have reflected an innate bent.

There were, in the town close by the Normal School, three daily papers, the *Morning Republican*, the *Local News* and the *Village Record*. The three composed the newspaper world that was closest to me. If I was to follow the admonition embodied in Russell Conwell's lecture, if I was to find "acres of diamonds" close to my feet, if I was to "dip down your bucket where you are," the little local dailies of West Chester were the well into which I must dip.

Writing this way, I may seem to imply that in my getting into newspaper work there was planning, deliberateness. I do not think there was, much. I suspect rather that I got into newspaper work much as the ground hog gets into the clover. I cannot now recall accurately how it happened, and nothing in the farm attic enlightens me. The earliest fact is that while still comparatively new in the school I was writing accounts of school activities for the *Village Record*. In the lack of confident recollection as to how this came about, I should say that probably I walked in to the town, went to the office of the paper, sought whoever was in editorial authority and asked if he would like to have me send him accounts of the Saturday night meetings of the literary societies and of other events at the school. That I approached the *Village Record* rather than the other two papers may have been because it, as the feeblest, did not already have a correspondent at the school, while the others did. I would have been likely to study the three and pick out the one that had a lack which I could fill.

My compensation consisted of a free copy of the paper daily, and gratis provision of the modest facilities I needed. There were some blank sheets of rough paper, newsprint cut to folio size, upon which I should write my contributions—the editor warned me to write on one side only; and some large envelopes of manila paper, ready stamped and with the address of the paper ready printed in heavy red letters, which impressed me as having an atmosphere of importance and immediacy—one of the attractions which, I think, lures young men to newspaper work and in some cases keeps old men in it.

That I received no material compensation weighed with me not at all. I suppose I must have been conscious of compensation of the less material yet essentially more substantial sort—the kudos among my fellows for being the author of the school notes in the town paper. So far as that existed and counted with me, I can remember it only in connection with reports of baseball games. Though I was athletic and not bad at games, my immaturity in years and growth denied me any possibility of a place on the nine. The players were heroes to me; I remember yet a famous pitcher the Normal had, a tall, slender, dark young man who used to bend his lithe frame into patterns more intricate than the curves he pitched. His name was Wagner; we called him by a name that suggested conquering might, "Bolivar." If I could not myself be a player, it was glory to be the Homer of the nine; the distinction of having a special place in the grandstand as official scorekeeper was sweet.

About the next step in my newspaper progress, the transition from amateur to professional, my memory is vivid. In the school, two classes ahead of me, was a young man who when he graduated became a reporter on the *Morning Republican*. While in the school he had known me and liked me; after he was a reporter he was familiar with the school notes I wrote for a rival paper. He brought it about that I should transfer my amateur connection and act as Normal correspondent for the *Morning*

Republican. In time he gave me opportunities to do other work, authentic newspaper work, in periods when I could take a few hours or a day off from my classes at the school. I have a letter from him dated April 9, 1891, when I was not yet seventeen and still a junior in the school:

Thursday 1 A.M.

MY DEAR MARK:

On Thursday, today, please attend the convention of the W.C.T.U. at the lecture room of the First Presbyterian Church. Confine yourself to two columns as near as you can. Put all reports in your pocket that you can get hold of, and I will see you before supper. Go to Miss Mary I. Stille, 128 West Gay, immediately after dinner, and she will give you any information that you may desire to have about the meeting.

We should like very much to have you work until nine in the evening if you can make it suit, as there is a great deal going on.

Very truly,

MAC

"Mac" was Edwin L. McKinstry. To him I am indebted for my start in newspaper work. After I graduated, in June 1892, he brought it about that I should have a regular job on the *Morning Republican's* reportorial staff, the other half of which was himself.

McKinstry spent his life in West Chester, in the work he began when he left school; he has reported nearly half a century of the town's doings. At the time I write this book he is editor of the town's one daily; occasionally he drives over to my farm and we talk about the experiences we had when we were reporters together, the personalities, the odd characters, the tragedies and comedies we encountered. Many of my contributions to our conversations begin "What ever became of——?"

Between us we could write a hundred novels about the cosmos that county-seat town composed. We knew, in the way every small-town reporter knows, something of almost every family in the town; about those that stood out for any reason we knew everything. McKinstry, remaining there, knows what happened to them; we can trace them, now, through three generations. We know what became of the congressman's son, the judge's

[*114*]

grandson, the clergyman's daughter, the bartender's boy. From our experience we can understand why some went one way, some another, why some were fortunate, others not; why the thing that seemed favorable fortune to the grandfather turned out to be different for the grandchildren, while in other cases the condition that seemed a handicap became a stimulant. We can see now why marriage made one man, marred another; why for one politics turned out an unfortunate career, why for others law or business or medicine turned out a good career or a poor one. We can understand why some took to drink, why others were happy, for reasons having no relation to the careers they led. And the element of fate, of chance and lot, that went through it all, and also the unescapable influences that flowed from inexorable change, the economic trends and new ways of thinking that came into the world and did not pass that little town by.

The sum of such firsthand observation of three generations in one small town is not unworthy to stand alongside the dicta of the philosophers and economists in any attempt to explain the world, to understand how it might be better directed and how the individual can most satisfactorily spend his days in it.

I am not sentimentally asserting that this wisdom is acquired by a newspaperman more readily than by persons in other callings; granted the right temperament and point of view, a physician may acquire it, or a lawyer, or a policeman or a keeper of a cigar store. But I do venture to suggest that as between two areas of newspaper work, small town and big city, the small-town experience is more likely to be fruitful of wisdom and understanding; more likely to lead to a well-ripened personality; more likely, too, to be fruitful of other rewards. I have done both, and on this point I am confident.

The four years I spent in newspaper work in two small towns of some eight thousand each were the years which many young men spend in college. I wish not to make too broad a generalization from a single experience, especially when that experience was my own; I merely say that, for me, spending those four years in small-town newspaper work was a better education than spending the same four years at college would have been. I should add a qualification: in my case, after the four years in local newspaper work, I went to college. For me that arrangement—from eighteen to twenty-two in small-town newspaper work, and twenty-two to twenty-six in college—turned out fortunately.

Each June young graduates of college come to me with letters of introduction. They want to do newspaper work. Invariably it is metropolitan newspaper work they long for. I have learned to ask them, "What do you hope to be at forty? How do you visualize yourself at that time?" Rarely have they thought of that. Neither have they thought, as a rule, of the possibility that their careers might be merely average ones; in almost all cases they think of "star" reporting, as they have seen it on the stage or in books. I try, without discouraging their enthusiasm, to lead them to consider that the chance of any individual to achieve one of the blue-ribbon positions in newspaper work is at least as small as the corresponding chance in other occupations. And I suggest to them that if their careers are to be merely average ones, an average career on a small-town newspaper—I include country weeklies—may be more fruitful of satisfaction than an average career on a metropolitan newspaper. And from the point of view of national good for America there are few things that would seem to me so promising as for a constant stream of thoughtful young men and women with good educations to become recruits on the small-town press.

To express all this by a concrete application which would have been understood by practically everybody who lived in America during the first third of the twentieth century, one might ask whether William Allen White had a more satisfactory career than Arthur Brisbane. Once White was solicited to the Brisbane kind of career; the Chicago *Tribune* offered him twenty-five thousand dollars a year. White said he preferred to spend his life in a town where he could water his own front lawn with thirty-five feet of hose. And from the point of view of national well-being, a thousand young William Allen Whites in a thousand Emporias would serve America well.

CHAPTER 15

I was young, less than eighteen; I was a newspaperman—relatively an important one, half the staff of the paper—in a town that was small enough to be within my scope, kin enough to my background to be within my understanding. For everyone there is a formula of living which for him is ideal, the precise fitting together of environment and personality that nature intended. I had mine, and had it young. It was sheer delight. The town, my work, my associations—the whole of my existence was one with the June trees on the Brandywine hills, the leafy roads of the countryside, the sun in the heavens.

A person who noticed me—I imagine there were few who did—says his principal impression was of a youth standing in front of the Turk's Head Hotel, somewhat alert, somewhat reflective, observing the flow of the town that provided at once his career and his lively enjoyment. The Turk's Head corner was to that little cosmos what the Paris Place de l'Opéra is said to be to the world, the spot where, if you wait long enough, you will see everybody you ever knew or heard of. It was the crossing of the two main streets, High and Market. Up or down, east or west or north or south, passed everybody in the town and everybody who came to the town. All were grist for my mill. Incoming passengers on the railroad came up Market Street; on Monday mornings in court term scores of jurymen from all over the county streamed up from the station; mingling with them, I got news of the outlying townships—there were practically no telephones and nearly all news from every source was got by direct contact.

Across High Street was the courthouse. From my vantage point I could see both front door and side door. The entrance or exit of the sheriff, or of the court clerk or prothonotary, or of the district attorney or a constable, had news potentiality.

[*117*]

A few doors up from the courthouse was Rupert's drugstore, where, late in the afternoon, elders of the town gathered for gossip.

If few observed me, I observed all. Diagonally opposite the Turk's Head was the Farmers' Bank. Its president was also the district's congressman. His name was Smedley Darlington, called—affectionately or derisively as the politics of the speaker might be—"Uncle Smed"; his grandson, Smedley Darlington Butler, years later had national attention as a general of the Marine Corps and also as a vociferous expresser of strange views and mighty utterer of esoteric expletives which the grandfather would have found shocking.

Uncle Smed was a heavy-set man with broad shoulders and a moderate paunch, not tall. Summer afternoons he would bring a deep chair out on the sidewalk, place it just around the corner of the building where the shade fell, and sit there, observing the come and go of the town, exchanging a wave of the hand with passers-by; sometimes, still sitting, accepting limply a shake of the hand from citizens of lesser station and ingratiating intent. If a farmer came in from one of the townships the congressman would make friendly inquiry about the neighbors and the crops; if the visitor were a constable or other figure in local public life the congressman would ask about township politics. As the shade receded around the corner he would move his chair to accompany it. A few doors down from the bank building was the office of the afternoon newspaper. When from the door the first newsboy erupted, crying, "Daily *Local News*, one cent," Uncle Smed would buy the first copy, set a pair of heavy black-taped glasses on his nose and read avidly, ignoring passers-by until he had devoured the news.

A different type was the ex-congressman—the "ex" represented several decades of time. His name was Washington Townsend; he had been born when "Washington" was a preferred name for parents to confer on children. Old Mr Townsend was in retirement; about two in the afternoon his tall, thin, erect figure would emerge from his home and walk down to the center of the town, to stop at the bank and look after matters of which he was custodian. He carried a cane, a straight one, and wore black clothes. I thought of him as a figure out of the past. With an exaggerated impression of his venerableness I associated his experience in Congress with that of Clay and Calhoun. To me old Mr Townsend and some others of his type, the judge and the older lawyers who used to come to court wearing silk hats, symbolized the stability of the town, its continuity with a rooted past.

The town was ancient, secure, serene. Its economic base was the leisurely trade of an incomparably well-tilled, fertile farming country, together with such business as went with the county seat. There were no factories to speak of. Nobody was poor, nobody rich. Hardly anyone had enough to make anyone else envious. Fifty thousand dollars was wealth; I doubt if more than two or three had a hundred. There was no inferior group, unless it were the colored settlement across Goose Creek, just large enough to provide servants for those able to have them. If the colored folks were underprivileged they did not know it, and no one told them; the political art of capitalizing quasi-pity had not yet been invented.

While the Turk's Head corner was my vantage point, I would, from time to time during the day, make several rounds I had: to the county offices along the courthouse corridor, where I picked up not only official information but also talk of county politics and miscellaneous gossip—some of the officials who spent Sundays at their homes throughout the county would on Monday morning bring me news of their communities; to the hotels, where I scanned the registers—if a guest had possibilities of a story I drew him out; to a row of one-story brick buildings which the occupants called "Lawyers' Row," but which persons who had been irritated by the lawyers' professional attentions called "Rogues' Row." The lawyers, summer afternoons, would emerge from their offices, draw chairs around one of the horsechestnut trees that shaded the sidewalk, and discuss the affairs of the day. Learnedly, too, and shrewdly— there were among them graduates of every important university, and that bar had a tradition of high concern about public matters, local and national. Among them were "characters," men of high intelligence but miscast in the law, who, from disappointment in their careers, took refuge in caustic humor or cynic wit. The county judge, who sometimes joined the group beneath the horsechestnut tree, but always stood, as if wishing to enjoy the companionship yet keep a detachment enjoined by his office, was the most impressive combination of dignity and benevolence I had ever seen. He was tall, erect, poised, yet suggested flexibility. In his judicial function he knew justice and knew mercy, knew the difference between the two, and practiced each in its place. From observing him, and what went on in the room over which he presided, I acquired a lasting regard for courts.

I dropped into the barrooms; I learned to know what hour in the afternoon the bartenders would have most leisure to gossip. That I did not drink was no detriment to the geniality of our relations. All bartenders, because their wares cause loquacity in their customers, are good sources of news. One of the West Chester ones had a special kindness for me; through me he expressed vicariously a creative instinct denied outlet by his own profession. Seeing me push open the swing door, if he was alone he would call out, "Hi, Mark, there's a good item around at the Fame engine house; better hop around and get it." I would ask what it was. "Now there you go," he would say, "askin' me; you hotfoot it around there and get it for yourself; pretty soon you'll want me to write your items for you."

At the livery stable Ed Hickman knew much of the comings and goings of the town, knew the reasons for hurried trips to neighboring towns, the errands of persons who drove in from the countryside. Officials hiring teams to go on legal errands— the sheriff on a trip to "sell out" a bankrupt farmer, a constable going to make a distant arrest, election officials distributing ballots—would take me with them; I recall those men with affection and the drives with pleasure.

Another good source of news was Gus Troutman's barbershop; barbers, if they are good conversationalists, hear much. Gus Troutman was smiling and friendly, took pleasure in being helpful to a young reporter, had zest for the news, lively curiosity about local affairs, was public-spirited. Coming from Germany some twenty years before, he had been absorbed by the democratic spirit of the community, and himself absorbed the community's ideals. He was elected three times to a county office, coroner; his son became one of the town's leading lawyers. In 1938 Gus, aged eighty-five, was still active at his trade and progressive in it; he had added a "beauty shop" to his establishment.

One stopping place on my beat, productive of fish for my net, was a hostelry where the guests were involuntary. Because the keeper's name was Haggerty we called his bastionlike building "Fort Haggerty"—we thought that was quite facetious. His guests we treated as a rule with a similar levity; most of them owed their incarceration to small breaches of the peace— drinking, brawls, petty thefts.

Of opportunity to write about criminals of a serious type we had little; a main reliance was what we called the "Welsh Mountain gang." That sinister phrase, eked out with some imagination, enabled us to feel like chroniclers of ferocious deeds. The ringleaders of the gang—so we called them—were Abe and Ike Buzzard. Their stature in crime was relatively about that of the Welsh Mountains in topography. These were a range of wooded hills; calling them mountains was more an expression of local pride than a measure of geological elevation. But they were covered with woods, there were few houses in them, and in those days of practically no telephones and im- passable roads in winter it was easy to see them as remote and to invest them with sinister mystery.

From cabins in the little glens Abe and Ike Buzzard used to sneak out in the dark of the moon and creep down to the neigh- boring farms, moved more by the necessities of an empty cup- board or a longing for the luxury of chicken meat than by any criminality more sinister. I doubt if they ever stole anything larger than a turkey, possibly on occasion a horse. If I here write about them in condonement it is because they enabled me to exercise my imagination and to enlarge my vocabulary with such words as "desperado," "bandits," "raids." Those who read what we wrote should be similarly grateful; in that quiet community, before movies or radio, drama was rare; newspapers of the time were rather expected to print occasional yarns of violence.

After I had not heard or thought of the Buzzards for more than thirty years, after they had slipped as far into the cellar of my mind as the stories of Red Riding Hood's wolf, I saw one morning, while sitting in the White House waiting for President Hoover to come to breakfast, a newspaper despatch which recorded one of those departures from normal that justify headlines. A man, the despatch said, who had spent much of his life in successive incarcerations in the Eastern Penitentiary of Pennsylvania, but who had been free for some time, came back and asked the keeper to take him in; he had been happier there than anywhere else, had come to think of it as home, and he wanted to die there. His name was Abe Buzzard. I felt a suffusion of glamor as warm as the memory of a boyhood expedition for arbutus in the spring woods. I hoped the keeper would welcome Abe and that he would be happy.

Another habitant of the Welsh hills, fellow denizen of the Buzzards, was the "Welsh Mountain bear." I should not like to swear that anyone ever saw him, but in the snows of winter the tracks of a cow might, in that faunally unsophisticated community, reasonably be mistaken for those of a bear, and farmers from the foothills were always willing to give us enough surmise to justify an eerie story. Another paper, about sixty miles away, on the other side of the Welsh Mountains, the Reading *Eagle*—it was printed half in Pennsylvania Dutch—practiced an accommodating reciprocity. They would quote our story about the bear marauding on the south side of the mountains. A little later they would print a story of their own about his emerging on the north side, and we in West Chester would quote that. Each paper achieved verisimilitude for its own stories by quoting stories of the other. Between us we enriched the local world by expanding the category of "fish stories" to include "bear yarns."

If these recollections of a young reporter's life seem to emphasize humor and exaggeration, that may be because vivacious experiences come back more readily. We took our work seriously. But editorial policy, interest in improving the town, civic reform, was for elders, the editors and the owners; an eighteen-year-old reporter would not be likely to be infected with concern about that; I accepted what was, as good.

We did devote ourselves earnestly to reporting the town's doings fully and accurately: the terms of court, the conventions of political parties, the sessions of the town council and of the school board. . . . Meetings of the temperance societies—the Knights of Temperance, the Women's Christian Temperance Union, the Christian Temperance League, the Loyal Temperance Legion, the Total Abstinence Beneficial Society. . . . Meetings of the many church societies: Epworth League, Christian Endeavor, St Agnes Sodality—there were a score of them. . . . The drills of the local militia company, Co. 1 Wayne Fencibles—the "Wayne" was for a local Revolutionary hero, Anthony Wayne, but why "Fencibles" I never knew. . . . The parades of the gorgeously uniformed West Chester Pioneer Corps No. 1—there was no No. 2 and I do not think it was anticipated there ever would be. . . . Meetings of the fraternal societies, Patriotic Order Sons of America, Junior Order United American Mechanics, Knights of the Golden Eagle, the Independent Order of Odd Fellows, and the sorority, Daughters of Rebekah. . . . Meetings of Post 31, G.A.R.—does a later generation need to be told that the initials stood for the national organization of Northern veterans of the Civil War, the Grand Army of the Republic?

But meetings of organizations yielded only routine news, elections of officers, resolutions passed. Always we searched for news in the sense of that which is not routine. Sometimes the harvest was slight. In the old pages of the *Republican* I find an item headed "Sprained His Ankle," another "Hurt His Thumb." An item under "Improvements" recorded that

[*123*]

"Abner Hoopes is having a hedge placed around his stable in the rear of Maple Avenue." In the gleanings of one winter's day an item recorded that

Ed Jackson and Joseph P. Eyre put in their leisure time yesterday afternoon in shoveling snow off the pavement in front of the West Chester Fire Company's house on Church St. Whenever there is a heavy snowfall, Ed and "Punk" always hasten to assist in cleaning it off the company's sidewalk.

Some news, heavily displayed to herald important innovations, became, not long after, quaint landmarks of a distant past. In 1892 we recorded that two boroughs of considerable population, Oxford and Coatesville, were about to have electric lights. Oxford, still without a telephone, was to get one. There were exciting rumors about a new form of transportation, trolley lines, to serve the town and connect it with boroughs ten and twenty miles away. They were built, they had their day, they became scrap iron, victims of the automobile and the bus.

For a period a zeal for attention-catching headlines resulted in an extraordinary collection of alliterations, sometimes entailing a regrettable flippancy. Deaths were recorded under "Death's Doings," interments under "Borne to Burial," marriages under "Matrimonial Mart," religious brevities under "Chat of the Churches." Changes of residence preceding moving day, April 1, were captioned "March Movings." A theft of a pig was "Hooked the Hog." A citizen's visit to Philadelphia was epitomized as "Took in the Town." News from a near-by village was "Mites from Mill-town." Tramps coming to police headquarters to ask for a place to sleep were "Loafers Long for Lodgings." Fox hunts were "Racing Reynard," varied with "Following the Festive Fox." A headline that would not be used now, and ought not to have been used then, achieved at once a triple alliteration and a pun; summarizing the capture of a raccoon by a colored man, it read, "Coon Catches 'Coon."

With the policemen I and the other reporter on the paper had an intermittent relation, sometimes cahoots, sometimes mutual suspicion; between the police and the newspapers of every town, small or large, there is this kind of partnership, curious in that it is never certain which partner is dominant. Each has a leverage upon the other; the police can withhold news, the newspapers can withhold glory. So long as the policemen furnished us generous harvests of news we praised their exploits—they were sleuths of incomparable acumen, heroes of magnificent courage. Describing the stopping of a runaway, we wrote that "the gallant officer, at risk of his life, firmly grasped the bridle." Describing the tracking down of a chicken thief, we wrote that the officer "successfully performed a difficult and dangerous piece of detective work."

But if we thought a policeman was "holding out" on us he found his name less frequently in print or his efficiency slyly doubted. Once when Officer Finnigan seemed less openhanded with news than we thought he might be, we printed a quip which we thought a masterpiece of humor. What basis of truth it had I do not now know, and I strongly suspect there was little or none; I am sure we did not pursue our inquiry to a point where excessive zeal for verification might destroy our story. Indeed memory, and consciousness of a trait of impishness I had, suggest that perhaps the story was an invention wholly. Officer Finnigan, our item said, was swinging his club along Gay Street, looking after the peace and safety of the citizens. There was a parade; to watch it some youths were standing on a wooden awning. Officer Finnigan thought they were a danger, to themselves and to passers-by who might suffer from collapse of the awning—he was a careful-minded official who took his responsibility seriously. "Come down out o' that," he ordered. They protested that their weight was not great, there were only three of them. Officer Finnigan was willing to ameliorate his fiat, but the dignity of his authority would not permit him to withdraw it wholly: "Well, the half o' you come down anyhow."

In my relation with the police, in part camaraderie, in part impish truculence, there was the beginning of an attitude toward authority, government. The police, and the personnel of government altogether, were a necessary and useful institution;

usually they were of high quality as individuals. But however worthy, they must be kept in their place, must never be permitted to feel they were superior to the citizen; once in so often they must be taken down a peg. When I congratulated the police force on having made headquarters clean as a new pin, I meant to praise the force—but meant also to suggest that policemen are not always in blue uniforms and brass buttons, that sometimes, like ordinary persons, they are in shirt sleeves, on their knees, with scrub brushes in their hands. I had a similar duplicity of intention when I recorded that an officer engaged in delivering delinquent tax notices had been worthily industrious—he had walked more than in six years before and was losing flesh. Report of a movement to present the force with an alarm clock and an umbrella was outright—and uncalled for —innuendo of somnolence and indisposition to patrol in the rain.

Where I acquired this attitude toward authority I do not know. Possibly it was inbred, possibly an infection from the American tradition about government. Perhaps, too, as a boy with six older brothers, I had had a surfeit of experience with authority.

II

After I had worked on the West Chester *Morning Republican* for about a year, and was still less than nineteen years old, I received an ambitious suggestion. It came from the bookkeeper on the paper, John Miller. He was a few years older than I and had qualities of sure-footedness coupled with modest enterprise. He had learned that in a town about fifteen miles away, Phoenixville, there was a daily newspaper, the only one, which had fallen upon evil days. The owner of it was elderly and discouraged, his discouragement had led to neglect, and the paper was in a condition in which the community looked forward to each day's issue, not with anticipation about what the contents would be, but with suspense as to whether it would appear at all. Miller had learned that there was a mortgage on the property, that the holder of the mortgage was the leading corporation of the town, the Phoenix Iron Company, and that the iron company was eager to put the property in charge of someone who would at once pay the interest and make a better paper for the town. Miller proposed that he and I should try to get hold of the paper.

Hiring a horse and buggy, we drove the fifteen miles to Phoenixville. It was a sunny August day, and the drive took us across one of the loveliest bits of country in America, the Chester Valley. The drive would have been enjoyable to anyone; to two young men bent upon ambitious venture it was thrilling. At our journey's end we saw the treasurer of the iron company and made a favorable impression; we could take the property subject to the five-thousand-dollar mortgage, without any cash payment. Imperatively, however, we must have a sizable amount to put the plant in even the minimum of working order.

I had some hundred and fifty dollars of savings—I had been receiving twelve dollars a week and boarding at the Green Tree Hotel for six a week. Miller had about the same. The sum of our slender savings was not enough. The money that made the difference between impossibility and opportunity came from an unexpected source. There was in the town where Miller and I were working a man of what was, in that time and place, some means; his name was Henry Buckwalter. Possessing perhaps a hundred thousand dollars, he was a capitalist, indeed a retired capitalist. In his leisurely strolling about the town he used to drop into the office where Miller and I worked. He observed us, chatted with us, came to like us; he would sit in the office and talk to us or read the newspapers while we worked. Noticing that we were putting our heads together about something, he asked us what was afoot. We told him, as a secret, for we were not yet sure we could swing the project, and if we did not go into it we did not want our employer to know we had contemplated it. Buckwalter asked questions, which our eagerness was very ready to answer and expound upon. After he had fully grasped the idea and all the details he said, "I figure you boys ought to have about two hundred and fifty dollars; I'll lend it to you if you like; you can give me a note for it." It was not business on his part, for he could have used his money else-where with equal or greater profit, and much greater safety. Neither was it benevolence in the merely sentimental sense, for he would not have loaned us the money if he had not thought we would be successful. It was friendly and practical encourage-ment to two young men whom he liked and whom he thought capable enough to do well.

In later years, after my work called on me to think about the nature of society, I have thought that Henry Buckwalter's lending us that two hundred and fifty dollars, and the episode as a whole, was a characteristic incident of American capitalism in operation, and at its best. Here were two young men who, emerging from school, had looked about for employment. They had found it in a kind of work they liked and which, because they liked it, they did well. They and their work came under the observation of a man who had capital, and he enabled them to go into business for themselves.

We bought the Phoenixville *Republican* in November 1893, I being then two months over twenty years old, Miller three or four years older. I went to Phoenixville and took possession—Miller could not come for a few weeks. From him, on Novem-ber 15, 1893, I received a letter which, as I read it after more than forty years, calls back our busy eagerness:

MARK, Suppose you take that list of display type we made out, and add to it one font Roman antique, long primer, for date line, and send it to Ayer and Son, asking them for a price on same and whether they would take it out in advertising. I believe they would, or at least a good deal of it. Send that right away. Arrange to have a machinist make wheel for that side gear of cylinder. Be sure to send those newspaper rollers down to Godfrey and Company to be re-cast, also write them that you have shipped them, giving name of press, also the time we must have them. We must get a new blanket for that press. We ought to be sure to start off with an unusually good paper. Call on Squire Howell, go around town just as much as you can. I will be over Tuesday for sure.

Miller had the business end; he was ideal for it. He was frugal, painstaking, methodically industrious, cautious, yet with an amount of imagination and ambition that was admirably in scale with the scope of our enterprise. Among his other qualities he had one that is desirable in the business end of a publication; he had no interest in writing, no wish to do it or judge it or concern himself with it. All that his happiness and pride needed from his editor-partner was a newspaper that would do credit to us and be liked by the community.

I loved it. Daily I went from end to end of Bridge Street, dropping into each shop and office. To this day I can remember the order in which they came, and see the features of the men to whom I called out one variation or another of "What's new?" Most fruitful of my sources was "Ellie" (short for Ellery) Miller's cigar store, a small, one-roomed frame building, which was a kind of clubhouse for several of the town's minor worthies and a few of its major ones. Its crowded furnishings were a dozen ancient wooden chairs and an equal number of immense spittoons—less than one per chair would not have been enough—together with a couple of checkerboards so long used that the squares were barely decipherable in such light as the dingy windows admitted, its sooty walls spotted with immense and lurid posters of tobacco brands—I recall Battle Axe and Star Plug. It was the gathering place for sundry of the town's personages: the chief of police in his hours off duty—he was called "Stony" Moore, the nickname supposed to denote intrepidity; the auctioneer, whose periods of occupation were irregular and brief, and therefore left him much spare time; the town's principal Civil War veteran—he bore, legitimately and creditably, the title "General"; two or three bosses from the iron mills who dropped in after work; various businessmen whose business was not too urgent; an insurance agent whose employment was at once elastic and ambulatory—he carried his office in his hat; two or three of the town nabobs spending the evening of their days in leisure; some lesser figures who, since their economic status did not permit leisure, had to be classified as idlers. In winter, sitting around the big-bellied coal stove stoked to red-hot, or in summer on the sidewalk, they heralded and discussed the doings of the town. I learned that by dropping in about noon, bearing news that I had picked up, I could, by contributing what I had to the common store, get still more news for myself, as well as salty views and pungent phrases useful for the paper. Later in the day, after I had finished getting the paper out, I would return, this time not for utilitarian purposes but as a sharer of the institution's leisure, recipient of, and perhaps sometimes neophyte contributor to, its wisdom and its humor.

My recollections of Ellie Miller's cigar store are more vivid than those of any of the more formal clubs to which I have belonged. Among the occasional spenders of leisure—and, I suspect Ellie Miller felt, not much else—was a Civil War veteran. He had a pension and wished a larger one. A law that would have increased his pension had just been vetoed by Grover Cleveland. I shall never forget my horror at the malice, the savagery of balked covetousness, with which he cried out, about the President of the United States, "the God damned potbellied son of a bitch." I shall never forget the greedy idler's venom. Once there came to the store a stranger, a traveling salesman of energetic and acquisitive bent. When I was introduced to him as the town editor, and he therefore saw in me one who might possibly be of service in his enterprise, he offered me a cigar. Upon my declining he urged, "Take it. It's good. It's a two-for," by which he meant that it cost two for a nickel and therefore was more recherché than the "three-fors" which were the usual limit of luxury at Ellie Miller's shop.

Editing implies writing editorials. I did as much of that as was done. I took no especial pleasure then, or ever, either in the writing of editorials or the dignity presumed to accompany that function. I much preferred reporting. That preference was, for the Phoenixville *Republican*, fortunate, for the editor was also the reporter, the only one, until, after a year or so, prosperity made an assistant possible.

Neither about national politics nor about local politics did I ever receive pressure or suggestion from the iron company, though they were at once our mortgagee, our landlord and our principal customer for job printing. Minor officials of the company sometimes suggested courses that would have served their personal ends in local politics. Left to myself, I took the side of the "kickers," the anti-organization faction, in the fierce fights within the Republican party which at that time composed the major part of Pennsylvania politics. Where I acquired the "anti" point of view I do not know; probably to some extent it was temperamental. Sometimes I wrote quite stirring editorials about local politics. During the first campaign after we had the paper I took a strong stand in favor of the kickers' slate of candidates for town council and county offices. The beneficiaries of my advocacy were pleased and grateful, but were mystified and a little hurt when, on Election Day, the climax of our common effort, I did not vote for them nor appear at the polls at all. I did not like to tell them that I was not yet twenty-one, so I invented a business errand to Philadelphia as explanation of my failure to vote.

CHAPTER 16

AT PHOENIXVILLE I lived in the "clubhouse," the former mansion of a local iron master, now turned into a boarding-house. Its patrons were mainly young executives of the iron company and the wives of such as were married. It was the quarters also of young engineers who came to Phoenixville for a few weeks or months, as inspectors representing railroads or other concerns from which the iron company had contracts. These engineers came to compose much of my companionship in recreation. They were a type with which I had not previously had much acquaintance, graduates of colleges or of the engineering schools of universities; they had experience of cities, and had ideas and interests broader and more varied than I had known. Contact with them stirred to greater energy the notion, never absent from my mind, that I ought to go to college.

To visit one of the young engineers came his fiancée, Miss Hope Cox, with her mother. Her father was dean of the University of Cincinnati Law School; he had been governor of Ohio, a member of Grant's Cabinet and a Civil War general. Her brother, Kenyon Cox, was an esteemed artist of the time.

To me the young woman became an important instrumentality of fate. She was of a type not likely to come within the experience of a small-town newspaperman, and indeed, any man might live a long lifetime without seeing many such. I did not know such beings existed, except in books or as paintings; I thought of her as a personification of the picture of Queen Louise, and it dawned on me as astounding that something which I had thought was merely an ideal of the imagination could actually exist. Hope Cox impressed that boy editor as much, and in much the same way, as if an archangel had been introduced to him and shaken his hand and said, "How do you do." When I heard her play the piano I learned that there is music and music; she playing and her fiancé singing was the first time I ever heard "On the Road to Mandalay." She loaned me a novel then new (and ever since important), Harold Frederic's *The Damnation of Theron Ware*, and talked to me about it, and I learned there were novels and novels; up to that time I had supposed that Ouida did not differ from William Dean Howells except that Ouida was more exciting, and therefore superior.

My unconcealable admiration, my looking up to her, would not have impressed her; adoration, I imagine, both from men and from awed boys, was an old story to her. She must have seen some latent quality in the boy editor and she took an interest in me. She did not bother herself with any correction of my gaucheries, she went to the heart of the matter. She told me I must go to college, I must go at once, the coming fall, and I must go to Harvard—no other would do. She gave me letters of introduction to friends on the Harvard faculty.

July 15, 1896, I wrote one of my brothers—apparently this letter is the second in a correspondence in which I had told him I was going to leave Phoenixville, and he had expressed some dubiousness about my breaking up a situation in which I was exceptionally fortunate. I did not mention to him the agency that had precipitated my going to college; I merely dwelt on the desirability of going. I print the letter complete, as I wrote it, for the flavor of it lies in its entirety, and I would not deprive the reader of the smile I got from it when I read it forty years after. If the letter reflects a young man intent on self-improvement, why, earnestness for self-improvement was in those days a virtue, and not a rare one. If it is sententious, even priggish, and seems more patterned after a Victorian model for letter writing than was my usual style, the reason is that I had been moved to high seriousness by Hope Cox's taking hold of me and insisting that I go to college, and I was justifying myself to a brother much older than myself, almost a parent.

My action in regard to a change here is inspired solely by my desire to take a college course. I have entertained the idea ever since I left the Normal School, my intention being to earn enough money to take me through college. I will be twenty-two years old in September. It is time either to go now or abandon the idea entirely. After this year it will be too late to start, and if I don't get to college the coming fall, I shall give up the idea utterly and buckle down to work. I have thought over the idea a long time and have viewed it from all sides, and I am thoroughly convinced that I would be doing the best for myself by leaving here and going to college. If you view the thing as a whole, apart from immediate necessities and considerations of expediency, you will have no trouble in seeing that the proper thing to do is to secure a college education. However, there seems to be absolutely no one else who sees the question as I do, and every person to whom I mention it advises me most strongly to stay in Phoenixville. Mr Miller [my partner] simply refuses to entertain any project looking to my leaving, and just insists that I stay.

The letter up to this point expressed my own ideas. In the rest of it I was clearly parroting something that had been said to me, I presume by Hope Cox—what would have been priggish in me would have been natural in her speaking to me:

There is no discounting the value of an education, and the acquaintances and associations formed at a big university. It simply transforms a man. After those four years are over, he looks at things from a different attitude. He is no longer the same man, and a man who fails to secure a college education never knows what he might have done, or have been, had he gone to college.

Yours very truly,
MARK SULLIVAN

With my partner I made a financial arrangement. He would advance me, from time to time, out of the profits of the paper, such amounts as I needed at Harvard, the advances to be never more than seventy-five dollars a month. Afterward, if I chose, I could resume my partnership by paying back the advances.

II

I packed my trunk, I took the train, I changed at New York and took the train for Boston—the train bore William Jennings Bryan on his swing around the circle in his Free Silver campaign for the presidency. I arrived at Boston in the evening, stopped overnight at the Thorndyke Hotel, and the next morning went out to Cambridge to arrange for admission. Because my preparation at the Normal School had not aimed toward college I was defective in my entrance requirements. I was obliged to register as a special student, with many conditions to make up.

About my experiences that first fall at Harvard I have no letters or other records, and my memory brings back only two incidents that are vivid. One was my first sight of President Eliot. It was in the forenoon. He was walking down the slope from the president's house to the university office. His physique, his vibrant bearing, his long legs and the lithe firmness of his step, the erect poise of his head, the distinction of his features, the combination of benevolence and strength in his countenance, impressed me instantly and powerfully.

In his physical endowment Dr Eliot was fortunate. Though it included a large, lividly purple birthmark on one side of his face, the defect served to call attention to his features, and the features bore well the notice that was focused on them. Anybody who looked frequently at President Eliot and at the bronze statue of John Harvard outside Memorial Hall saw resemblance between the two, Eliot the sculptor's ideal reproduced in life. I reflected that Dr Eliot's birthmark had been an asset to him. It marked him off from other men, it called attention to a countenance that would bear inspection; and, I reflected, its influence on him as a child may have been a stimulus to achievement; he may have thought that he must overcome by distinction of mind and by achievement what to a weaker character might have been a handicap.

To say that Charles William Eliot was one of the very great men of his time is to repeat what thousands have said before. I, contemplating Dr Eliot, realizing the effect his mere presence had on me, the enlargement of my mind that came through him—I could affirm an epigram more extreme than the old saying that a log with a student on one end and Mark Hopkins on the other, is a college. I could say that Charles William Eliot walking down the slope from the president's house was a university education.

I can recall the particular form in which one of Dr Eliot's

qualities dawned on me, and affected me in such a way as to compose a landmark of intellectual expansion. It occurred to me, observing Dr Eliot's utter freedom from servitude to the habitual, that he was a man who would approach any subject or problem as if it had never been considered before. If he addressed himself to what kind of clothes human beings should wear, he would gravely consider the needs involved in the problem, warmth in winter, coolness in summer, weight of garments, convenience—and might arrive at a type of clothes never seen before.

While in college I saw little of Dr Eliot. Soon after I graduated and was writing, I became aware that he liked me, and that was a powerful stimulant to me. He approved the unorthodox views I was expressing in my writing and talked with me about them. Once, entertaining a concern about my health and suggesting a trip to Bermuda, he advised characteristically, "One may get there a very desirable sense of isolation from the hustling world, particularly if one lives in a boardinghouse, or lodging house, and not in one of the large hotels."

The "hustling world" was much in Dr Eliot's mind as he grew older. Once he came to my office at *Collier's Weekly* to enlist my aid in a project he had—this, oddly, was for a preservation of the old, a defense against the new. He wished to prevent automobiles from being permitted on Mount Desert Island; he said they had been banned by Bermuda and thought it could be done elsewhere. I sympathized with his wish to keep Mount Desert attuned to a slower tempo, but was obliged to tell him I doubted if the automobile could be resisted. In any event, I told him, newspapers and periodicals could not help him; the economic basis upon which they existed was advertising, and at that time about half of all advertising was of automobiles and accessories.

One other incident of that first October at Harvard remains vividly with me. I can see the scene and identify the time. It was a sunny afternoon and I was hurrying across the Yard with as many books as my two arms would hold. I had read, soon after arriving in Cambridge, a novel by William Dean Howells. It was *The Landlord at Lion's Head;* it had been recommended to me by Hope Cox because it dealt with Harvard. Finishing it, I had felt elation; here was something new to me, and entrancing. I then had rushed to the college library. I asked how many books I could take out. I looked up the titles of Howells' novels and I took all I was permitted. Going toward my room with them, my mood was one of hurry, of anticipated delight. Yet something in the sight of the westering sun on the walls of Holworthy, something in the green of the grass and the falling leaves of the elms, something in the quiet of the hour—it was a Saturday and few students were about—something in it all arrested my hurry and altered my mood. The spirit of excited anticipation inspired by the books in my arms calmed to a mood of serenity inspired by the college yard. I had a moment of quiet rapture. I was in a new world, an enlarged and elevated world; I was glad I had come to it, I was going to be happy here.

CHAPTER 17

I FINISHED my college work at the midyear examinations in 1900, about the middle of February. (I would not get my degree until the following June.) I was uncertain about my future. I knew that my partner in the Phoenixville *Republican* would not wish me to come back; he had been managing the paper alone for nearly four years, he had done it successfully, he had no real need of me; if I came back he would be obliged to divide the earnings with me and I could make no material addition to the paper's income, for the field would not permit expansion. He was in a position, if he wished, to insist on his point of view, even if I did not agree, for he had advanced to me while I was in college an amount of money that was about as much as my half interest in the business was worth.

Though I felt sure my connection with the *Republican* must come to an end, I put off doing anything about my future. At times I gave thought to remaining in the college community, perhaps to seek some kind of foothold on the lowest rung of teaching, though my record as a student had no such excellence as would justify that hope. But I had learned to like learning; I recall going through the college catalogue and finding that the total number of courses, including remote ones about the history of Assyria and of the Bagdad Caliphate, was roughly two hundred. To take all those courses, at the rate of four a year, which was the college requirement, would consume fifty years; and I thought it would be a nice way to spend one's life, living in a college room and covering the whole world of learning. The inclination to remain at college comes to many young persons, I think. If hesitancy about going out into life came to me, who had already had contact with the world, much more must it come to those younger and less experienced than I.

II

In my looking toward the future I considered returning to newspaper work, usually in terms not of going on a city newspaper, but of operating, and in time owning, some small-town newspaper. That was the experience I had had. Because I had done well in it I thought I was adapted to it. Because I had enjoyed it in a small town I thought I would like it also in a somewhat larger one.

I thought mainly of making a start in some young city in the West that had promise of growth, for at that time, about the turn of the century, "going West" was still a lure to many young men in the East; Horace Greeley's aphorism, "Go West, young man," was still quoted. There were still recent examples of Western cities, such as Seattle, that had grown rapidly, carrying to position and fortune those who had been in at the start.

Considering this, I used occasionally to send out broadcasts for copies of Western newspapers. From a newspaper directory I would make a list of the papers in a section of the West, and send requests for sample copies. These I would study to find what combination of paper and locality might be most inviting. A considerable number of Western towns would be surprised to know how narrowly they escaped seeing an ambitious young man drop in upon them with a view to starting a new paper or making an existing one better. Always in my contemplations I tried to pick a city favorably situated for growth. The one that I thought about most was Cheyenne, Wyoming; I recall being fascinated by the pictures of cattle brands in the advertising columns of Cheyenne papers. As it happens, had I gone to Cheyenne in the year 1900, I would have hit upon the one city in the West that was destined to have almost the least growth.

Without coming to any conclusion I decided to use the three months of idleness I would have before receiving my college degree by taking a trip to the West. Nineteen hundred was still a time when anyone having a newspaper connection could get railroad passes, and my partner in the Phoenixville *Republican* would be glad to accommodate me. He got me transportation on the B. & O. Railroad that would take me to Chicago, and on the Chicago, Milwaukee and St Paul that would take me to what was then the Western terminus of that road, Fargo, North Dakota. Of the journey the details that remain most vividly in my mind include staying in an inferior Chicago hotel, in which the rooms were rented in two shifts—for fifty cents I had occupancy from the arrival of a morning train until the departure of an evening one. At Minneapolis I was impressed by features of the still remaining frontier: employment offices with placards offering jobs to railroad workers on the roads that were still extending long fingers of new lines into virgin land; trainloads of immigrants—upward of a hundred thousand went into one state, North Dakota, that year.

My journey yielded me much of interest, but nothing in the form of newspaper opportunity. Returning to Cambridge, I took my degree from the college in June 1900. I arranged my separation from the Phoenixville paper, as I knew must be. I had no plan for the future. I went back to the farm for a few weeks; always, to me and to my brothers, the farm was a refuge and a sanctuary in times of indecision or other disturbance of spirit.

I am glad now that my after-college Western trip did not result in my becoming a newspaper publisher, and glad that that ambition never came to fruit on the many other occasions when I entertained it. Until I was upward of forty, hardly a year went by but I was fingering the notion of being a publisher, sometimes on my own account, sometimes in association with others. I was frequently in tentative negotiation for newspapers, during my early years in small cities, later in New York, Washington and other large cities. That I never took the step was due in large part to my wife. She, understanding me better than I understood myself, knew that the routine and complexity of a publisher's life would deprive me of happiness. She did not argue about it. By a passive resistance so unobtrusive that I did not then realize it existed, indeed by no more than merely not abetting me, she eased me past my recurring fits of disquieting ambition for the wrong thing. She serenely took it for granted that it would never happen, and it never did. She was wise. I would have been miserable. That a person with capacity to write should willingly deprive himself of the detachment and concentration that are essential to writing would be a mismanagement of life.

III

After I had graduated from college I was in a situation that caused me something approaching dismay. I had been, while still in my teens, an important figure. The fact that the pool was small did not too much diminish the young frog's pride—to that particular young frog, the pool had not been small at all, it had been large, the largest he had ever known. I had been half owner and editor of a daily newspaper, and my income had been materially more than a youth in his teens commonly commands. Both income and position I had abandoned to go to college. Now I had my college degree, but no greater access to a livelihood and career than any other young college graduate without connections. During a month or two after graduating I moped on the farm. "Moped" is perhaps too strong a word; while it has been my nature to make a thorough job of discouragement when I was in it, the mood has rarely lasted long.

Looking about for a new foothold, I turned to a newspaper that was then making a stir in Philadelphia. The *North American* had been, through many decades, perhaps the staidest paper in the city, with a small circulation chiefly among conservative families. But it had been bought recently by a wealthy man of the city, a department store merchant, Thomas Wanamaker, who wanted it not primarily as a newspaper but as an organ to fight the Republican machine of the state. Newspapers are about the only form of property men buy for purposes other than profit. Wanamaker, for his purpose, wanted a large circulation, and a popular kind of circulation. Like most rich men who buy newspapers, especially those who buy them for other than newspaper purposes, he wanted circulation quickly. Wanamaker and the manager he employed, Edwin A. Van

Valkenberg, having much money and impatience, were throwing a fury of energy into the *North American*. The effects, apparent in the paper, suggested to me that here I might find an opening. I found one, as a reporter of rank hardly above cub. The salary was twelve dollars a week.

By the experience I now had I came into contact with one of the striking American phenomena of my times, one that has had much effect on newspapers, and therefore on every area of life.

Wanamaker and Van Valkenberg, impetuous for quick circulation, looked about to find the means by which quick circulation was being achieved elsewhere. They observed what William R. Hearst had done in New York. Since the way to get circulation seemed to be the Hearst way, they decided to adopt the Hearst methods. And since the quickest way to adopt Hearst methods was to hire Hearst men, they imported into sober Philadelphia several Hearst-trained editors and writers. The chief editor, Arthur McEwen, had been one of Hearst's head men from the time he started in San Francisco. Several of the more important executives on the *North American* and some of the star reporters had been Hearst men in New York or San Francisco. My employment on the *North American* was, so to speak, a Hearst experience once removed. I did not like it.

Once I was detailed to shadow the venerable Catholic archbishop of the city. Bishop Ryan had been helping in an attempt to settle a strike. In the effort he had frequent meetings with the parties to the strike. If news of these meetings got out, settlement would be retarded. The bishop tried to keep his engagements out of the news—and that made them more sought after as news.

I was told to station myself where I could watch the door of the bishop's residence, and to follow him wherever he went. The bishop that day did not emerge until three in the afternoon. Furtively I dogged his footsteps while he made two calls at near-by residences, followed him into a streetcar and seated myself where he would not notice me, alighted behind him when he got off at the railroad station, bought a ticket to the same suburban station for which he entrained, followed him as he walked to a residence, lurked outside while he remained there, took the same train with him when he returned to the city. As he walked up the steps of his home I approached and stopped him. I asked if his movements during the day had had anything to do with the strike.

The bishop's distress made me thoroughly ashamed. He seemed like a man utterly appalled. "Oh, my dear boy," he said, "I have only been dining at the home of a friend." The way he said it, the gentleness of his voice, his manner of protesting and yet not reproaching me, made me sympathize with him and like him—and dislike myself. He was one of the sweetest and most trusting of men, and his recent experiences with reporters had been outrageous violation of his trustfulness. Not long before, a man had come to him, representing himself as a devout member of the bishop's faith who was traveling through the city and could not think of returning to his home without seeing and speaking to so distinguished a prelate of his church. The visitor steered the conversation into channels having to do with a subject of current and controversial interest, and the bishop talked informally and frankly. When the visitor was ready to go he took from his pocket a book the bishop had written and asked the bishop would he make the book more precious by autographing it. A few days later there appeared in a newspaper a sensational statement of the bishop's views on the topic he had talked about, authenticated by a facsimile signature of the bishop.

Much of my work on the *North American* had to do with getting photographs. Progress of the arts of photography and stereotyping to a point where it was practicable to print photographs in newspapers had coincided with Hearst's entrance into the newspaper business, and lavish use of photographs was one of the innovations by which Hearst established his type of paper. His former employees had brought the innovation with them to the *North American*. "Pictures, pictures, pictures," the city editor would say to reporters as he sent them out for stories—the command was a routine of the daily giving out of assignments. A story too trivial in itself to be printed would be given space if a photograph accompanied it. A story in which the facts took two lines of space would be accompanied by a photograph two columns wide.

From the instructions of older reporters, lore handed down by the expert to the neophyte, I was told the knack of getting photographs from persons not willing to give them. "You know the bluff," one of them said as I went out on a story about a fifteen-year-old girl who had run away to be an actress. "Tell her mother the police department has asked us to print a photograph of the girl to help them find her." Another time he said, "If they don't want to give you a photo of the bride, tell them we already have one in the office but it's an old tintype and we'd rather have a good one—that generally works." One of the seasoned reporters had a rule: when sent to a home to get a story, while waiting alone in the parlor for the person he had asked to see, he would slip into his pocket any promising-looking photographs that were on the mantel or elsewhere in the room, on the chance that one of them might be a photograph of the person involved in the story, or of a member of the family close enough to warrant publishing. The professional photographers of the city had been so often victimized by the bribing of their employees and by divers ingenious false pretenses that they were on their guard. A stratagem so frequent as to be commonplace was to go to a friend of the subject of a coveted photograph and tell a plausible story about having been sent by the subject to get a photograph because the latter had no more left. This was practicable in the days when telephones were still comparatively rare, and the duped person could not readily communicate with his friend.

One night a superior called me to his desk, introduced me to one of the staff photographers and gave the two of us a joint assignment for the following day. There was to be a parade in Fairmount Park. Riding in the parade would be the mayor, against whom the *North American* was conducting a campaign. So the photographer and I were to go to the park in advance of the parade, find a clump of bushes or other concealment along the route, and there wait and take a photograph of the mayor. Our clump of bushes must be on the right side of the parade, and our photograph must be so taken as to bring out a patch which the mayor wore over the socket of his missing right eye, a defect about which the mayor was believed to be sensitive.

When this assignment was given us it was late at night. The photographer and I made an appointment to meet the next morning, and I left the office. I never went back. Whether the photographer kept the assignment, and whether the *North American* got the picture it sought, I never knew. For within twelve hours I had left Philadelphia and was on my way to Boston. Somewhere, I suppose, on the account books of the *North American*, which some thirty years later ceased to exist, is a balance of about three days pay due a reporter who had worked on the paper a little over a month and had departed, without explanation, in the middle of a week.

My departure from the *North American* was in late September. It coincided with the opening of a new year at Harvard, and I suspect this coincidence was part of the inspiration for my action. In my distaste for the sordidness and febrility of the work I had to do on the *North American*, I thought longingly of the quiet serenity of Harvard. And in my reaction against this particular kind of newspaper work (with which I had had no contact before) I thought of studying law. The impulse to go back to Harvard was strengthened by the fact that while I had graduated in 1900 several of my close friends were in the class of 1901 and would still be at Harvard. Yet others of my class were staying at Harvard to enter the Law School. Those youths were very dear to me. The combined pull of the several allurements drew me back to Harvard and to registration in the Law School.

CHAPTER 18

For paying the expenses of my three years in the Law School I had no money and no provision for money, and I knew of no place toward which I had any right to turn. But I persuaded myself that I could get along by a plan I had.

In Boston was a fine old newspaper—half newspaper, half magazine, and wholly an institution. It printed, twice a week, on Wednesdays and Saturdays, a magazine section made up of features so well written and of such elevated standards that almost they might have appeared in the *Atlantic Monthly*. From the time I had first come to Boston four years before I had read the *Transcript* so diligently, and with so much liking and understanding, that I, from the outside, knew its policies and needs practically as well as the editors on the inside. I believed that I could write articles for the *Transcript* which would so impress themselves on the editors that they would ask for more; and that from this source I could get enough income to carry me through the Law School.

I had begun a siege of the *Transcript* already. The spring before, while I was still in college, I had written for them an account of my trip to North Dakota. But it was not that that I relied upon to impress myself on the *Transcript* editors. That was a travel article; all travel articles were, to all editors, mere "run of the mill"; mine from North Dakota had no striking importance or novelty.

The article which I relied upon to impress the *Transcript* and get me a foothold there was the second I wrote for them. The conception of it represented a requisite for the career of journalism—a flair for the interesting and the timely. The preparation of the article represented the quality that is indispensable to success in any career, hard work. To find a career to which you are adapted by nature, and then to work hard at it, is about as near to a formula for success and happiness as the world provides. One of the fortunate aspects of this formula is that, granted the right career has been found, the hard work takes care of itself. Then hard work is not hard work at all.

About this time, the year 1900, Theodore Roosevelt was coming to an advanced stage of conspicuousness in the public eye. He was governor of New York and had been nominated as the Republican candidate for vice-president. Hence anything written about him would have, to editors, the valuable newspaper advantage of timeliness; and anything new about him would be sure-fire.

Roosevelt had been a student at Harvard some twenty years before—that fact had been abundantly exploited in the current outflow of print about him. But none of this, I knew from avid newspaper and magazine reading, had gone more than superficially into his Harvard years. Any new facts, I reasoned, would be certain to interest the *Transcript.*

I set about a thorough search. The search, like all newspaper work of this kind, had the fascination that goes with the work of a mining prospector. I talked with as many of Roosevelt's former classmates as were reachable in the neighborhood of Cambridge and Boston—a mere recital of the names and their present activities would now be made interesting by reflected eminence. I talked with such former teachers of his as were still members of the faculty. From the files of the college periodicals of his time I dug up college activities, the clubs he had belonged to, his contributions to the *Advocate,* of which he had been an editor. I found the house in which he had lived, and his room. I talked with his former landlady—from her I got entertaining stories. One was about a large turtle from the South Seas which young Roosevelt's interest in natural history had led him to keep in a box in his room, and which escaped one night and proceeded to the nearest equivalent of the South Seas in that neighborhood, to the consternation of one of Roosevelt's fellow roomers who stepped on the turtle in the bathroom in the dark. Another story was about an occasion when young Roosevelt leaped in his nightshirt from the window of his second-story room to quiet a disturbance caused by a horse in a near-by stable. I found what of itself would make an irresistible appeal to any editor, an unpublished photograph of Roosevelt, showing him without the mustache that was now conspicuous in current cartoons of him—but with generous side whiskers.

In my thoroughness I searched for background in articles dealing with Harvard in the magazines of the time when Roosevelt had been a student. I found one which served me well. In *Scribner's Monthly* for 1876 I found Harvard described as being characterized by "repression or even distaste for enthusiasm, that emulation of high-bred cynicism and arrogant coolness which in a young man do not betoken the healthiest enthusiasm; the divine fervor of enthusiasm is openly or by implication voted a vulgar thing." That was written about Harvard as of the year when Theodore Roosevelt was a freshman—and Roosevelt in maturity was called a "steam engine in trousers." The contrast between the common conception of Harvard and the qualities which brought fame to its most distinguished graduate would, I felt sure, add interest to the article I was writing.

I took my article to the *Transcript*. They bought it. Some penciled figures in my scrapbook indicate that the article was forty-six inches long and that I was paid a column rate which worked out as thirty-five cents an inch, in all $16.10. If this fell short of exalted compensation for the time and work involved, yet my remuneration in the form of the favorable impression made on the *Transcript* editors was abundant. It was a long step in my start as a professional writer.

II

The next article I wrote for the *Transcript* grew out of something within myself, a concern I felt about a matter of public interest. About 1900, and during some years preceding, it was widely assumed that the buffalo was about to become extinct.

The condition came to my attention through occasional allusions I encountered in my voracious newspaper reading. The newspaper mention was infrequent and casual. There was no great public interest in the subject, the approaching extermination was taken for granted. To me the condition seemed terribly to be deplored. My concern was mainly of the same nature as the average man's interest in wild life, only more intense. In the groping exploration into the facts which I presently began there was not, at first, any definite expectation of making the subject into newspaper copy. I was, as respects this matter, a reformer; the threatened fate of the buffalo, in addition to stirring that intellectual curiosity about the interesting which must be part of the make-up of every person born for newspaper work, aroused in me personal poignancy. Yet the spirit in which I began to collect the facts did not include any expectation of changing the facts for the better. At the first, like nearly everybody else, I accepted the approaching extinction of the buffalo as an unavoidable fate. That one of the largest animals, one having romantic associations, was about to perish from the earth, was an interesting fact. I wondered what was the exact number of buffalo still living, where they were, and how and where the last one might roam. To find out, I began to read systematically. As I looked up articles in popular magazines I was moved to push my reading on into scientific periodicals. The statements I discovered were fragmentary, and in many cases contradictory. I decided to make investigation beyond the printed material.

I started with a list of all the places—Western public parks, zoos in Eastern cities, and a few areas still wild—which the reading I had done had mentioned as containing buffaloes. To the heads of those, or to persons familiar with them, I wrote letters. I had no tyepwriter and of course no stenographer. From my Harvard room, in such periods of leisure as I had, I wrote longhand letters. To all my letters (without exception, I think) I got replies, for all to whom I wrote were interested in the subject and could recognize from my letters that I was interested.

Those who felt a concern about the fate of the buffalo were a kind of fraternity, with no organization except the letters we exchanged, but united with more zeal for a common interest than most fraternities have. We thought of ourselves as the company of mourners for a great animal about to cease to be, for a romantic aspect of American life about to disappear.

The replies to my letters, as they came in, mentioned other persons to whom I ought to write. The head of Yellowstone Park, which contained the largest herd, knew of smaller herds or individual animals elsewhere, and suggested the names of persons who might have exact information. In time—the enterprise lasted many weeks—I wrote to the head of every zoo in every American city, to the game commissioner in every Western state, to several private citizens who had saved small herds, to the head of Banff National Park in Canada and the head of the Northwest Mounted Police. I wrote to Carl Hagenbeck, who from his *handels-menagerie* in Hamburg had supplied buffaloes to zoos and private estates in Europe; I wrote to the Duke of Bedford, who had a small herd in Woburn Park, Bedfordshire.

As the replies came in they necessitated further letters to the same persons. Since the question was how near the buffalo was to extinction, not only was the number of each herd important but the number of each sex, and, as near as could be judged, whether the females were still of bearing age. Also it transpired that at some points in the West breeders had crossed buffalo with ordinary cattle, resulting in a hybrid called a "cattalo." The attempt had not gone far, for an ordinary cow could not give birth to a half-breed bison, because of the latter's hump; consequently the only crossing that could be fruitful consisted of breeding an ordinary bull to a female buffalo. Since female buffaloes were now scarce, and valuable for bearing full-blood buffalo calves, the attempt to produce a race of cattalos had been given up. But the effort had resulted in a number of half bloods; hence it was necessary to write yet again to my correspondents, asking them to tell me, with certainty, how many in their herds were unquestionably full blood.

My research had a startling result. The number of living

buffalo was materially larger than had been supposed. Contemporary estimates had put the number at between four and six hundred. My investigation showed the number was 1024, of which a normal proportion were female.

With prospect that the buffalo could be saved, interest turned from antiquarian repining to reformatory zeal. I busied myself —though my activity was as yet confined to letter writing—with suggestions to heads of zoos that they exchange animals, to offset inbreeding, and with projects for setting up small herds in every part of the country and at varying altitudes so as to achieve diversity of environment.

With reformatory zeal came also a capacity for literary objurgation. In the *Transcript* article in which I embodied the results of my researches I used the term "wanton ruffians" for hunters who poached on the herd in Yellowstone Park, and I asked the public to visit "merited contempt upon persons who bought heads and hides from the poachers." Because a proposal to set aside twenty thousand acres as a buffalo range had been resisted in Congress by the territorial delegate from New Mexico, I indicted, with an inclusiveness common to reformers, every person west of the Mississippi River: "Your true Westerner reverences nothing but utility; he would use his grandmother's tombstone for a doorstep."

My *Transcript* article, by the surprisingly and pleasingly large number of buffalo which my census discovered, created widespread interest. By the obvious thoroughness of my research, and by the interest I showed, I got the approving acquaintance of distinguished naturalists and lovers of wild life. For me, and for the *Transcript*, the article was a striking success.

I now had secure standing with the *Transcript*. I could count on their printing something from me every week or two. The compensation I received was not large but it would go far toward supporting me while I was at the Law School. The compensation in satisfaction was immeasurable. If ever I am indicted for the crime of vainglory, the damning proof will recite the spirit in which I used to go into Boston on Wednesday or Saturday forenoons, walk down Washington Street, stand in front of the *Transcript* office and read on a large bulletin board the words: "By Mark Sullivan."

I continued my association with the *Transcript* throughout my three years at the Harvard Law School and for some months after graduation. I wrote scores of articles, the topics almost always of my own choosing. The *Transcript* editor with whom I dealt—his name was Rollin Lynde Hartt and I am under great obligation to him—learned what most of my employers and associates have learned, that they got the best out of me when I was left to pick my own path. Since the topics were of my own choosing, a collection of the titles would seem an index to my bent, my interests. As I look through an old scrapbook I am impressed by the number which reflected the same kind of interest as my article about the buffalo. In article after article I was saving wild life. In "Protecting the Birds" I supported a measure in Congress limiting commercial shooting of game birds and the sale of feathers of ornamental ones—I illustrated my plea with the story of the extinction of the passenger pigeon. In "Vanished Forest Folk" I wrote of the animals and birds that once were common in Massachusetts but had disappeared. In "Saving the Gulls" I praised a Massachusetts citizen who had endowed the Thayer Fund for the Protection of Gulls and Terns. In "Wanton Slaughter of Big Game" I advocated legislation to limit bags. In "Happy Days for the Whale" I gloated over the dwindling of an industry, due to lack of demand for whale oil, which resulted in safety for a picturesque mammal. I lauded the order of Elks for passing a resolution pledging themselves not to use elks' teeth as watch charms—"the species is in imminent danger of extermination."

I prowled about Boston in search of the picturesque. I wrote "Before His Honor," an account of a day in the Boston police court; "Strangers at the Gate," a trip down Boston Harbor with the immigration officials to meet an incoming steamer; "Joining the Army," a day in a recruiting office; "An Expounder of the Oraculum," an account of fortunetellers and the venders of "dream books."

In a more conventional area of interest I reviewed books, interviewed local authors and reported the lectures which visiting scholars delivered at Lowell Institute. One of these, Frederic Harrison, the exponent of positivism, I described for Boston understanding as a "composite of Charles Eliot Norton and Theodore Roosevelt." And I wrote much about politics, always with reformatory zeal.

III

So great was the latitude permitted me by the *Transcript* that I was able to fulfill a writer's dream, travel, with assurance of acceptance of enough articles to defray my expenses. One journey, taken in a summer vacation from the Law School, was to Nova Scotia and Newfoundland. Much of the way I walked, carrying, for days at a time, no more luggage than could be bundled into a folded red sweater. By this simplicity of travel I had contacts with types of persons and points of view which journeyers more pretentious do not have.

At Halifax, sitting in the park and observing the ships pass in and out of that long, bottleneck harbor, a stranger sat down beside me. He was a man of good dress and cultivation, wholly sensible so far as I could tell until he got on the subject of the Catholic Church. He was of Protestant and British birth and he told me his fear that Canada would be dominated by the Catholic French. The population increase of the French, he said, was due to a practice devised by the Catholic Church and carried out by the priests—the priest in each parish maintained a standing award of a hundred dollars for every pair of twins born. "It isn't that so many twins are born," he told me, "it's the everlasting trying for twins." His prejudice and misinformation were incredible, and gave me an insight into how a man's mind may be warped by bigotry. Gravely he informed me that if I would observe the houses into which I went, both in Canada and in the United States, I would notice that in every room where there was a chimney there was a considerable space between the outer wall of the chimney and the flue. This space, he informed me, was created, carefully and secretly, by the building contractors who, in both Canada and the United States, were mainly Irish Catholics. The purpose, he said, was to provide room for a man to stand—in every chimney there was a spy of the Pope, listening.

I did not argue with him. It has been my way not to argue with individuals—I do not think a writer should. He can address a million individuals—to argue with one is a waste. Besides, a writer who listens gets more material for his trade than one who argues.

When I landed at Port au Basque in Newfoundland I could have taken a narrow-gauge train for the thirty-six-hour journey which spans that immense island. But I was in a mood to walk. One afternoon, approaching a tiny farmhouse solitary by the sea to ask for lodging for the night, I was cheered to hear a woman's voice singing:

> *Where you be-en a' this day,*
> *Bonnie Hieland laddie, O?*
> *In the mountains gathering hay,*
> *Bonnie Hieland laddie, O.*

and I felt that anyone who sang so blithe a song would give me welcome. She did. I ate supper, for which the family wanted no more pay than the talk an outsider brought to their remoteness. The father had an intelligence and cultivation which puzzled me, and led me to probe tactfully into his background. I learned that he had been educated for the Catholic priesthood, but in the senior year of his seminary course had fallen in love, married and gone away to this secluded spot. As the time for bed approached, the mother and children got a blanket, spread it on the kitchen floor, spread hay on the blanket and on top of the hay another blanket, upon which I passed the reposeful night that youth can always command.

In the morning, after breakfast, as I started on my way, the father walked a little distance with me. After we were well away from the house he, with an abruptness which startled me, addressed me very earnestly: "You're a personable young man"

—it was the first time I had ever heard the word "personable"— "you can marry well; be sure that you do; don't take the first love that presents itself." He turned abruptly and left me. I was sorry for him, yet shocked by his bitter worldliness.

In the hotel at St John's, as I went in and out upon my work collecting material for my articles, I observed in the lobby two middle-aged Americans whom I judged to be businessmen, of somewhat less than high standing—I inferred they were in Newfoundland on some enterprise which, when completed, would result in loss of money by inhabitants of that unsophisticated island. I did not speak to them except to nod as I passed through the lobby. One day one of them called me and asked me to sit down by him. To my quite extreme astonishment he said, "My partner and I have been noticing you around here for a couple of weeks; I'd like to tell you we have noticed the way you go about your work; we like the way you carry yourself. You have the makings of success. If you make no mistake you should do well in life, and I thought I'd just like to tell you, above everything, always be honest—never take any short cuts." He expatiated in a way which, in words, revealed nothing of himself or of his life, but which in manner and the circumstances told me much. Worldly age contemplating carefree youth is always engaging to observe; when the worldliness has not resulted in success it can be tragic.

In a deep, narrow bay along the north shore of Newfoundland I walked through four tiny villages, the location and names of which suggested that they must have been successive stages in the flight of some harassed mariner seeking sanctuary from storm at sea. The village farthest out in the bay, at the tip of the cape jutting into the ocean, was Heartbreak. Down the side of the bay, in successive advances toward safety, were Heart's Ease, Heart's Content and, finally, Heart's Delight.

In one of these charmingly named villages I learned the lore of sealing; this was not the season for it but the life of the community was colored with it. These Newfoundland sealers were of west-of-England stock; through two centuries of isolation they had preserved the Devonshire tongue which permitted their name for their occupation to rhyme with "islan'," in a ditty about their calling:

> *Way out on Pigeon Pond Islan',*
> *When Daddy comes home from swilin'—*
> *Maggoty fish hung up in the air,*
> *Fried in maggoty butter—*
> > *Cake and tea for supper,*
> > *Loaf and tea for breakfast,*
> > *Pork and beans for dinner,*
> *Way out on Pigeon Pond Islan',*
> *When Daddy comes home from swilin'.*

From a Heart's Ease fisherman I heard what few have heard in its natural background, a "come all ye" ballad. Of the first stanza I preserved only the opening lines:

> *Come all ye friends and neighbors*
> *My story for to hear. . . .*

The ballad told of a trip of a fishing schooner, which began in early July. After the stocking of the ship and other preparations,

> *The next day bein' the Fifth, my boy,*
> *The great King William's day,*
> *We hove her anchor to the bows*
> *And then we bore away.*
> *Folla de lura lura lay,*
> *Folla de lura lura lay.*

On the trip, one day

> *We opened a tub of butter*
> *And it were an awful smell.*

On another day their luck was bad; the failure was recorded in a couplet in which "sea" was pronounced in the old English way:

> *All we got was sculpins,*
> *The scrapin's of the say.*

From a skipper who gave me a lift on a little boat called, charmingly, The Pearly Gates, I heard a ditty that to this day I occasionally hum:

Lukey's boat has cotton sails.
All she wants is pleasant gales.
Hi-diddle-i-dee.

A lively lilt I picked up on this journey, and which I still repeat when some mood summons it up, was a narrative of a trip of a trading schooner:

Up she goes to Mir-a-ma-chi
With a load of sugar and tea.

At a little landlocked harbor called Tilt Cove I stayed over Sunday with the businessman of the place, an Englishman in exile for the sake of trade. As we sat down to Sunday dinner he looked up at the clock, observed it was twelve and remarked, "It's teatime now at home." I could see it was a rite with him. He had not been back to England in twenty years, but when it was five o'clock in England, it was teatime, regardless of what any alien clock might say.

At a spot called Snook's Arm, on a long peninsula that sticks out like a pointing finger toward the Arctic Ocean, I fell in with some Norwegian whalers. The captain had caught whales in every sea from the Persian Gulf to Baffin Bay. He had now given up the ancient way of his calling and had established a fixed depot on the coast of northern Newfoundland. Each morning he steamed out twenty or thirty miles, and each nightfall he brought back his catch. I asked if I could go with him for a day; he, glad to have company, said I could. The catch that day was two whales. Late in the afternoon the captain swept the sea with his glasses and saw no sign of another "blow." He glanced at the sinking sun and measured with his eye the twenty miles to the harbor, dropped his glasses and gave a quiet order. The deck was made shipshape, and the stocky little whaler, her trophies grappled close to her sides, set her bow toward the mainland, like a chubby, happy boy with a big bundle under each arm, hurrying home at the end of the day.

Coming south through Nova Scotia, along the Bras d'Or Lakes on my way back, I arrived at the village of Baddeck.

There a number of Americans had summer places. The American newspaper most convenient to them was the *Transcript*, and they had been reading the articles which I had written from Newfoundland. For a writer, his writings are, to most who read them, a sufficient introduction. The Americans at Baddeck took me to themselves with great kindness.

One of the little American colony was Dr Alexander Graham Bell, inventor of the telephone. I inquired if it would be possible for me to call on him and was told to come to dinner. The trip to his house was made by rowboat propelled by the arms of one of the permanent residents of the community, who talked with a Scotch accent—practically all the permanent residents of Baddeck were descendants of Scotch immigrants. On the way across the lake the boatman talked about Dr Bell—with complete respect, yet with the tolerant half pity with which one discusses a well-intentioned but eccentric acquaintance. Some of what the boatman said I wrote down and printed later in the *Transcript*, from the files of which I here reproduce it:

He's the queerest mon ever you see in all your life, that Mr Bell. He goes up there on the side of yon hill of a sunny afternoon, with a lot of queer thing-a-ma-jigs, and there he fools away the whole livelong day, flying kites and doing things like that. Flying kites, mind you! Now what do you think of that! And him with that much money he might be spending every day of his life on a yacht enjoying himself. He sets up a blackboard on the hill there—you can see it 'most any day—and he marks down figures about those kites and the queer machines that he keeps bobbin' around in the wind. And God knows the kites are poor things! I could make better kites myself. He must have fifty of them of all kinds of queer shapes. And these men that comes to visit him—they goes up there with him, and there they do be spending the livelong day flying these kites—old men, mind you, that you'd think would have some business of their own to attend to. It's the greatest nonsense I ever see in all my life.

At the house Dr Bell introduced me to two of the venerable kite flyers. To suggest that I must be discreet about what I printed he introduced them smilingly as "Mr Smith" and "Mr Jones," but did not seriously try to conceal from me that they were two of the most distinguished scientists in America, Dr

Samuel P. Langley of the Smithsonian Institution and Dr Simon Newcomb, the astronomer.

During the evening Dr Bell talked about his kite flying and about the possibility of aviation—though in my record of his talk, as printed a few days later in the *Transcript*, I did not use the word "aviation," for neither the word, nor the thing the word describes, was yet in existence. To appreciate the prophetic interest of what Dr Bell said, and the extreme skepticism with which I listened, the reader should bear in mind that the date was October 16, 1901. (It was the day President McKinley was shot; news of the crime came to us during the evening.) Dr Bell talked freely about the experiments conducted by himself and his guests; they included a frequent spectacle even more queer than the kite flying that had mystified and disgusted my Scotch boatman—three learned men, two of them old and all of them very dignified, standing on a grassy lawn, dropping a kitten from a height of three or four feet onto a pillow, and taking a photograph of each stage of the process by which a cat accomplishes the feat of always landing on his paws.

"In my experiments [Dr Bell said, and I printed in the *Transcript*] I have simply been trying to satisfy myself whether such a thing as a flying machine is possible, and to discover the principles which must govern such a means of communication. I approach the subject with the absolute conviction that a practical flying machine is perfectly possible. It is purely a matter of speed of propulsion. Once we get a machine that will go through the air sixty feet a second, we can pick up anything on earth and fly away with it."

In my account in the *Transcript* I wrote as I here quote, "pick up anything on earth." What Dr Bell actually said was "pick up a church." I used the other phrase because I felt that "anything on earth" was vaguer, less concrete, than "a church," and would therefore be a slighter shock to credulity. I felt I was to some degree saving Dr Bell from seeming too ridiculous, and myself from seeming absurd to my readers. About the possibility of a practical flying machine and the value of Dr Bell's experiments I was as skeptical as the Scotch boatman. I felt vicarious shame for Dr Bell, thought he was fatuously deluded.

My impudent young skepticism failed to reflect that a man who had caused sound to conquer space might be entitled to consideration for his views about conquering gravity. As a necessity of my occupation I would record what he said, but I would not believe it:

"The future changes in the flying machine [Dr Bell declared] will be less and less use of the balloon, and more and more rapid motive power for the propeller. Ultimately we shall certainly have a perfected flying machine. When my scientific friends say it is impossible for heavy machinery to float in the air, I merely point to the birds and call attention to this important fact—the heavier the bird, the smaller the wings, the less the supporting surface. The mosquito has forty-nine square feet of wing to one pound of mosquito; the duck has only one half of one square foot of wing per pound of duck. Ultimately we shall discard the balloon utterly. None of the flying things of earth have balloons. A balloon swims like a fish, it does not fly. In the past, the line of development in flying has followed the fish, not the bird. This is wrong. We want aerial locomotion, not aerial navigation, which is an incorrect, unscientific thing. We want greater velocity."

I printed what Dr Bell had said, and did not reread it until a quarter of a century later. About 1926, writing about aviation in my *Our Times*, I recalled my conversation with Dr Bell and went back to the files of the *Transcript*. I knew now that his prophecy had been fulfilled. The first flight of an airplane took place on December 17, 1901, at Kitty Hawk, North Carolina, just three months after my talk with Dr Bell.

My last work for the *Transcript* represented a gently romantic adventure. I felt that the West—the thing that old America meant when it said "the West"—was passing rapidly. The last great land rush, in Oklahoma, had taken place fifteen years before; the last Indian uprising seventeen years before. Railroad building had passed its peak. All that remained of the frontier was fragments, fast becoming relics. Of the old West I had never had but a glimpse, on my trip to North Dakota in 1900. I felt that with the disappearance of "the West" one of the most picturesque phases of our history would be gone forever. I disliked to think that I should have lived through its passing and failed to see what remained of it.

Reflecting upon this, I observed that there was one place where some of the old West still remained. In Canada, between Winnipeg and the Rockies, and to the northward and westward —the country then called Northwest Territory—there was under way, just at this time, the opening up of new land, the pushing through of new transcontinental railroads, the rush of settlers. That region was just experiencing what had been completed in the United States—the passing of the old, the coming of the new. There was still a chance for a glimpse of the old West while it was still authentic, of the new West while it was still new. I asked the *Transcript* to send me there. They did. What I saw bore out what I had hoped.

"The cowboy," I wrote from Calgary, "rides his cayuse in all the glory of fringed leather trousers. Indians, real Indians in picturesque blankets, jostle you on the street. In this little city of Calgary, Frederick Remington's pictures are still contemporary art. One hears the term 'remittance man' as often as one hears 'college man' in Boston. And there is all the bizarrerie that one associates with the West. There are little towns near here named Whoop-Up, Stand-Off, Moose-Jaw and Man-Who-Stole-The-Coat." These names, I assured Boston, "are not local slang, they are actually on the map."

In the year in which I write this book, 1938, it had been a quarter century since I heard the term "remittance man." To readers born after 1900 the phrase may mean nothing; certainly few of them had ever seen a remittance man in the flesh. Once he was commonplace in western Canada, and familiar in our own West. He figures in many English novels of the nineteenth century, and in at least two of Kipling's poems. I described him in an article written from Calgary:

The remittance man is an Englishman who neither toils nor spins, but lives by virtue of a friendly mail that once in so often brings him a check from home. About the size of that check, there is no fixed rule, but this can be said: it is always less than enough to buy a ticket from Calgary to London. At home in England, the remittance man is said to be in Western Canada for the sake of his health; in Calgary he is commonly supposed to be here for the sake of the family reputation at home. I am inclined to a more charitable view of remittance men than the common Calgary opinion. They are the fruit of social conditions in England rather than damned by original sin. The remittance man is a by-product of the English system of primogeniture. You can read the whole story in Kipling's "Gentleman-Bankers," or "Lost Sheep." The eldest son inherits the landed estate, the younger must fend for themselves. It is no favor to the younger son to raise him in an environment that means champagne and truffles, the Carlton and Mayfair, and all that goes with it; and then turn him loose with just about enough income for beer and frank-furters and all that goes with that. His education doesn't fit him for any career whatever; there isn't an occupation open to him that would pay him more than twenty shillings a week, and if he goes to work in any but a few selected callings, he loses caste. If he's of very rare caliber, he may go to the colonies, become an empire-builder, and later be heard from. In the more frequent case, he falls into ways that make him an eyesore at home; and by-and-by his people make a more or less definite bargain with him; if he'll go to Western Canada and stay there, they'll send him enough money to keep him. His family gives him enough to set him up on a ranch, and cheerfully announces to friends at home who inquire for him that he's running a ranch in Western Canada. As often as not the money that should have started a ranch goes over the bar of the Royal Hotel. . . . These tales of profligacy are the commonest talk in Calgary. They say you can find in the local pawnshop silver-mounted, ebony-backed hair brushes and all the paraphernalia of a London clubman's dressing table. But there is one thing the most profligate will cling to as firmly as to hope of final social redemption. You will find dress suits bearing a Bond Street tailor's trademark in prairie shacks that contain little else to suggest civilization. Not all the remittance men are such as this. Some have gone about the way of the country with excellent spirit and business method. They have become prosperous ranchers, and with a complement of Chinese servants, serve dinner in courses in their bachelor ranch houses.

CHAPTER 19

THROUGH MY ASSOCIATION with the *Transcript* I came into some contact with what was left of the Boston that had once been the country's literary hub. Mainly they were elderly or aged persons, such as Thomas Wentworth Higginson and Louise Chandler Moulton, whose distinction, not very important and somewhat melancholy, was that in their prime they had known the authentic New England gods—Lowell, Longfellow, Whittier, Emerson. They could have paraphrased Holmes, could have said: "Now the mossy marbles rest on the hands that I have pressed."

One New England deity still lived, Sarah Orne Jewett. I did not meet her. Once there was a plan for me to meet her at the home of the poet, Mrs Moulton, but it missed. I have always been sorry. Miss Jewett's books are approved by the usual canons of literary judgment; for me they are an individual taste; my liking for them is an essential part of my personality, as definite as the color of my eyes.

Miss Jewett and a few other authors—W. W. Jacobs (*Many Cargoes*), Somerville and Ross (*All on the Irish Shore*), Mary E. Wilkins (*New England Nun*), Bret Harte (*The Luck of Roaring Camp* and *Jack Hamlin's Meditation*), W. E. Hudson (*Long Ago and Far Away*), Willa Cather (*My Antonia*), Joel Chandler Harris (*Uncle Remus*), Harry Stilwell Edwards (*Eneas Africanus*)—compose the library that I would take with me to exile on a solitary island. For certain of my moods Miss Jewett's books are perfect solace; they can bring me serenity of spirit as surely as a drug can bring sleep. I first read *The Country of the Pointed Firs* while at Harvard; read it again, and repeatedly, while working in New York; read it between dosings while a patient at Carlsbad; read it on long shipboard journeys; read it after hard days of work in Washington, and while at ease on the porch of my Pennsylvania farm; I have read it, and still read it, again and again. My liking for *The Country of the Pointed Firs* was in part a fruit of the New England part of my education. I had never seen New England until I went to Harvard; the years I spent there gave me strong liking not only for New England people but for the New England landscape. Both, landscape and people, are vividly and lovingly portrayed in Miss Jewett's books.

Of what was left that was vigorous in literary Boston, easily first was the *Atlantic Monthly;* almost it stood alone in sustained vitality. The associate editor of it in 1901 was William Belmont Parker. Him I met in a boardinghouse on the south side of Louisbourg Square, on the slope of Beacon Hill. To him I told stories of Pennsylvania politics, which entertained him vastly.

One of the stories I told him was about an experience I had had while on a visit to a remote Pennsylvania county. I had been staying with a family whose head was the principal banker of the county seat and leader of one of the county political factions. Driving with him on a country road, we met a shirt-sleeved farmer, an acquaintance of the banker. The farmer was a man of directness. No empty conventionality about the weather for him, he came to business at once.

"Well," he said to the banker, "I suppose we'll be able to do a little business together next week."

"I'm afraid not, Henry," replied the banker; "there's no money at all floatin' around, this campaign."

"A-a-l-l right," said the farmer truculently as he slapped the reins on his horse's back. "No money, no votes, I guess. Get ep, Jinny."

"There's a case for you," said the banker. "That man owns a two-hundred-acre farm clear, and he's got four thousand dollars' worth of bank stock; but he's mad clean through because I won't give him five dollars for his vote and his hired man's. I wouldn't mind if he was a poor man; you can't expect a man to leave his cornfield and go two miles to vote for nothing. But that fellow's an old skinflint. He counts on five dollars for his family's vote twice a year just as certainly as he depends on the sale of his wheat crop and his hogs."

On another occasion I went with my banker friend to the polling place. He leaned against a porch stoop a little distance from the booths, his pockets filled with packages of dollar bills. To him, so frequently as to be almost a stream, came those rural and village voters, some with simple directness; some shambling a little, with eyes averted; some accompanied by a minor political leader who vouched for them. To each the banker gave two dollars.

Across the road the head of the other faction did the same for his crowd. Between the two there was no tension, hardly even a rivalry.

About midafternoon both streams slowed up. Voters sat on the fences, a little sullenly. Minor lieutenants of the leaders reported that the electorate was conducting what would have been called, a few decades later, a "sit-down" strike; they felt they should have more money. Thereupon the two disbursers, dismissing all rivalry for the moment, consulted together. They agreed not to outbid each other. For a while the disbursers conducted the political equivalent of an industrial lockout. They left their posts, acted as if there was not to be any more paying. After a half-hour, as the sun began to get low and the close of the market was in sight, the voters began again to approach the leaders. Amiably the leaders resumed paying out.

After the polls closed, my host, raking the bottom of his coat side pockets with the fingers of both hands, brought out the residue of the several hundred dollars with which he had begun the day. His calculation of what he would need had been accurate; there was but a handful of bills left. Turning to me, he thrust them into my coat pocket: "Here," he said, "I had a little more than enough, you take it, a young fellow at college can use a few dollars."

When I told these stories to the *Atlantic* editor he said I ought to write them, together with other stories and reflections I had told him about Pennsylvania politics; they might make an article for the *Atlantic*. Pennsylvania politics was then much in the national eye; the Republican boss of the state, Matthew S.

Quay, was a national character, outstanding symbol of the boss system everywhere. He was by far the ablest of all the bosses in either party; as a boss on a national scale, with paramount influence in Republican national conventions, and as a United States senator, he was at the zenith of his power.

I wrote the article, captioned it, "The Ills of Pennsylvania," and gave it to Parker. After a few days he sent for me, told me he liked the article, that the editor of the *Atlantic*, Bliss Perry, liked it also, and that they would print it and pay me forty dollars. But they had a suggestion. Because the article was provocative it would excite acrimonious discussion; some of the heat would focus upon the author; and if it should turn out that the author was an obscure young student in the Harvard Law School, much of the force of the article would be lost. So, would I object if they printed it anonymously, signed merely, "A Pennsylvanian"?

II

For my opening, with happy journalistic technique, I quoted a litany chanted at Quay-controlled Republican state conventions in Pennsylvania: the delegates' hoarsely roared question, "What's the matter with Pennsylvania?" and the deep-toned, exultant response, "She's all right."

Taking that question as my text, I gave a less complacent reply. I described the widespread vote-buying; and the likewise widespread fraudulent counting of voters whose names had long before passed from the polling list to the tombstone, or who had never existed. I cited a recently notorious bribery of a public official, the favors given to businessmen who supported the Republican machine, the oppression of those who did not; the willingness of the respectable—trustees of hospitals and the like—to "stand in with" the Quay machine for the sake of state appropriations for their institutions.

From this I deduced a conclusive generalization of odium: Pennsylvania, I declared, was "politically the most corrupt state in the union." And Philadelphia, I declared, was "the arch-hypocrite of cities; you are virtuous in Philadelphia by appearing so, not by being so; appearances are everything, respectability is a thing wholly divorced from conduct." Defying Burke's dictum that it is impossible to indict a whole people, I declared that "You can't have corrupt politicians without some moral deficiency in the mass of the voters."

To sustain so broad an indictment I had necessarily to get into my bill of particulars every unfavorable aspect of the Pennsylvania ethos that my memory or research could assemble. In addition to the ordinary and familiar faults, I departed from Senator Quay and his machine to charge snobbishness to the superior caste, quoting a story told by a Philadelphia author, Owen Wister, about a descendant of an old family of the city who had written some verses. The manuscript, shown to his friends, elicited approval; but when the writer said he was going to publish the verses, he encountered shocked surprise: "Publish a book! Is that the sort of thing one does?"

To convey the Philadelphia point of view I invented three business letters of introduction which, I said, would illustrate the differing spirits of three American cities:

In Boston: "Permit me to introduce Mr Jones, who graduated with highest honors in classics and political economy at Harvard; he speaks and writes French and German, and if you employ him I am sure his learning will make his services extremely valuable to you." In New York: "The bearer, Mr Brown, is the young fellow who took hold of Blank and Company's Chicago branch when it was so run down, a few years ago, and built it up to a hundred thousand a year; he's a hustler, all right, and you'll make no mistake if you take him on." But in Philadelphia: "Sir: Allow me the honor to introduce Mr Rittenhouse Penn; his grandfather on his mother's side was a colonel in the Revolution, and on his father's side he is connected with two of the most exclusive families in our city; he is related by marriage to the Philadelphia lady who married Count Taugenichts, and his family has always lived on Spruce Street; if you should see fit to employ him, I feel certain that his desirable social connections would render him of great value to you."

Searching deep into the Pennsylvania mores to sustain my indictment of the people's morals, I excoriated a Philadelphia household gadget, called the "busybody," which a less censorious observer might have seen as more amusing than wicked:

Just below the second-story windows of row after row of Philadelphia houses projects a three-sided mirror, designed to reflect doings on the sidewalk into the room above. In the case of your own acquaintances, of course, this serves a legitimate purpose. Madam in the second story can tell, without leaning out the window, who her caller is at the door below, and can decide whether or not she is at home before the maid goes down. But the universal name "busybody" suggests a less worthy use of these mirrors—in families other than your own acquaintances, of course. The busybody is distinctly a Philadelphia institution. I know no one who has seen it in any other city. Fifty thousand women spending their afternoons in fifty thousand rocking chairs, observing the callers at their neighbors' doors, the passers-by on the sidewalk, and even happenings in their neighbors' second stories—this is perhaps an even more depressing feature of a city's life than stolen franchises and bribed councilmen.

In my philippic I made comparison between Pennsylvania and Massachusetts. Invidiously I weighed the respective contributions of the two states to literature and public life, contending that the comparison was as that between a blank page and a full one. To Pennsylvania I credited only Benjamin Franklin and derided him as "pre-eminently the apostle of 'brown-stone front' respectability." "All Poor Richard's maxims," I said, "are but variations of one exhortation: 'Young man, put money in thy purse.' . . . Compare that," I invited, "with any epigrammatic summing up you may attempt of the career and teachings of Whittier, of Sumner, of Phillips, of Adams, of Garrison. By all means, if there be any dispute about it, give Pennsylvania one niche in the Hall of Fame; Massachusetts has enough and to spare. Credit Franklin, not to the land of his birth, Massachusetts, but to the congenial soil of his fruition, the enthusiastic and literal disciple of his worldly wisdom, Pennsylvania. . . .

"While Pennsylvania wallows in corruption," I said, "Massachusetts is the best-governed commonwealth in the union." In my search for reasons for this distinction I went far back into history. Between the Puritans of Massachusetts and the Quakers of Pennsylvania I made a comparison which, while it contained some truth and was not unworthy as the scholarship of a young student, would not unreservedly command my more mature assent. The Quakers, I said, were too meek:

It is one of the anomalies of history that when the Puritan hanged the Quaker, both were happy—the one to hang a man for his belief, the other to die for his belief. This brings out strongly the distinction between them. The Puritans were a church militant. The Puritan went to church with a Bible in one hand, and in the other a musket for hostile Indians. The Quaker settled his difficulties with the Indians by reading tracts to them. When the Quaker came to the Puritan commonwealth to spread a doctrine which the Puritan didn't like, the Puritan beat him and drove him out; and when the Quaker came meekly back to turn the other cheek, the Puritan hanged him. The point is, the Puritan insisted on governing his commonwealth in his own way. He founded his commonwealth to carry out a certain set of ideas, and he never let his eye wander from that purpose. What the Puritan resolved upon was to be done; he would have no objector, be he Roger Williams, Anne Hutchinson, or Quaker. The Puritan formed the dominating habit, and to this day Puritan ideas dominate the essentially non-Puritan population of Massachusetts.

Among the Quakers, on the other hand, meekness was the cardinal virtue. Their creed forbids them to bear arms. It does not, in so many words, forbid them to take part in politics, but certainly the rough and tumble of actual party contest is hostile to the ideal which the Quaker seeks to follow. The early Quakers, instead of strangling doctrines not in agreement with their own, instead of casting out the apostles of strange creeds, welcomed them, tolerated them. They soon came to the point where they were tolerating intolerance. Lacking the strenuous dominating spirit of the Puritans, the early Quakers soon let the control of the colony pass into the hands of the less desirable elements, and there it has always remained.

My "Ills of Pennsylvania," it will be observed by those who read these extracts, was a tour de force in malediction. It excoriated not only Senator Quay but the whole people of the state. Much of what I said was true and penetrating—but much of it was farfetched and distorted. It was my first attempt at a magazine article and I was overeager to make it arresting.

As the *Atlantic* editors had shrewdly anticipated, the anonymity of "The Ills of Pennsylvania" increased its piquancy. The furore was even more acrimonious than the *Atlantic* editors had expected, and included the form they had guarded against. There was instant search for the author, that he might be subjected to appropriate contumely. Attempts to penetrate the veil of the anonymous "A Pennsylvanian" resulted in attribution of undeserved opprobrium to a considerable number of eminent and innocent Pennsylvania citizens, not all of whom regarded it as opprobrium; some of them neglected to deny authorship. The surmises, after some months, narrowed down to mainly two: "The Ills of Pennsylvania" was written by the Rev. Floyd Tompkins, prominent pastor of a Philadelphia church. It was written by Wayne MacVeagh, a Pennsylvanian who, some twenty years before, had been allied to the Republican machine and had been attorney general in the Cabinet of President Garfield, but whose present relation to the Republican organization was that of gadfly.

Along with search for the anonymous libeler of Pennsylvania went composition of replies. Indignant manuscripts deluged the office of the *Atlantic;* editorials in Pennsylvania Quay organs scourged the anonymous recreant who had smirched the fair name of the state, "fouled his own nest." Pamphlets of defense were composed and widely circulated.

Among the repliers, one was outstanding, and his reply made not unimportant history.

Among all who were outraged by "The Ills of Pennsylvania" and by the invidious comparison of Pennsylvania with Massachusetts, there was one whose indignation was especially deep. He was a judge in Philadelphia. His last name, Pennypacker (originally Pannebakker), derived from one of the oldest and most conservative stocks in that state (or any other), the Pennsylvania Dutch; his first names, Samuel Whitaker, tied him to a mainly English and Scotch strain that had been almost equally long in the state. Of both lineages Judge Pennypacker was proud, and had good reason to be; a strikingly large proportion of his forebears had occupied high place in practically every area of early Pennsylvania life, military, civil, business, the professions.

Pennypacker's self-consciousness about ancestry, and his local pride, escaped the dilution they might have suffered had he the misfortune to go outside the state for his education—all his training had been in small academies near his birthplace. As a young man his principal excursion from home was of a nature to increase his regard for his native state, his low esteem for all outlanders; when twenty years old he served as a private in a Pennsylvania regiment in the Civil War, from which experience he returned with a sentiment that led him, throughout his life, to speak always of the "War of the Rebellion." "I decline," he wrote fifty years later, "to use the euphemism of the Civil War, no such thing having been ever."

Along with Judge Pennypacker's pride of locality and ancestry went emphasis on individuality. He was pleased that he had five incisor teeth in his lower jaw; and with another uniqueness: "I have," he wrote, "the power of voluntarily using the muscles which dilate the nostrils; I likewise have control of the muscles which spread the toes of the feet, thus, to some extent, making them prehensile."

About this distinctiveness of physique Judge Pennypacker, so he recited in his biography, wrote a letter to the naturalist Darwin. In the pattern with his other traits was persistence in the ways of his youth; all his life he wore knee-high boots.

The sum of Pennypacker's traits composed a strong and salient individuality, with a powerful mind and absolute intellectual integrity. If his mind sometimes expressed itself in views and actions that seemed eccentric, that was, in part, perhaps, because of the gaps which are sometimes left by an education that is largely self-acquired. Yet let not Pennypacker's education be demeaned. It was very thorough and very sweeping. He was self-taught in several modern languages and read habitually in them. He kept a meticulous record of his reading year by year. In 1904, although busy with public business, he read 27,434 pages, of which 1321 were in German, 48 in Dutch and 216 in Italian. He was the author of many books and pamphlets on local and colonial Pennsylvania history, including: *Rittenhouse's Orrery; Johann Gottfried Seelig and the Hymn Book of the Hermits of the Wissahickon; Address of the Honorable Samuel W. Pennypacker upon Pennsylvania Day, August 20, 1904; The Pennypacker Reunion; The Pennypacker Pedigree; The Pennsylvania Dutchman and Wherein He Has Excelled.* He was an industrious and discriminating collector of Americana, having more than ten thousand volumes, with emphasis on colonial Pennsylvania specimens. He was a trustee of the University of Pennsylvania, a founder of the Pennsylvania Society Sons of the Revolution, president of the Historical Society of Pennsylvania.

Before the eyes of this fervidly if parochially patriotic Pennsylvanian, in the quiet of his judicial chamber, came the copy of the *Atlantic Monthly* of October, 1901, containing "The Ills of Pennsylvania."

He read it. He reread it. He read it yet again. Then he took his pen in hand, jabbed it in the ink and wrote. "It is extremely difficult," he began, "to regard the article with any seriousness." Then, himself taking it with the utmost seriousness, he denounced it as "absolutely discreditable and unworthy." He subjected each part of it, and the whole of it, to angry refutation, a refutation not always as relevant as it was thunderous. Pennsylvania, Pennypacker said, had a library, a medical school, a law school, a hospital, an academy of arts and a philosophical society—before Massachusetts had any. "The English Bible and Testament, Milton, Shakespeare, and Blackstone, were all reproduced, for the first time in America, in Philadelphia." He recited Pennsylvania's leadership in the antislavery movement. He compared Pennsylvania's and Massachusetts' contributions to George Washington's army, to the detriment of Massachusetts. In the War of 1812, Pennsylvania's part was noble; she contributed "a greater number of troops" than any other state, while "the attitude of Massachusetts toward that war can only be condoned and forgotten."

Similarly in the Civil War: Pennsylvania had done nobly, but "Will some one tell us what great captain or what significant event in this most fateful of American crises is to be credited to Massachusetts?"

Finally Pennypacker came down to date. "There has been some commotion in public affairs in Pennsylvania since 1895," he admitted, "but it is neither deepseated nor important and does not call for invidious comment. . . . Pennsylvania," he declared pontifically and conclusively, "Pennsylvania has no ills that are worthy of mention."

Having thus conclusively exculpated the state, he finally gave a paragraph, the concluding one of his article, to Senator Quay. Quay likewise he exculpated, eloquently:

Little inquiry [Pennypacker wrote] is needed to ascertain why men in Pennsylvania are attached to Mr Quay and proud of his accomplishments. . . . Mr Quay is a plain, simple, modest and kindly man, with a taste for books and literature, with no propensity for the acquisition of riches, and with a genius for the organization and control of men in masses, such as, like the gift of Shakespeare, comes but once in centuries. Without prating about honesty, he has this essential of the highest integrity that he meets every obligation and keeps his every word. He fails in no duty and he is never beaten. During the last twenty years no Republican President could have been elected without his consent, and no national policy successful without his support. Helpful, sagacious and strong, a knightly and picturesque figure, Mr Quay's fame is assured as a statesman who deserves well of his country, and in whose achievements even Massachusetts may properly take a pride.

To Quay personally Pennypacker's panegyric about him meant little—Quay was a redoubtable person, as indifferent to defense of him as to charge against him. But to Quay as a political leader Pennypacker's defense was valuable and timely. Quay and his party organization had been under cumulative attack for several years; about all the so-called "better elements" in the state were against him. And while the better elements could not alone defeat him, they were just now aided by schism within Quay's own ranks. Quay needed to divide the better elements, get some of them for himself. For that purpose the defense of him by one of the most respected men in the state, an incorruptible judge and high-minded scholar, was an asset. It was an asset, and Quay saw how it could be made a larger one. Quay, ignoring his organization, to the dismay of his own lieutenants and the astonishment of the state—Quay made Pennypacker his nominee for governor. Quay was acquainted with Pennypacker, was indeed a distant kinsman of his; but everybody knew Pennypacker had not written his answer to "The Ills of Pennsylvania" with any expectation of reward; and everybody knew that Quay's nomination of Pennypacker was a happy thought that came after Pennypacker had defended him and his machine.

In the campaign Pennypacker's literary defense of Quay and Pennsylvania had an important part. Millions of copies of it were printed. One sentence from it became, curiously, a slogan for both sides. Uttered seriously by one side, jeeringly by the other. "Pennsylvania has no ills that are worthy of mention" resounded from every stump.

Pennypacker won the election, served as governor. In time he learned that the author of the article which, by provoking him to reply, had elevated him to the governorship, was an obscure young law student. To find that his adversary had been so diminutive seemed to provoke him. Years later, in his autobiography, he wrote:

There appeared in the *Atlantic Monthly* a paper upon "The Ills of Pennsylvania." It was published anonymously and was sufficiently dull and stupid. . . . The paper set forth that it was written by a Pennsylvanian, which, of course, gave its confessions of iniquity an added zest. I have since learned, however, that it was really written by Mark Sullivan, the son of an immigrant from Ireland, who, after living a short time in Chester County, went away to seek his fortune and became the editor of *Collier's Weekly*. Indignant that the *Atlantic Monthly* should do anything so indecent, I wrote a historical parallel upon Pennsylvania and Massachusetts, pointing out the great comparative importance of the former in American affairs. It was published in many shapes and I really believe had an influence in giving me a representative position among the people of the state.

THE EDUCATION OF AN AMERICAN

I should like to record here that, among other judgments of public men which I have revised, some upward, some downward, I think Governor Pennypacker was one of the ablest men in American public life during the early part of the century, one of the best equipped for statesmanship. The lowness of the common estimate of him was due to the newspapers. He paid no deference to them, and they "ganged up" on him; he was more jeered at and lampooned than any other public man of his rank. As an object of satire he was a national character; his integrity, ability and rugged-mindedness were appreciated only by a small circle. Certain features of his appearance—his solid body, head set squat on his neck; his small, sparse, Asiatic-looking chin beard and his knee-high boots—lent themselves to the cartoonist; his mannerisms of speech and thought, his combination of parochialism and pedanticism, of Pennsylvania Dutch homeliness with extraordinary erudition, invited the comic versifiers—a skit by Wallace Irwin in *Collier's* called him "Samuel Whangdoodle Pennypacker" and began:

> *Like Noah Webster, he reclines*
> *Within his easy chair,*
> *A-talking wisdom's sacred mines*
> *And culling here and there . . .*
> *And he can speak in French and Greek*
> *On topics of the day*
> *Like Moses, Plato, Socrates,*
> *Himself and Matthew Quay.*

Pennypacker gave as good as he got, took a dourly humorous pleasure in defying and frustrating the newspapers, flaunting his contempt for them, his intellectual superiority over them. Once when he was governor a newspaper he disliked—he called it "a worthless sheet published in Philadelphia, the *North American*"—sent a reporter

to pry into some action of the government supposed to be then in contemplation and asked me for an interview. I had learned by experience that whether I saw him or not an interview would appear in the paper, since the discipline of the office required that something must be brought back in his bag. Therefore, I told him I would give

[*175*]

him an interview. He took out his pencil and memorandum book and made ready, and I proceeded:

"Celerity ought to be contempered with cunctation."

"Won't you please repeat what you said?" he asked.

"Certainly. Celerity ought to be contempered with cunctation."

"Would you object to spelling that last word for me?"

"Not at all. C-u-n-c-t-a-t-i-o-n."

He went back to the city, hunted up his dictionary and wrote two or three columns, and the paper has not yet entirely recovered from the shock.

The newspapers, making facetious copy out of the more superficial of Pennypacker's strongly individualistic traits, ignored, or did not understand, other expressions of his individualism that were as valid as original, and might have been valuable to the country had they been persuasively presented to it. From his autobiography, which I reread while I was writing this volume, I copied some views of his which excited my enthusiasm for their vigor and originality, regardless of my disagreement with some of them. They should be read, not in the light of the present, when some of them are accepted or tolerated, but in the light of the time Pennypacker held them, when they were so unusual as to add to Pennypacker's reputation for eccentricity.

The modern tendency to create new crimes by act of assembly ought to be curbed. . . . There are entirely too many technical crimes and too much creation of crime by legislation. . . .

The most important questions which arise in the courts are those which concern personal liberty. . . .

The worst of crimes are those which involve brutality to man and beast, and the abuse of women and children.

The failure to pay customs duties to the government may cause it inconvenience, but this does not constitute a crime. To call it so only leads to confusion of thought. . . .

I very much doubt the efficacy of the effort to prevent wrong-doing or to elevate the standards of life by punishment. . . .

I have had a distrust and even a sort of a horror over the ways of the detective, and no man was ever convicted before me of any offense upon such testimony alone.

The power of corporations to take private property . . . by the exercise of eminent domain should be carefully restricted. . . .

The state is interested, within reasonable bounds, in bringing about a condition in which, in the distribution of rewards resulting from business ventures, capital shall have less of profit and labor more of compensation.

No man should be permitted to interfere, upon any pretense whatever, with another who may choose to sell his labor, and violence should be promptly and rigidly suppressed.

Newspapers ought to be held responsible for the want of reasonable care in what they publish, and to be required to publish the names of their owners with each issue. . . . The whole doctrine of liberty of the press is a harmful anachronism.

The commotion over "The Ills of Pennsylvania" went on over my head. If it and its consequences elevated Pennypacker to the governorship, me it did not elevate at all, except in the view of my fellow students at the Law School. The article brought me no elevation in the eyes of the public, for the public did not know who had written it. The surprise and pleasure of my family and friends was all the kudos I got from it. But magazine editors, the whole periodical publishing fraternity, were not likely to overlook an article which gave rise to such furore. They were alert to probe beneath the anonymity of the author. One who took especial pains was Samuel S. McClure, publisher of *McClure's*, the most alive and energetic magazine of the time. One expression of *McClure's* enterprise was their employment of a scout, whose function was to travel about looking into promising young writers. The scout sought me out, and I suppose a report on me went to McClure's office. At the time I heard nothing of it, but some three years later it had consequences important to me. Meantime I remained in the Law School and continued my work on the *Transcript*.

CHAPTER 20

THE EVENING after my final examination at the Law School I was sitting in my Harvard room, reading a volume of Stevenson. What volume it was I do not recall. I read all of Stevenson about that time; he was used as a model by the classes in English, and besides, I enjoyed much of Stevenson. Whatever the volume, it contained an allusion to the docks of London. The phrase, a picture it conjured up, and perhaps something in the context, perhaps Stevenson's spirit-moving style—and perhaps also something in the June night in Harvard Yard outside my window—caused my imagination to leap. I had never seen the docks of London! It was an intolerable lack. I had never been to Europe! It was an unbearable deprivation. It must be remedied, at once. Within an hour I was busy with ways and means.

I made inquiry about going as a hand on a cattle boat, but found no cattle boats would go for some weeks, and I was in one of my fits of imperative impetuosity. I borrowed a hundred dollars from my roommate, borrowed two hundred dollars from one of my brothers, who were by this time becoming prosperous, and arranged for passage on a second-class steamer.

Before I sailed I went to the farm to visit my parents, by this time quite old. They took my enterprise with the combination of sympathy and concern which was their habitual attitude toward many of my impulses. My mother, the night before I left, came into my room, after I had gone to bed, and asked where was my coat. "I want to put something in it," she said. The next morning I found it was a roll of bills with some coins in the center, twenty-six dollars and fifty cents. I told her I did not need it. "Ah," she said with the affectation of impatience that was her way of defending herself against being thanked, and the deepening of her Irish accent that came to her when she was embarrassed, "Ah, sure ye can use it, take it along with ye."

I asked her where she got it. "I sold the ingrain carpet," she said. I remembered the carpet, my brother had brought it to her fully ten years before. She had never used it, but saved it against the day of poverty, fear of which never left her. Besides, she felt that any ostentation, even so mild a one as a new carpet on the floor, might tempt the fate that sends poverty as punishment for pride. Now she had carried the roll of carpet across some fields to a neighbor, to whom she had showed it, and who, she knew, wanted it and would buy it.

II

I saw the London docks, stood on London bridge and saw the boats go down the Thames; I looked up the haunts of Dickens and the scenes of Thackeray's novels; I followed the trail of Dr Johnson; I visited the Shakespeare country. I saw as much of England, Ireland and France as could be covered with funds so scant.

At Liverpool, as I boarded the boat on which I was to return, I noticed a porter in contentious expostulation with a passenger, a young American woman whose tip the porter had regarded as niggardly. I shooed him off, took the bag and carried it to the young lady's stateroom. She told me her name. It was Marie McMechen Buchanan, and she came from Baltimore. I thought her voice the loveliest I had ever heard. On the homeward journey I became well acquainted with her, later very intimately acquainted indeed, and found her throughout a lifetime of matrimony neither contentious nor niggardly. Our marriage took place four years later, in 1907.

III

On my return to America I was faced by necessity of decision. Throughout my three years in the Law School I had thought vaguely I might follow law as a career; the writing I was doing I looked upon as a means for paying my way through the Law School. I had now got my degree; I must decide whether I should make use of it. I went so far as to take and pass the bar examinations in New York City (in 1904)—I could practice law if I wished to, and if the wishes of clients coincided with mine. Halfheartedly I took desk room in the office of a friend in a canyon of downtown New York. I got one case—more accurately, a minor part in one case. I was assigned to serve a subpoena on a defendant who, as is the way with many defendants, preferred not to be served. My principal present recollection of my career at the bar, as brief as it was briefless, is of a kindly young woman telephone operator in a Vermont village who, her friendliness exceeding her discretion, kept me informed of the movements of the defendant as he fled in a chase through several New England villages. For my services I received fifty dollars, gross—I paid my expenses.

That fifty dollars is the only payment I ever received from the law, or from any other occupation or source except writing. Payments from newspapers and periodicals which printed my articles, from publishers who published my books, and occasionally from lecture committees who, with whatever soundness of judgment, have paid me to talk, have been the only compensation ever given me for services.

That I should practice law was never in the cards. The certificate of admission to the bar, the Harvard law education, and the Harvard law degree were stowed away in the background of my mind as equipment for the calling that at all times had the stronger pull on me. Excepting the period I spent at Harvard, and the few years of my youth when I was a publisher myself, the career, beginning when I was not yet sixteen, has been lifelong and uninterrupted.

It became part of the fiber of my being. Once, in Antwerp, walking along an old street, I felt suddenly a sense at once of pleasure and homesickness, of alertness and longing. Stopping, I recognized that it came from something in the air. Walking forward a few feet, I lost it. Walking back, I felt it again faintly. It came from a smell, one that hardly one person in a thousand would have noticed. The source of it was not visible. Trying to track it down, I walked back a block to find where it might come from, but could find no door or building that seemed likely to be its source. When I reached a point where my sniffing could no longer hold the faint clue, I again retraced my steps. Half-a-dozen times, like a hound upon a scent, I walked back and forth on that city block, jostled by persons talking French or Walloon, without being able to identify any source of the smell that intrigued me. Finally my coursing narrowed down to a tiny foot alley, with an arched opening not more than two and a half feet wide, literally a hole in the wall. I entered, found the smell stronger, and followed the dark little passageway to a court hidden away behind high buildings. As I entered the court, I felt like a traveler who in a strange land comes miraculously upon blood kin. Before me, in an ancient building, with the smell of printer's ink suffusing the air, was the oldest printing establishment in the world, now taken over by the Belgian government for preservation, the Plantin Museum. Hundreds of times, in cities and towns and villages, in a score of countries, I have had that experience—to sniff the familiar smell, to look about, to see a newspaper office, and there find fellowship.

IV

During the period when I was in New York to take the bar examination I had, as always, to support myself by writing. Seeking opportunity to contribute to New York newspapers, I had an experience which illustrates the element of timeliness in finding a market for writing. A New York judge, Alton B. Parker, was the Democratic candidate for President, and therefore ranked with the Republican candidate, Theodore Roosevelt, as the two men in all the country about whom editors would like to receive good articles. One morning during the campaign I read of an experience Judge Parker had had. His habit at his home at Esopus, New York, was to rise in the morning, put on a bathing suit and go to a pool back of his house for a swim. A photographer, learning of the judge's custom, concealed himself behind some bushes and took a photograph of the candidate for President attired in a limp and dripping bathing suit, to the serious distaste of the candidate.

Reading of the incident, I recalled that while in the Law School I had studied a case in which Judge Parker had written the decision. It was a suit involving the right of privacy; the photograph of a young woman in Rochester had been used, without her consent, in an advertisement of a flour manufacturing firm, and she had sued for damages.

To tie together Judge Parker's opinion in that old suit about the right of privacy, and his present involvement while a candidate for President in a controversy over his own privacy, was certain to appeal to any editor. The article must be for a daily paper, for quick timeliness was of the essence of the opportunity.

I took the suggestion to the editor of the New York *Sun*, Edward P. Mitchell. He was pleased, told me to write the article and bring it in. He liked it, bought it, asked me to do more work for him.

The incident illustrated my conviction that to ask for a job is not the best way of getting one; that to ask an editor to give you a topic to write about is wrong. An editor must feel dismay when anyone asks him to assign a topic and to give a commission to write about it. As a source of topics an editor frequently feels like, and often is, a squeezed sponge. What an editor appreciates and is sure to remember is a good suggestion for an article presented to him from outside. And if afterward the article turns out to be well written, the editor will not forget the writer.

My way was not to ask an editor for anything but to present him with something. If a writer is to acquire any right to consideration by an editor he must be able to know for himself what the editor is likely to want. My way was to study a paper until I knew what the editor wanted as well as he knew himself; then to suggest a topic that was within the editor's general field, but new; one that would not occur to the editor but which would interest him when it was brought to his attention.

CHAPTER 21

BEFORE I could take advantage of the *Sun's* suggestion that I write more articles there came to me, out of the air, an opportunity which determined my future. Not quite out of the air, either; it was a result of work I had done before.

One day in 1904 I received a letter from Edward W. Bok. That, to a young journalist, was an event, and it betokened a yet greater event, for Bok said he wished to call on me on a certain day and hour. He said that if I did not expect to be in I should write him, and he would come another time; but that if I expected to be in I need not trouble to acknowledge his letter, but should merely await him. I imagine that Bok was fairly confident I would manage to be in.

But I suspect Bok did not give thought to it. He had markedly individual ways of doing nearly everything. When, early in his career, he first practiced them, he may have worked them out as the best technique for effectiveness; or they may have been spontaneous expressions of his unique personality. In any event his ways were strikingly effective. To call upon a young journalist instead of asking the journalist to call on him was certain to give the occasion an emphasized impressiveness and cause the younger man to have an especial regard for the older one. If Bok's way cost him time and a trip to downtown New York, that pleased Bok rather than otherwise, for he was of that temperament which gets a kind of pleasure out of the hard way, and he felt—not necessarily correctly, I think—that that which is done with difficulty is by that fact well done, that what is done with ease is suspect.

When Bok called he said that he had a task for which he needed a journalist, that the task was of such a kind that it would be better if the journalist had had legal training, that he had spoken of his need to Samuel S. McClure and asked McClure if he knew anyone he could recommend; that McClure had told him there was a young fellow named Sullivan; that McClure had never himself met Sullivan, but that a scout he employed to look up promising young writers had surveyed Sullivan and reported favorably on him.

Bok explained to me what he wanted. He had started, in his *Ladies' Home Journal*, a crusade against patent medicines. In one of his articles he had asserted, without adequate investigation as it turned out, that a certain patent medicine, Dr Pierce's Favorite Prescription, contained sixteen per cent of morphine. The Pierce Company sued him for libel, and Bok discovered, in the belated investigation he now made, that the Favorite Prescription did not contain sixteen per cent of morphine, nor any. But Bok thought it possible, again mistakenly as it turned out, that the medicine's innocence of morphine was recent, that perhaps the company had changed its formula out of deference to laws some states had lately been passing, and as a safeguard against attacks that were being made upon the whole patent medicine industry. Bok surmised that perhaps if he could get hold of a bottle of the medicine five or six years old, morphine might be found in it; and that possibly an old bottle could be picked up somewhere, perhaps in some remote country store which did not change its stock frequently.

Bok wanted that search made. In addition he wanted information about the chemical formulas of all patent medicines and about the companies that made them, with a view to carrying farther his campaign against the industry.

I said I would take the job, and Bok asked me to come a few days later to his office in Philadelphia. There he introduced me to his father-in-law, the proprietor of the *Ladies' Home Journal*, Cyrus H. K. Curtis. Curtis was a man of slight figure with a white beard and soft brown eyes. He had more the face of a musician than of a businessman. Throughout my presence in his office he sat leaning back in his chair smoking a large cigar. He did not say a word beyond a friendly greeting and a kindly good-by; but he conveyed an impression of undemonstrative warmth which made me like him, and of quiet power which made me respect him. His part in the present ceremony was merely to size me up, a detail of his function of checking Bok's habit of rather headlong urgency with his own sure-footed judgment of men. Approval of the young man Bok had picked up was conveyed by some quiet look or gesture which I imagine had developed as a kind of code between publisher and editor.

Bok took me back to his own office, put me on the pay roll at fifty dollars a week, took me out to the leading banking house in Philadelphia—Bok would always patronize the best—got me a letter of credit for a thousand dollars for expenses, and sent me off. Because my job would involve some secrecy, indeed some sleuthing, I was not to be attached to the *Home Journal* office, nor to report except by occasional letters and by meetings with Bok on the frequent trips he took to New York. I was to make my headquarters in the office of a young New York lawyer, a classmate of mine. Bok would not address any letters to me direct, he would enclose them in envelopes addressed to the young lawyer.

The sleuthing I had to do came to have zest for me, for as I probed into the patent medicine businesses I found many to be nests of reeking charlatanry. In my amateur detective work I had to attain professional excellence, for the patent medicine industry had an espionage staff of its own, and presently I became aware that two strange men were showing curiosity about my movements. They turned up at the West Twenty-third Street Y.M.C.A., where I was living, scraped acquaintance with members and made carefully casual inquiries about me: what was my occupation, where had I come from, what had been my occupation before I came to New York? They turned up also at the office of the young lawyer with whom I had desk room and where I received my mail. Flatteringly they told him they had important legal work, for which they might want to engage him. This led to lunches and conversations with the young lawyer in his office, in which the patent medicine detectives directed the talk toward the young man who had a desk in the office but seemed never to occupy it. The young lawyer was a shrewd person and had humor. So also did some young friends of mine who frequented the office. Those patent medicine detectives were told, miscellaneously, that the young man was the discarded scapegrace son of a well-known millionaire, that he was the agent of South American revolutionists secretly buying arms in America, that he was a young man who had inherited a large fortune and was going about the country secretly to find good causes which he might endow, that he was a brilliant but unfortunately dipsomaniac youth who had been put in the care of the young lawyer. Since these explanations did not jibe with each other, nor with what the detectives had been able to find out about me, the hawkshaws ceased to appear at the office, but did not cease to follow me.

After some weeks I adopted, for occasional phases of my investigation, the device of an assumed name. Once in Boston I advertised in the newspapers for a chemist "experienced in patent medicine work, good salary." In other cities my advertisements called for experience in the correspondence department; in others experience in the advertising department. Then I registered at a hotel under the name of Jones and awaited replies.

As I anticipated, subordinate members of the staffs of about all the patent medicine firms in the country answered one or another of my advertisements. To several I sent replies asking them to call on me at my hotel. To each, when they came, I represented myself as counsel for a man who had recently fallen heir to a patent medicine business and wished to expand it. My callers, eager to get employment with an expanding firm, devoted themselves to telling me how expert they were in the jobs they already held. They told me the tricks they had invented or that were practiced by their firms. From them I learned the formulas and other details, nearly all sordid, of many of the patent medicine businesses of the country. Thus equipped,

I set out to collect concrete evidence which would be the exhibits and illustrations for what I should write for Bok.

One of the meanest practices in the industry was the sale, by some firms, of the letters of the deluded sick persons who answered patent medicine advertisements. A company would advertise to cure "female troubles" and would solicit sufferers to write letters describing their symptoms. To these victims a patent medicine company would sell as much of its nostrum as it could dispose of by a technique of ingenious "follow-up" letters to the patient. After the patient ceased to buy any more of the medicine her letters would be packed with others in bundles of five hundred or a thousand. These bales of women's intimacies would then be sold to another company, and by the second to a third; there was an auxiliary business of dealing in such letters, clearinghouses of the recitals of the symptoms and other confidences of the deluded. From one of these dealers I bought several packages, paying five or ten dollars for each. These packages I photographed, and Bok printed the photographs together with extracts (omitting the names of the writers) from letters which naïve and trustful women had written and which had been sold from firm to firm of the harpies.

A patent medicine firm that was important and which had altogether higher standards than much of the industry was the Lydia E. Pinkham Company. It solicited letters but did not sell them. Its advertisements in newspapers and magazines of the time, each accompanied by a picture of a wise- and benevolent-looking woman, joined promise with adjuration: "Mrs Pinkham, in her laboratory at Lynn, Massachusetts, is able to do more for the ailing women of America than the family physician; any woman, therefore, is responsible for her own suffering who will not take the trouble to write to Mrs Pinkham for advice."

When I learned that there was no Lydia E. Pinkham living, that the Lydia E. Pinkham of the flesh had been dead for more than twenty years, I sought a friend who had a camera, went with him to Pine Grove Cemetery near Lynn, Massachusetts, and took, and later published, a photograph of the impressive tombstone which bore the inscription:

LYDIA E. PINKHAM
Died May 17, 1883

I discovered that the patent medicine makers of the country were organized into a trade association, the Proprietary Association of America, which held annual meetings, for the discussion of matters of interest to the industry. I felt that those discussions, if I could get access to them, would disclose more of the secrets of the industry than any other source. Everywhere, cautiously, I led conversations toward the annual meetings of the Proprietary Association. Presently I got hold of a copy of the minutes of one meeting. From it I got not only confirmation of what I had already learned or come to suspect. I discovered also a sordid practice hitherto unknown to the public, and discovered it in a form which best lent itself to my journalistic purpose, the verbatim words of the patent medicine makers themselves, as taken down by a stenographer.

The meeting was presided over by F. J. Cheney, maker of a catarrh cure. In his address he told his fellow members that, as they all knew, the principal threat to their industry was hostile legislation, laws which would require them to print their formulas on their bottles or otherwise handicap them. For preventing such legislation, Cheney reminded them, the association had been maintaining lobbyists—"there is hardly a year but we have had a lobbyist in the different legislatures, one year in New Jersey, one year in New York, and so on." This, Cheney reminded them, cost money, big money. Then he told them he had invented a better way, and a less expensive way. "I have used it in my business for two years and I know it is a practicable thing."

Cheney explained. He had inserted, in his contracts with some fifteen thousand newspapers, a clause which, he confidently said, "is pretty near a sure thing." The clause read: "It is hereby agreed that should your state, or the United States government, pass any law that would interfere with or restrict the sale of proprietary medicines, this contract shall become void." Then, whenever a bill to regulate patent medicines was introduced into a state legislature, Cheney would send to each newspaper in the state carrying Cheney's advertisement a telegram calling attention to the cancellation clause.

The device thus recommended had been enthusiastically adopted by the Proprietary Association for its members. "I think," said the proprietor of Pierce's Favorite Prescription, "a great many members do not appreciate the power that we can bring to bear upon legislation through the press." And the system had been improved. Added to the contracts of many of the concerns was a second clause, reading—this was the version in the contract of Ayer's Sarsaparilla:

Second, it is agreed that the J. C. Ayer Company may cancel this contract . . . in case any matter . . . detrimental to the J. C. Ayer Company's interests is permitted to appear in the reading columns or elsewhere in the paper.

For facilitating the operation of this scheme the patent medicine makers had set up a central office, called the legislative bureau, which kept track of each state legislature and, whenever an anti-patent medicine bill was introduced, notified all the makers and let loose a flood of telegrams to newspapers. The legislative bureau had the co-operation of a national association of newspapers. "The American Publishers' Association," said a member of the Proprietary Association, "has rendered us valued aid through their secretary's office in New York, and we can hardly overestimate the power brought to bear at Washington by individual newspapers."

All this I learned from the annual report of the Proprietary Association meeting. Then, painstakingly, I set out to get the documents which would most convince the public. By various devices and by co-operation of a few newspapers which would not accept contracts limiting their freedom, especially William Allen White and his Emporia, Kansas, *Gazette*, I procured copies of the contract forms of the leading patent medicines. And I procured originals of telegrams and letters sent to newspapers—one sent by Swamp Root to the Taunton, Massachusetts, *Spy*, read: "House Bill 829 discriminating against proprietary medicines passed Lower House. Up in Senate Monday. Quick work necessary. Use your influence."

All this I told, in an article, and then proved it by an example. In the Massachusetts Legislature the preceding spring there had been a debate on a bill requiring that every bottle of patent medicine sold in the state should bear a label stating the contents. The debate had been long: it had occupied a whole afternoon. It had been lively: more than twenty members had engaged in it. It had been dramatic: a member had told of a young woman now in an institution for inebriates as the end of an incident which began with patent medicine dosing for a harmless ill. The debate had contained humor: the secretary of the State Board of Health stated that Peruna was merely a "cheap cocktail," and upon that titillating suggestion a member sent a page out to buy a bottle, which the member passed around for fellow members to taste and decide for themselves. In short, the debate was interesting and important, two qualities which invariably insure big headlines in the daily newspapers. But that debate was not celebrated by big headlines, nor any headlines at all, though Boston was a city and Massachusetts a state where the proceedings of the legislature figured large in public interest, and where the newspapers responded to that interest by reporting the sessions with great fullness. Had that debate been on prison reform, or Sabbath observance, or the early-closing saloon law, or any other subject, there would have been, in the next day's papers, overflowing accounts of verbatim report, more columns of editorial comment, and the picturesque features of it would have ensured the attention of the cartoonist. "And yet," I wrote in my article, "I invite you to search the files of the daily newspapers of Massachusetts for March 16, 1905, for an account of the patent medicine debate that occurred the afternoon of March 15 in the Massachusetts Legislature. You will find none, except in one paper, the Springfield *Republican*."

All this, and many other details picturesque and picaresque, I wove into an article which I called "The Patent Medicine Conspiracy Against Freedom of the Press" and which I sent to Bok with the rest of the fruits of my work for him. This article, however, was not adapted to the *Home Journal;* Bok's standard of length was short, two or three thousand words, and this article was long, about seven thousand words, and it was so tight-woven that it could not readily be cut. Bok, impressed by the article, wishing to see it printed, and eager to have other periodicals co-operate in his patent medicine crusade, took the article to *Collier's Weekly* and offered it to them for seven hundred dollars.

The *Collier's* people were as impressed as Bok had been. Indeed, I think, probably more so, for the editor of *Collier's,* Norman Hapgood, had a special appreciation of any writing about a public matter that was austere and factual, which made its effect not by emotion but by massing of facts. *Collier's* decided to buy the article from Bok. As a precaution, however, they felt they should talk with the author. From Hapgood I received a letter requesting me to call. He satisfied himself of the authenticity of the article and the accuracy of its details.

Just what followed never came within my knowledge, but I surmise that Hapgood spoke to the publisher of the paper, Robert J. Collier, perhaps to the effect that the paper might be helped by having on its staff, already strong with some of the best talent of the country, a younger journalist with the obvious bent for digging that my article reflected. Whatever it was that went on between Hapgood and Collier, I received an invitation to lunch with them at The Players. The two belonged in the very highest journalistic level of the America of that time. I was extremely impressed.

CHAPTER 22

THAT LUNCHEON with Collier and Hapgood I have always identified as a definite upward step, indeed a whole spiral of steps, in my career. I can identify the moment of the boost even more definitely. Before lunching we went into the downstairs washroom, to attend to that preparatory rite which The Players, in their unique and charming club house, identify by a quotation from Shakespeare painted on the wall above the place where the rite is performed:

Nature her custom holds,
Let shame say what she will.

I think that, either out of nervousness or from having taken pains to prepare for an event by which I was so greatly impressed, I did not myself participate in the preliminary ceremony. While Hapgood and Collier bent over the bowls of the washstand I stood a few feet behind. With the awe of a neophyte toward masters I watched their faces in the mirror, Hapgood's extremely distinguished, Collier's both distinguished and handsome. As I studied Collier's face I observed that he, while his hands were busy with soap and water, was using the mirror to look with some concentration at me. As our eyes met through the mirror, in the split second that passed before both of us dropped our eyes, I knew that he liked me, felt that we would know more of each other, sensed that we would participate in many experiences and emotions.

From Collier in a few days there came to the cubicle I was occupying in the dormitory of the West Twenty-third Street Y.M.C.A. a letter saying he would like to have me on *Collier's* staff, and that he would be glad to pay me seventy-five hundred dollars a year. He could have had me for half that. What I was earning at the time was a third, and that was as much as I had ever earned. Collier as a publisher followed a policy of high pay, and as a man was generous. Besides, he, I am sure, had shared that curious instant of psychic recognition in The Players' washroom. He knew he would like me; and he was, perhaps and so to speak, impressed by my being impressed by him. He was but a year or two older than I, and probably my awe toward him was pleasant to feel.

I told Collier that I would like to come with him but that I was embarrassed. For, a little while preceding, immediately after I had completed my work with Bok, and before I had been called to Collier's attention, I had gone to work for *McClure's Magazine*. I told Collier that I felt under obligation to McClure, for it was he who had recommended me to Bok, and he had otherwise befriended me. I told Collier that I did not feel it would be decent for me to leave McClure so soon, especially since I was engaged in some special tasks for him.

I imagine Collier could see from my manner that I wanted very much to come with him, for that was the way I felt. Indeed, if Collier had been peremptory, if he had said I must come at once if at all, I think I would have overcome my compunction about McClure, even at some cost to my conscience. The invitation to *Collier's* was one of those occasions when I knew what I wanted to do, knew it instantly, and felt it with such overwhelming imperativeness that there could be no question about my doing it. I think Collier knew how I felt. He told me it was quite all right, that he would wait, that I should finish my work with *McClure's*, that he knew Sam McClure very well, and that after a decent interval he would arrange with McClure for a friendly divorce for me.

II

Samuel S. McClure, I thought at the time and still think as I look back, was the pre-eminent magazine genius, easily first, in a period in which magazines flowered as never before. I do not overlook the editors and publishers who lasted longer than McClure and had greater success. That McClure and his magazine did not endure was due mainly to the very virtues that made McClure unique, the intensity of his preoccupation with ideas, his helplessness to resist his own impulses—impulses which usually were the very yeast of magazine genius, but which tumbled out over each other in such profusion that often they crowded each other out of life. With his perpetual immersion in ideas and impulses, and the hectic activities they led him into—activities so numerous, diverse and often mutually destructive that he could not always carry them to fruit—with that went utter lack of interest in money or in the material details of presses, paper and balance sheets. He was a Scotchman (actually born in the North of Ireland) who cared nothing for money, and regarded economy, if ever he thought about it at all except as an abstraction of economics, as an irking brake on spontaneity.

He was a queer bird, but he was a great editor. Not a great editor, either; not at all, for editing implies patient sitting at a desk, minute reading and emendation of manuscripts. That McClure could never do. That was for lesser men. But as a geyser of ideas, as a sensitive barometer of the moods of the time he lived in, as a supernatural senser of what people felt and thought—as that, McClure—how shall I express it? I cannot say he sat at the head of the table, for he was too volatile and impetuous to sit through any meal. To McClure ideas were everything. Once, he complained to me—complain is too strong a word, it was rather a gentle plaintiveness—of the repression with which his associates and subordinates tried to check and control that gusher of all the intellectual oils, gasolines and detonating explosives that ever burst from the mind of man. "I get an idea," he said. "It comes to me in the night. I lie awake until morning. I rush to the office with it—and they throw cold water on it."

I could see the point of view of his associates, trying to get a magazine printed once a month and delivered to the readers with some reasonable approximation to scheduled dates— against the undisciplined impetuosity and at times almost maniacal errant energy of a publisher who, not just once in a month but five times in a day, would have discarded an article that was in the works, often in the process of printing, for a new idea that he thought better. Often McClure's new idea was better, but a magazine must have a deadline, and it is no wonder McClure's associates and editors took on toward him a protective manner of coldness, and were only warm to him on the occasions—they were, happily for his staff, frequent—when he came to the office at nine in the morning to announce that he was sailing for Europe at twelve. Facilitation of the hurried getting of tickets and other preparations for departure was about the only function in which McClure's associates served him with unqualified cheerfulness. Yet, though I could sympathize with the harassed editors, I knew that McClure had the surer wisdom when, completing his gentle plaint, he said: "You know, Sullivan, a new idea is like a newborn child; the first thing is, keep it alive, feed it, make it grow. Afterward, if an idea does not turn out well, you can drop it."

McClure's eccentricity—no, that is not the word. With McClure eccentricity was the true man; conformity or regularity, if ever for a moment he practiced it, was the aberration. His, let us say, concatenation of unusualnesses extended into every relation he had with the world. Once, traveling together on a steamboat down the Mississippi, he, with no relevancy to anything that had happened before, poked an urgent finger into an opening of my buttoned coat, pressed his exploration between the buttons of my waistcoat, pressed on between the buttons of my shirt and groped about between shirt and skin. "Ha," he said exultantly, "I supposed so; you're wearing an undershirt; no one should ever wear undershirts." What reason he gave me I do not recall, if indeed I grasped at the time.

Possibly the longest and most continuous consistency McClure ever practiced was about a theory of diet. One of the most indispensable chores of the editors and associates who aided in getting him off on his trips to Europe was to assemble enough bottles of milk to last as his only food during the voyage, and to arrange for keeping them fresh, a process not easy before the days of mechanical refrigeration. Once I sat with him at breakfast at the Hotel Adlon in Berlin. His order to the waiter was for fresh lettuce and tomatoes. It was an extraordinary order for breakfast but the waiter preserved a stoic calm. As he wrote the order on his pad he, with a sang-froid which had suffered a shock but would not show it, asked McClure the question that has been heard by every diner who ever ordered a salad in any restaurant from Greenland to Little America, "French dressing or Russian dressing, sir?" McClure, with the resignation of a man who has long endured that discipline of waiters which makes them the sternest ritualists of all mankind—McClure, with gentle patience, replied: "Neither, thank you: just as nature made it."

McClure was a queer bird, but a lovable man and a great one. He, under fiction names, is the principal character in several novels by major authors of the 1890s and later. The authors had come to know him in an ordinary way, as purchasers of their literary output—and they found him stranger than any fiction they could invent.

While I was writing this book it happened that McClure came to see me. In his eighty-first year he was busy with what he called "The Principles of the Organization of Human Beings." That, he said, is what we must understand before society can get anywhere; he felt sure America had not given sufficient thought to it, and he was seriously upset about the country's future. I diverted him from his concern about the organization of society, led him to talk of the times when we were associated. I told him I was writing some pages about him in my memoirs, and mentioned some things I was saying about him. He said it was true that he was the original of Pinkerton in *The Wrecker.* The other legend about him he said he doubted; he believed that the hero of Howells' *A Hazard of New Fortunes* was not himself but was a variation of one of Howells' other fiction characters, Silas Lapham. McClure added that another author, Alice Hegan Rice, once put him in a book, but made him talk like a South-of-Ireland Irishman, whereas McClure in fact came from the North.

More authors than these, I imagine, put McClure in their

[*196*]

books, if not the whole of McClure as an identifiable portrait, yet traits of his; a single facet of McClure would be a whole character in a novel. And even more authors than put him in their books got inspiration from him. Practically every author of the time knew him, liked him, received stimulus from him. Kipling, in his autobiography, said that McClure was "far more original" than the character whom Stevenson modeled after him. Kipling "liked and admired" McClure, prized his "genius and simplicity."

McClure, while a young child, was brought to America by his widowed mother, who in the early 1870s, in a town in northern Indiana, worked as a servant for two dollars a week, at a time when cost of living was high, brown sugar was twenty-five cents a pound. Young McClure worked at about every chore known to boy or man; he tended furnaces, mowed lawns, did washing, was a cook, a farm hand, a peddler, a clerk in a grocery store. Supporting himself thus, he managed to get a good education, the latter part of it at an excellent college, Knox, at Galesburg, Illinois, where he was distinguished in Latin and Greek. After graduating he edited a bicycle magazine, the *Wheelman;* started a newspaper syndicate which bought popular fiction and sold to newspapers the right to publish it; and, in the depth of the depression of 1893, with a capital of seventy-two hundred dollars, started *McClure's Magazine*, which, three years later, was the leader in its field and extremely prosperous.

The thoughts and ideas that sparked out from McClure's mind, the impalpable emanations of his personality, became, by some process of nature undirected by him, material things. They became presses, offices, staffs, editors, paper, ink, hundreds of thousands of copies of printed magazines, hundreds of thousands of readers, millions of readers. It was not that McClure created these things, it was rather that they gravitated to him, came out of the air, to attach themselves to McClure's thoughts and make the immaterial material. They grew like coral, formed themselves into orderly structures like a cathedral of stalactites, except that they had life, which begat more life, multiplied itself, became an immense and complex living mechanism.

Journalistically McClure was an idea-man only. His gift was idea-origination and, in occasional moments of calm, idea-valuation, a valuation usually achieved, like most of his functioning, by instinct. Editor he was not, writer he was not. If any writings by him are extant I do not know of them (except his autobiography). In the magazine office, when I was on the staff, there were remarks, not generous I felt, to the effect that the only direct contribution ever made to the contents of the magazine by the man to whose name it gave fame was a few dull paragraphs of statistics and comment about something or other, I think it was the increase in crime. McClure's lack of facility in writing was strange, for in conversation he was magnificent. In talk he was a great reporter, gave character, drama and humor to the life. One conversation between McClure and Kipling, so Kipling recorded, "lasted some twelve—or it may have been seventeen—hours." Much must have been said, for, Kipling added, "McClure was one of the few with whom three and a half words serve for a sentence."

The editing of *McClure's* consisted largely of screening the one most practicable idea out of a hundred of McClure's suggestions, and seeing that the chosen idea was well and thoroughly developed and written. It was a formidable business. While the older magazines—*Harper's, Scribner's,* the *Atlantic Monthly,* the *North American,* the *Century*—were still following the placid paths of the past, selecting from the daily batch of manuscripts voluntarily submitted enough gems about literature, art or abstract public questions to fill an issue, and paying the conventional stipend of a hundred or two hundred dollars—while the older magazines were following that comfortable routine, *McClure's* was originating ideas, sending out not one man but half a dozen to get the material, digging and checking and compiling and composing; often a single article in *McClure's* represented the work of half a score investigators and writers, consumed many months of time, and cost as much as ten thousand dollars. The work of directing all this, keeping the strings clean of tangle and seeing that a magazine was printed once a month fell mainly on McClure's partner, heaven-sent for that combination, John S. Philips, even-tempered, sure-footed, with a strong critical faculty combined with a strong affirmative liking for whatever was fine and sound.

Of McClure's staff the one who became best known for the longest time was Lincoln Steffens. He had been city editor of a New York evening newspaper, and *McClure's* made him managing editor. Then McClure, feeling that all his office men ought to know America, sent Steffens on a Western journey. One of the public men whom all traveling reporters called on at that time was Joseph W. Folk, then prosecuting attorney of St Louis, later governor of Missouri. Folk told Steffens about municipal corruption in St Louis, and Steffens wrote an article about it. Then Steffens went to Minneapolis and wrote an article about corruption there, which *McClure's* captioned "The Shame of Minneapolis." Still later, St Louis having willfully neglected to reform itself after Steffens had exposed and admonished it, he wrote a second article which the editors captioned "The Shamelessness of St Louis." From the start with St Louis and Minneapolis grew a series dealing with several cities, which made "The Shame of the Cities" a familiar phrase, and Steffens a famous person.

His fame lived until his death, in 1937. Nothing he wrote afterward attracted widespread attention. His long tenure on fame was due, I think, to the fact that he was a radical, and, living on into a period in which much of the writing was done by radicals, he was more written about than some others who had similar claim to fame. To the younger generation of literary radicals who succeeded him, Steffens was the old master, and they celebrated him.

He was called a great reporter. In his younger, obscure newspaper days he may have been, but in his better-known writings

I rarely saw a paragraph that I would have called great reporting. Hardly would I have called it reporting at all. Some of the articles that made him famous, his accounts of political corruption in cities, seemed to me to be primarily not reporting at all, and not objective at all, but at once psychic and subjective. He probed into, or surmised, the inner mind and motives of a mayor or a boss; then he wrote what Lincoln Steffens thinks about what Lincoln Steffens conceives to be the mind of the mayor of Minneapolis, or Philadelphia, or wherever.

I saw Steffens often, talked with him much, but never had understanding with him or of him. I felt that when one tried to hold him down to any orderly sequence of logical argument he took refuge in some evasive, grinning paradox. It was on one repartee of evasive paradox that some of his later fame rested—I tell the incident from memory: Asked by a finger-pointing inquisitor, "Are you a Communist?" he replied, "Oh, much worse—I'm a Christian." To me it seemed that so far as he had any philosophy it was fatalism, which is not a philosophy at all; it is an acknowledgment of inability to attain a philosophy, it is intellectual defeatism.

There is much evidence that some young writers found Steffens stimulating and helpful. I did not. I was never free from feeling that he was in part a poseur—possibly a sincere poseur, that is, a poseur to himself. Once, during the Progressive party convention at Chicago in 1912, Edward G. Lowry lunched with him. Afterward Lowry said, "And there sat Steffens, talking revolution and blood—and sucking the guts out of a chocolate éclair impaled on an upright fork."

One reason for my failure to achieve comradeship with Steffens was my feeling that he did not appreciate the head of the magazine, Sam McClure, and my observing that Steffens was rude and arrogant to McClure. I felt also, as McClure did, that Steffens was an egotist and a frustrated dictator. Once McClure said to me, with allusion to Steffens' close-set stockiness of head and body, "All tyrants have short necks."

More admirable than Steffens' work, I thought, was the writing of other members of McClure's staff: the restrained, unexcited, soberly factual exposures of Standard Oil by Ida M. Tarbell; of the insurance business by Burton J. Hendrick; of the railroads by Ray Stannard Baker. As in their writings they were simple, direct and unpretentious, so in their personal contacts were they kindly, tolerant, modest, gently humorous. I liked them and learned from them.

My connection with *McClure's*, lasting less than a year, was not long enough to get past the stage of apprenticeship. It was hardly of the nature of apprenticeship, for I did no office work, nor did I write any articles nor attempt any. Yet the experiences I had were valuable and interesting.

When I went to the magazine there was in the office a manuscript that later became a remarkable series of articles in the magazine and still later a book with a comparatively enduring life. A woman in upstate New York who, I think, had not attempted authorship before, Mrs Georgine Milmine, wrote a life of the founder of Christian Science, Mrs Mary Baker Eddy. It was a biography in somewhat the new manner, then the very new manner indeed. Mrs Milmine had painstakingly grubbed for facts, reaching back many years into the early days of Mrs Eddy, and into her ancestry, and covering with much completeness of detail the whole of her extraordinary life up to that time —Mrs Eddy was still living. In this method, what was new was mainly the thoroughness of the search for facts. Though Mrs Eddy and her circle and her followers showed some apprehension about the approaching publication, it did not seem to me, as I read it in manuscript, that Mrs Milmine had approached her subject in any spirit of malice or other preconceived interpretation. I surmise that the apprehension of the Christian Scientists may have been caused in part by the fact that *McClure's*, in its treatment of politics and business, practiced a technique called "exposure," later designated by President Theodore Roosevelt "muckraking." The Christian Scientists may have assumed that the biography of Mrs Eddy would be an extension of the method and attitude into religion.

With whatever went on between *McClure's* and the Christian

Scientists I had no contact. I had come on the staff, I was being paid fifty dollars a week, and something should be found for me to do. In that spirit, and because I had had legal training, the manuscript was turned over to me with no instruction except that I should subject it to an ordinary checking of facts. The seriously controversial points in the manuscript were covered, I suppose, in other ways, and after I left *McClure's*. The work carried me into remote points in New Hampshire and elsewhere in New England, the scenes of Mrs Eddy's early experiences and birth and ancestry, to hamlets far from the railroads, which could only be reached by horse and wagon, and at least one which could not be reached at all, for it had disappeared—I recall an elderly New Englander pointing to some depressions in the earth which he said had been the cellars of houses, in one of which Mrs Eddy had lived as a child. It is episodes of that kind that now chiefly remain in my memory: a long drive on a May morning to a village in the eastern New Hampshire mountains; another drive up a long hill somewhere near Franklin, New Hampshire, and on the ridge at the wind-swept top a gaunt house which struck me as a good setting for a gloomy novel—one of many impulses toward fiction writing which I never followed.

My second assignment at *McClure's* was to subject to a similar checking a manuscript that had been turned in by a Montana lawyer named Christopher P. Connolly, a story dealing with the feuds of the copper kings, Daly, Heinze and Clark, and with the manipulations of Montana politics, bizarre almost beyond credibility. My checking of Connolly's "Story of Montana" went little beyond going to Missoula, Montana, where he lived. His fineness of character, intellectual integrity and exactness of mind were so readily apparent as to leave me little to do beyond a nominal search of the court records and other documents upon which his book was irrefutably based.

My last assignment took me to Louisville, Kentucky. That city had been reported to *McClure's* as a proper subject for inclusion in the series on municipal corruption which Lincoln Steffens was writing, the "Shame of the Cities." Steffens was so busy finding shame here, there and elsewhere that he could not cover all the cities that clamored for his attention. "Clamored" is the suitable word; a remarkable feature of that series was that cities, or many citizens in them, seemed to take a morbid pleasure in being included. They wrote letters to *McClure's*, crying, "Expose us next!"; many enclosed briefs or fragmentary manuscripts or "leads" to the mine of shame.

It was in response to some such request that I went to Louisville. The shame was there, as it was in practically every American city; whether Louisville's was more gross or less so than that of other cities, whether it lent itself in greater degree or less to magazine treatment, was a matter of comparison and journalistic judgment. I remained there some weeks and made reports to *McClure's*. What part of the experience remains most in my memory is a Christmas dinner, and other kindnesses, given me by Mrs George Madden Martin, author of the "Emmy Lou" stories, who lived outside Louisville at a place called Anchorage; acquaintance with a picturesque editor of the day, Colonel Henry Watterson; and the hotel I stopped at, the Galt House, last, I think, of the old-time, big-roomed, high-ceilinged, ornate hotels of the old South—in most cities they were called The Planters.

CHAPTER 23

IN THE EARLY PART of 1906 I began my work with *Collier's Weekly*.

Collier's Weekly was the elongated shadow of the man, still living, whose name it bore. Everybody in his own generation called him "Pat"; younger men spoke of him as "P. F."; his name was Peter Fenelon Collier. He had come to America as a lad, with twenty-five cents in his pocket; had studied at St Mary's Seminary, Cincinnati, Ohio (with some thought of becoming a priest), had driven a streetcar and worked with his hands at various trades. About the middle of the 1870s he sold Bibles from door to door of Catholic households. His Irish customers were poor. One day a woman told him she would like to have the Bible but "I have no dollar; if you want to leave it here, I'll give you ten cents, and you can come back sometime and get the rest."

By that incident was born, in Collier's resourceful mind, the notion of selling books on the installment plan at a cost adapted to people of moderate means or less. Presently he had a collector working under him, then an agent, then more agents and more collectors; finally an army of them, with branch offices in some twenty cities.

Selling books on subscription is a perilous business; more so when the price is low and the installments small. Since the difference of a few cents in price made the difference between getting along and going under, Collier decided, in 1879, to start his own printing plant. After a few years he was selling some three million volumes a year, all reprints of standard sets; Dickens was his best seller, about a tenth of the whole.

In 1888 he started a weekly periodical, at first called *Once A Week*, later changed to *Collier's*, no doubt in imitation of the two great weeklies of the 1880s, *Harper's* and *Leslie's*.

Collier's, under the elder Collier, was edited casually; it aimed to be a combination of pictorial and literary—drawings (and later photographs) of current events, summaries of the news, and essays about books and public questions. The circulating of it depended almost wholly on the Collier agents, who sold it in combination with sets of books; the paper had, to some extent, the somewhat demeaning status of what the subscription book business called a "giveaway proposition," a premium thrown in with a set of books.

In 1898 Collier wrote "and son" after his name. The son was Robert J.; he had completed his education at Georgetown University, followed by a year at Oxford. He was a son for any father to be proud of. In looks he was a handsome Irish type; many kinds of persons are called "typically Irish"—they range from deep black hair to bright red. Young Collier was an indigenous racial type—almost blue-black hair; eyes deep, soft blue, with a quick twinkle. He was tall, with long, well-proportioned legs, with shoulders made broad and a chest made deep by outdoor games. He played polo lustily, and wrote poetry that reflected a trait of mysticism—while at Oxford he had been in the circle of Wilfred and Alice Meynell. He had taste in art and in books, was at once sensitive and strong, sentimental and high-spirited, quick to range from serious to gay, but usually gay. My wife and I, through a long association with him, believed, from our separate points of view, that Robert Collier had the most charm of any man we ever knew.

To young Collier was given charge of the *Weekly*. He set about making it such a paper as would reflect his classical education. In the first issue of which he was editor he printed, as the cover, a full-page drawing of a Greek figure, to the symbolism of which the public was given no clue other than the title, which was printed in Greek letters: ΑΩΣΟΜΕΝ. As a serial fiction feature young Collier printed the first installment of one of the most esoteric novels ever written by an American, Henry James's *The Turn of the Screw*—in a periodical which aimed to have a large popular circulation!

But soon young Collier got a grip on his problem. What he

had was an amorphous review; what he wanted was a popular weekly—to the title *Collier's* he added a subtitle, *The National Weekly*. Aiming toward a union of essential merit and popular appeal, he sought out the best artists of the day, ones who had at once high distinction and also the common touch. With as many of these as he could he made contracts to work for *Collier's* exclusively.

He got Frederick Remington with his Southwestern scenes of cowboys, Indians, horses and cattle—Remington "reproduced the high colors of the desert with a fidelity which, to the ordinary observer, made his paintings seem unreal but made old desert dwellers homesick"; Maxfield Parrish, who pictured Arabian Nights and other storybook fantasies in colors at once gorgeous and delicate; Jessie Willcox Smith, who could draw the precise turn of a child's knee better, I think, than any other artist who ever lived; A. B. Frost, whose pictures of homely American rural life gave nostalgic pleasure to farm-born city dwellers; E. W. Kemble, who preserved forever a type then common but swiftly passing, the old-time colored folks with the ragged clothes and simple ways of recent slavery.

To these artists Collier paid high salaries and fees—not merely because he was an impatient young man who wanted what he wanted and wanted it quickly; and not merely because he was generous, but also because part of his problem was to attract attention to *Collier's* and do it quickly; and he shrewdly knew that a good way to make *Collier's* talked about was to pay high prices, and let the public know he paid them.

The most popular artist of the time was Charles Dana Gibson, then drawing for *Life*, and reluctant to leave it. To Gibson, Collier offered an unheard-of price, a thousand dollars a drawing for a hundred drawings to be delivered during four years. When Gibson wrote a letter of acceptance, in which the startling figures were set out, Collier reproduced the letter far and wide, and sent Gibson, with *Collier's* editor, on a tour through the country, to give out interviews and otherwise make the country *Collier's*-conscious. By similarly lavish offers Collier secured other eminent artists and authors, and advertised them and

Collier's with similarly widespread publicity. He secured Sir Arthur Conan Doyle, and his Adventures of Sherlock Holmes, then sensationally popular. He paid Richard Harding Davis a thousand dollars a week to report the Russo-Japanese War.

Collier's illustrations—lavishly displayed on cover, frontispiece and double-page center spread—were admired. So were its photographs and illustrations of the Spanish War and the Russo-Japanese War; so were its typographical distinction and its treatment of the news.

But young Collier wanted something more, he wanted to achieve a leadership in thought. He dreamed of having the best editorials in America—best in the sense of at once high level of thought and at the same time readableness. Of the two requisites he put power of thought first. Readableness he thought he could achieve himself, in part by attractiveness of typographic layout. He planned two pages facing each other, each to contain six to eight editorials, each editorial to be a single paragraph of five hundred words or less. Such brevity would be a daring innovation—in the common estimate of the day, and in much of the writing profession, the force of an editorial was supposed to be in proportion to its length and weight. And Collier would give the editorials prominence; he would print them on the first two pages of the paper—in a time when, in most papers, the editorials were retreating toward the want advertisements on the back pages.

Young Collier had his blueprint but he needed the substance to build upon it; he had his layout but he needed contents for it; he had a saddle and a bridle and a bit but he lacked a horse. Inquiring for an intellectual steed, he was told by one of his friends to look up a young man named Norman Hapgood, then unknown to Collier.

Hapgood had been brought up in a well-to-do family in Alton, Illinois, had gone to Harvard, had graduated in the college and in the Law School, and then spent a year in a Chicago law office. Giving up law, he had gone to work on the Chicago *Evening Post*—where his most important achievement was to make the acquaintance of a young man named Finley Peter Dunne, then receiving forty dollars a week for writing all the paper's editorials, and fifty dollars a week more for a weekly humorous feature purporting to be the views of an Irish saloon-keeper on Archey Road named "Mr Dooley."

Hapgood, after a short and not very successful experience on the Chicago *Evening Post*, went to Milwaukee to work on the *Sentinel*, edited by the father of one of Hapgood's college friends. After a few months there he went to New York, where he made a place for himself as a dramatic critic. In periods of leisure he wrote some bookish biographies, of Washington, Webster, Lincoln. That was what he liked. To do more of it he resigned from his newspaper connection and went to Italy. He regarded himself as embarked on a life of leisurely, scholarly writing. Nothing in his career suggested that he could write editorials, except that Peter Dunne thought so.

Peter Dunne's thinking so meant much. It was Dunne to whom Collier went for advice when he was looking for an editor. To the public Dunne was known as a humorous philosopher, "Mr Dooley"; to his circle of intimates, when he could be led into seriousness—and he could be by any troubled friend—he was one of the wisest and shrewdest advisers on almost any sort of problem. For Collier, Dunne's suggestion that he employ Hapgood was conclusive.

To Hapgood, browsing in Rome, giving most of his thought to Michelangelo and Raphael, came a cable from Robert Collier, offering him the editorship of *Collier's Weekly*. Hapgood, moved by a contagion from Collier's personality that projected itself across the ocean and managed to express itself through the stark condensation of a cablegram, started back to New York.

Hapgood and Collier sat at lunch in the old Holland House, on Fifth Avenue, the first of many lunches they were destined to take at a table to which came, one time or another, over a period of ten years, practically every important literary, artistic and political character in New York, and the rendezvous for similar figures when they were visiting the city. On the first occasion Collier and Hapgood were alone. Terms they did not talk—the salary Collier offered, twenty-five thousand dollars a year, was of a size that short-circuited discussion. Coming together was merely a matter of making clear what was needed, that *Collier's Weekly* should have the most distinguished editorials in America. Hapgood took the job. Quickly Collier had what he had sought. Within a year, Collier's editorial pages were what the idiom of a later America called "tops."

Young Collier's equipment was now complete. In art, in photography, in fiction, in editorial writing, he had the best attainable. And in himself he had the quality that co-ordinated them into the best weekly in America. With it all he had, also within himself, enormous resourcefulness in presentation, enormous energy in exploitation.

Collier, in short, had everything except success. More accurately, he had everything except the recognition of success. *Collier's* still lacked public esteem. While every week it was put by Collier's ubiquitous book agents into the hands of three hundred thousand persons, that list did not include the level of reader that Collier desired. When Collier had asked Hapgood to be the editor, Hapgood had been obliged to reflect, to himself, that "nobody of my acquaintance read the magazine, or even knew its name." What young Collier needed, and ardently wished, was that just that type of person should know the *Weekly* and read it; read it, like it, be moved by it. And to bring that about he needed some dramatic impact upon the public consciousness. This he might, perhaps, in time have devised, for he was inventive and daring. But while he thought about it, it came to him from outside, by an unplanned incident—perhaps also in fulfillment of some mystic law which says that if a man wishes something greatly and strives for it ardently, he is likely one day to see it coming toward him on the road.

II

There was published in New York a weekly called *Town Topics*, a paper of the sort that, a generation later, were spoken of as "scandal sheets"—though, in the esteem in which "society" was held in the early 1900s, such a demeaning term would hardly be applied to a periodical that recorded society's doings. In the *Town Topics* of 1904 the aroma of social elevation and authority was borne out by its typography and format; it was austerely simple, the headlines like a row of brownstone fronts, the type selected for the plainness of its face, no illustrations. The principal owner and editor was an elderly Southerner, who printed "Col." before his name, the title having come to him through service in a Confederate regiment; and whose full name and title had the effect of a grandiose flourish, Col. William D'Alton Mann. With a florid face and sweeping white whiskers, Mann was a striking figure when one observed him seated in front of a broiled lobster at a corner table which any of the fashionable restaurants of the time felt honored to reserve for him on the rare occasions when he ate in public.

Town Topics printed paragraphs of gossip about persons socially prominent; the first page or so about society in New York, other pages or parts of pages about society in Philadelphia, Boston, Chicago, Washington and such other cities as were large enough to have local and miniature four hundreds. On the tables of the leading clubs in practically every city one saw *Town Topics;* it had almost official sanction for the authority it claimed as "the journal of society."

Readers who took *Town Topics* at its face value saw its paragraphs as mainly the records of balls, weddings, engagements, comings and goings to Newport and Europe. But persons who read it with sharper discrimination observed that interspersed among the perfunctory items were paragraphs dealing with individuals, paragraphs that were pointedly personal—some pointedly fulsome, others pointedly malicious. One observed also that interspersed among the paragraphs about persons of assured position were allusions to persons on their way up; and that among these latter *Town Topics* seemed to practice discrimination, some being fulsomely boosted, others jeeringly pushed back. One noticed also that *Town Topics* arranged the order of its paragraphs in such a sequence as to create a kind of ranking, as in the court gazettes of European monarchies; so that a reader who accepted such grading as authoritative could infer the precise social rank of the person mentioned by the distance of the paragraph from the top. This court gazette impression was borne out by giving a leading paragraph or two to the family of the President, whoever he might be, on the theory that the occupant of the White House had, by that fact, a kind of brevet headship of American society.

One day Robert Collier, picking up the current *Town Topics*, saw a paragraph about President Theodore Roosevelt's daughter Alice. Collier knew that Alice Roosevelt was a spirited young woman, even a daring one. But the extreme measure of her daring consisted of smoking cigarettes, which, by the standards of 1904, was very reckless, but not so reckless as to give the faintest justification for what *Town Topics* implied about her. *Town Topics*, indeed, did not mention the cigarette smoking; it alluded to unconventionalities more serious, and imputed something more than unconventionality:

She is looked upon by the men of the Newport set as an example of all that is smart. If her Dutch ancestors knew what that included they would turn in their graves. During the last week of her Newport visit this past season there was considerable gossip. From wearing costly lingerie to indulging in fancy dances for the edification of men was only a step. . . . Flying all around Newport without a chaperon was another thing that greatly concerned Mother Grundy. There may have been no reason for the old lady making such a fuss about it, but if the young woman knew some of the tales that are told at the clubs at Newport she would be more careful in the future about what she does and how she does it. However, it is admitted that she is a smart girl, and smart girls are supposed to be clever enough to take care of themselves without the aid of chaperons.

Young Collier, reading the lines with mounting anger, came to his Irish boiling point as he took in the outrageous innuendo hinted by the closing sentence. Carrying the paper to Hapgood's desk, Collier, with a firm-lipped seriousness that anger brought to him, suggested that *Collier's* ought to do something about it. Hapgood, as angered—in his Puritan way—as Collier had been, wrote an editorial. About *Town Topics* and its editor he used his strongest adjectives of objurgation:

The most degraded paper of any prominence in the United States. . . . It is a weekly of which the function is to distribute news and scandal about society. The editor lives a secluded life, and well he may. With a little caution such a man can escape the criminal law, and of course he is worth nothing in a civil suit. A recent issue of his sewer-like sheet contains as its leading feature, an attack on a young girl who happens to be the daughter of the President. It uses her first name only. That is a little way it has. It charges her with all the errors that hurt a woman most, and it makes these charges in the most coarse and leering way.

By this denunciation Hapgood satisfied his indignation. Then, for the conclusion of his editorial, he considered what should be done by way of remedy. The reformer that was indigenous in him, and also the faint trace of pedagogue, would not let him be satisfied by mere excoriation; there must be reflection about the relation of the incident to high public policy. And Hapgood, in his role of guide to public policy, was always detached, even-tempered, Olympian. In that spirit he wrote:

That any legal steps could or should be taken to suppress such unclean sheets we do not believe. Paternalism, official regulation, once started, goes too far. We can trust only to the people, to business standards, and social sanctions. To suppress this weekly would contradict democracy. The remedy of arbitrary control is worse than the disease of evil license. We can only say that whoever refuses to read the journal we refer to, or to advertise in its columns, performs a public service.

Thus, with unexcited recommendation about civic policy, Hapgood concluded the editorial he had begun in hot anger against a "coarse and leering" act committed by a "degraded, sewer-like sheet."

To Collier, when he read Hapgood's editorial in proof, the ending seemed inadequate. Collier, reaching for his pen, added some sentences of hot Irish anger, and Irish recklessness:

As to personal recognition, we can hardly imagine that many decent men would consent to meet the editor. His standing among the people is somewhat worse than that of an ordinary forger, horse-thief, or second-story man.

Collier's words were more a thermometer of the heat of his indignation than carefully chosen as the accurate portrait of a scandal-sheet publisher. Indeed, Collier's words were not chosen at all; no product of weighing and selecting were they; he wanted to throw a ton of bricks at the editor of *Town Topics*, and the ones that came to his hand were the simple epithets of primitive emotion; the words just erupted in the geyser of his indignation, and he wrote them.

Had Collier consulted a lawyer, for the express purpose, not of avoiding a lawsuit but inviting one, had he asked an expert in libel to tell him the particular words that would most certainly bring a libel suit, and be most likely to result in conviction —and Collier was capable of doing that had he thought of it— the lawyer would have told him that just about the most dangerous words in the English language are "forger," "horse-thief," "second-story man" and their equivalents.

In due course the libel suit came, a criminal suit, with Hapgood as defendant, and therefore to stand in the dock, accused of a crime. Hapgood was disturbed, to a degree that puzzled me a little. For months preceding the trial he was apprehensive. Part of his disquiet sprang, I think, from intellectual precision; he did not like to be made conspicuous as having written words that actually he did not write, words which he primly felt himself above writing. It was not that he resented having to take responsibility as editor for a libel that had been written by Collier as publisher; Hapgood was too fond of Collier to feel that way. But he felt that "forger," "horse-thief" and "second-story man" were crude words, and he did not like to have the public think he had used them, especially the intellectual part of the public, college teachers and others, to whom Hapgood was a kind of accepted guide.

Hapgood feared also the obvious danger inescapable from any criminal libel suit. Peter Dunne, half in teasing, half in worldly wisdom, told him that if he were convicted, all that anybody would remember about it ten years later would be that, "Hapgood? Oh yes, he was in jail one time, for some kind of a crime or other, something about forgery, I think it was."[1]

I tried to reassure Hapgood, told him that even if by any chance he were convicted, even if by any remote possibility he should be given a prison sentence, what of it! A man does not fear an experience of jail—so I, in the security of my immunity, told him—merely because of jail as such. What a man really fears, I said, is seeing his friends turn their faces from him after he gets out. And that, I told him, would not happen to him if he should go to jail in so good a cause as defense of a President's daughter against a scandalmonger; on the contrary, he would be a hero. My vicarious equanimity did not carry as much peace to Hapgood's mind as my generosity intended.

Nor did Hapgood take comfort from the fact that the prosecuting attorney who, by reason of his public office, would conduct the case against him, the district attorney of New York, William Travers Jerome, was his personal friend. Jerome, and also his assistant, Frank P. Garvan, an able, racy, salient Celt, shrewd and loyal, were both intimates of the Collier coterie. Both Jerome and Garvan, in their contacts with Hapgood and the *Collier's* group, after the suit was started, treated the matter with the sobriety that should exist between a prosecuting attorney and an indicted defendant. That their ostentatious propriety was in part inspired by their consciousness of the humor in the situation, Hapgood could not know. For Hapgood's own sense of humor was not acute; in this respect he was rather a babe in the woods to the Irish who composed much of the Collier circle. They liked him and respected him extravagantly, but they did "kid" him.

[1]This is my recollection of what Dunne said to Hapgood. Hapgood's recollection, given in his autobiography, differs:

"It is all right now," Dunne said, "when people know what it is about, but ten years from now they will think you were arrested for writing an article in *Town Topics* libeling Alice Roosevelt, and many of them will remember your name without being sure whether you were the editor of *Town Topics* or the man who jumped off Brooklyn Bridge."

Hapgood added: "Dunne's humor had in it so much of actuality that a man on a pullman once told me he remembered me as the editor of *Town Topics*."

Hapgood felt that Jerome was capable of doing what Hapgood himself would have done in analogous circumstances, of taking the puritanical line, of leaning over backward to convict his friend, rather than bending to save him. And indeed Jerome was capable of just that, had the circumstances really called for it; Jerome one time or another subjected a considerable number of members of his clubs and of his own caste, the highest in New York, to the sternest rigors of his official function.

In preparation for the trial Collier was at his generous and energetic best. To be Hapgood's lawyer he employed the best in New York for the kind of tactics that were needed.

The traits that made James W. Osborne superb as a jury lawyer included a large and homely body, features likewise large and homely, a fundamental simplicity of personality, expressed in part by a mellow drawl brought with him from North Carolina; an indigenous kinship with many kinds of human nature; a native, effortless, automatic conformance to whatever any dramatic situation called for, and tremendous absorption in whatever role any given condition cast him for. The very intensity of Osborne's preoccupation with his art, the completeness of his absorption in each case as it came up, prevented him from exploiting his remarkable talent to the degree it would have borne, though his fame was sufficient to label him as the greatest New York trial lawyer of his time. At once he was a force of nature and a child of nature.

On some later suits he defended for *Collier's* I sometimes collaborated with him in collecting and arranging evidence. Night after night, in his office downtown, or in a room in the Bar Association Building on Forty-fourth Street, we worked until after midnight, on occasion until dawn. After we had gone over the evidence, detail by detail; after Osborne had absorbed it; after, in his mind, he had arranged it in dramatic sequence—he always conceived of a trial as a dramatic performance—after all that, Osborne, more to clarify his own mind than enlighten mine, would tell me, step by step, just how he would present the case in court. Always the final step, the climax of the drama, was to be the complete demolition, the utter extinction from the surface of the earth, of whoever, whether defendant or plaintiff in the particular case, was the opposition to Osborne's client. With an intentness that at first almost horrified, and never ceased to fascinate, Osborne would lean forward, his eyes boring into mine, his fists clenched and held together. Then, wrenching his fists violently apart, he would say, "and then—we'll snap his head off his God damn neck."

Having thus arranged the drama in his own mind, Osborne would proceed to rehearsal, a rehearsal in which he and I were the only participants; he as star, I as stooge. With his large eyes rapt, glaring at me through the big lenses of old-fashioned spectacles with ill-fitting and twisted ear-holds, he used me as every character; stormed at me as the defendant, browbeat me as an unfriendly witness, beamed on me as a friendly one, cajoled me as the jury, was deeply respectful to me as the judge. Throughout all this I could be no lay figure, no mere dummy. Something in Osborne's personality, resistless when he got under way, compelled me to be the character for which he cast me. I must look scared, or pleased, or arrogant, or complacent, or resistant, or appreciative, as the role called for. And I could not get by with mere looking it; under the compulsion of Osborne's titanic personality I must be it. And throughout everything I must, in addition to being the stooge, be also the audience, must emanate appreciation and approval.

Those midnight sessions with Osborne were a physical drain beyond the lateness and length of the hours; I was obliged to pour out for Osborne a quantity of nervous energy which left my stores low, until sleep and rest could refill the reservoir. But, exhausted as I was, I could not be off to my recuperation. He, pleased with his grasp of the case, his very saturation with it, would express his feeling of command of the situation by reciting an adaptation of a verse, Osborne's adaptation being rather more vivid and effective than Scott's original:

> Oh, Countie Guy, the hour is nigh.
> Beast, bird and flower proclaim the hour—
> But where is Countie Guy?

"Countie Guy," he would say, pointing his thumb to his breast proudly, "Countie Guy is going to be right there on the job." Cheerful with the anticipation of success, he would relax, falling into a mood in which he recited passages from Dickens. Later, when the actual trial came, Osborne liked to have me in the courtroom where, when he felt the need, he could look at me and get from me some addition to the store of magnetism that he was prodigally pouring out.

Years after I had ceased to see him frequently I read one morning that while in a game of chess at the New York Athletic Club he had toppled over—victim, I think, of his tremendous intensity of concentration, the torrential pouring out of vitality that seemed limitless, but was not.

With Osborne to appeal to the jury, Collier engaged, for appeal to the judge about such legal points as might arise, one of the city's most scholarly lawyers and high-minded public men, Edward M. Shepard. To supply this legal battery with ammunition Collier lavished money on investigators who read every line *Town Topics* had printed during many years, who talked with the persons who had been mentioned, fulsomely or maliciously, in *Town Topics* paragraphs; dug up details of *Town Topics* finances and scouted patiently back over the past of Colonel Mann.

By the material thus assembled, Hapgood and his lawyers were able, when the trial came, to show that fulsome paragraphs in *Town Topics* were sometimes associated with financial transactions between *Town Topics* and the individuals praised; that, contrariwise, disapproving paragraphs in *Town Topics* sometimes dealt with individuals who had failed to see the advantage of advertising in *Town Topics*, or subscribing to its stock, or loaning money to its proprietor.

Collier's counsel held up before the jury a sheet of paper over six feet long, containing two columns of clippings of *Town Topics'* paragraphs, arranged in a "before and after" manner. One column, all derogatory, was about O. H. P. Belmont during the period in which he had refused to lend money to Mann;

the other column, all praise, was about Belmont after he had loaned $4000.

Collier's counsel showed that Colonel Mann had been loaned $10,000 by a wealthy promoter and speculator, Thomas F. Ryan, for a reason which must have been something other than commercial, for, when *Collier's* counsel asked Mann, "At that time you did not own a dollar in your own name?" Mann answered, "No."

Collier's counsel showed that Mann had been loaned $25,000 by a member of one of New York's wealthy families, W. K. Vanderbilt; $3000 by George Gould and $3500 by Howard Gould, two brothers who were heirs to a railroad empire; $2500 by J. Pierpont Morgan (the elder); $5000 by a railroad magnate, Collis P. Huntington; $90,000 by a stock market speculator, James R. Keene; $20,000 by a new-rich plunger, John W. Gates; $10,000 by the head of U.S. Steel Corporation, Charles M. Schwab.

Collier's counsel showed that *Town Topics* had conducted an enterprise called *Fads and Fancies*, a book, a monumental and sumptuous book, which was to contain appreciative accounts of the avocations and diversions of Americans of sufficiently deserving eminence—and able to pay from $500 to $2000 for a copy of the book. It was brought out that in office correspondence of *Town Topics*, the persons solicited to subscribe to *Fads and Fancies* were referred to in the terminology of pursued game, sometimes as "'coons," other times as piscatorial quarry, "fish."

This evidence doubtless would have been sufficient to get from the jury a verdict of acquittal of Hapgood. If further reason for acquittal were needed it was supplied abundantly, and rather humorously and sensationally, by a question which Jerome asked Hapgood, and Hapgood's reply. Jerome, sternly as became a prosecuting attorney examining an accused criminal, asked Hapgood where he had learned certain facts damaging to Mann and *Town Topics*. Hapgood, with complete simplicity, with genuine concern, asked whether he was required to answer this question. Upon being told by Jerome and the

Court that he must answer, Hapgood replied that he had got the information in a conversation with Jerome.

That this disclosure was entirely agreeable Jerome showed when, in his address to the jury, he said: "The defendant in this case is an old-time friend of mine; I have known him for years and we have sat down and talked for hours together. Only the best of motives could have actuated Mr Hapgood in writing what he did, from information obtained in talk with me, and therefore in a measure I was the expurgated author."

All of which explained and justified the gently humorous opening paragraph of the account in which the New York *Tribune* described the conclusion of the trial:

So convincing was the argument of District Attorney Jerome as the prosecutor of Norman Hapgood, editor of *Collier's Weekly*, on the charge of criminal libel, that it took a jury in the criminal branch of the Supreme Court just seven minutes to agree on a verdict acquitting Mr Hapgood yesterday. A broad grin was on the face of the foreman of the jury when he announced the verdict of "Not guilty."

"Get out of here, now, you criminal," laughed Mr Jerome, slapping Mr Hapgood on the back in a most friendly manner. Mr Jerome and Mr Hapgood left the courtroom arm in arm, after the members of the jury had paused on the way out to shake hands with Mr Hapgood. . . .

The *Town Topics* suit did for *Collier's* what Collier most desired and needed. The first-page stories and heavy headlines with which daily newspapers reported the trial, the parade of names of the best-known figures in New York yielding to intimidation or occasionally resisting it; the feeling that *Collier's* had done a worthy job and done it, as the New York *Sun* said, "with courage, celerity and artistic thoroughness"—all combined to give *Collier's* esteem, éclat, kudos. It became, and for years remained, the most influential periodical in the country, in many respects the most distinguished America has ever had.

CHAPTER 24

AFTER I HAD BEEN with *Collier's* a few weeks Collier and Hapgood went one week end to Collier's camp in the Adirondacks. Because the weather there was lovely while the city was stifling, they decided to stretch their holiday into a week. This meant that the editorial pages would be put to press in their absence. To Collier this occasioned no great concern; he was by temperament one to take a chance. But Hapgood was anxious. The one thing that made him willing was his feeling that in me he now had, for the first time, an aide about whom he could be free from serious worry. I would not, of course, write with his distinction, but I would make no serious blunder; he could rely on my not committing any glaring error of taste or judgment. He wrote me a letter, in which he enclosed some paragraphs he had written, and he asked me to write enough to fill out the pages, O.K. them, and send them to the composing room.

The commission was one to awe me, and it did, for we all had extreme respect for the editorial pages. The public prestige which Hapgood had built up for them was felt in the office, by me even more than the others, for I had a special appreciation of Hapgood's quality.

Though awed, I felt that I had an opportunity to make a contribution. I would, I decided, introduce lightness into the pages. This good intention Hapgood would have approved, for he had talked with me about the desirability of lightening up the pages —he was aware that the one criticism most often made of the *Collier's* editorials was that they were heavy, a heaviness due in part to appearance, two pages of solid type facing each other, and in part to the importance of the topics Hapgood discussed, and the seriousness of his style. He was aware, too, that he lacked lightness of touch and was not strong on humor. His notion of lightening up the pages was to do it typographically, by breaking one of his solid paragraphs with two or three lines of verse, usually chosen from Wordsworth or Browning.

Setting myself rather seriously to the business of being humorous, I turned to two speeches I had read in the *Congressional Record*, by Congressman Augustus Owsley Stanley, of Kentucky. Aptly chosen quotations from those speeches, I decided, would give *Collier's* readers a smile. But just to print, baldly, two quotations from the *Congressional Record*, even if one was very funny and the other amusing, would not comport with the *Collier's* editorial pattern. The quotations must be aptly introduced, there must be editorial generalization about them, they must be presented in their relation to cosmos, they must be built up into one of those literary disquisitions which *Collier's* editorials were supposed to be. Addressing myself to the necessities of the occasion, I produced this:

Every Kentuckian is born to the literary purple. His first articulate cry is a dactyl; he prattles in hexameters. We are not often deeply impressed by what Colonel Watterson says; but the way he says it—his verbal pyrotechnics, his lingual chiaroscuro, his sudden swoops and pirouettings, the rumbling thunder of his polysyllables, the rippling tinkle of his penults—these delight us perennially. The Colonel is a fountain of words; they flow from him with the murmuring gurgle of bottled-in-bond from a Pendennis Club jug, the gentle tinkle of ice in a julep glass.

A worthy brother Kentuckian, entitled even more than the Colonel to the appreciation of the fastidious, is the Honorable Augustus Owsley Stanley, Member of Congress from Henderson County. Congressman Stanley was endeavoring to picture to his fellow-statesmen the more subtle and recherché qualities of a beverage which is one of the chief commercial products of his district. "It will," said he, describing the local brand, "turn an anchorite into a howling dervish, and make a rabbit spit in a bulldog's face."

Now, there is real literature for you. Picture the scene. Was the quality of inspiring to reckless daring, of filling with death-defying, fate-scorning courage, ever so concisely, so aptly, so vividly expressed as by picturing the timid, shrinking, and pusillanimous bunny spitting defiantly into the menacing countenance of the fierce and terrible bulldog? Beside this, how inept and futile those clumsy figures of speech with which Homer tried to tell how brave his

heroes were! How tame and tautologous Shakespeare's description
of the courage-inspiring virtues of sack: "Warming of the blood;
which, before, cold and settled, left the liver white and pale, which
is the badge of pusillanimity and cowardice." It is no disappointment
to our pleased anticipations to learn that Congressman Stanley is an
emeritus professor of belles-lettres in a Kentucky college.

Why is a Kentuckian, in common with most other Southerners,
habitually less restrained in the expression of high-pitched emotion
than most other folks? Congressman Stanley was denouncing the
Tobacco Trust, dwelling especially on its lowering the price which
it paid to the Kentucky farmers for their crops. "There was not,"
said he, "in all the world, not in the jungles of India, nor on Siberia's
frozen plains, in no pest-haunted, penury-cursed hole in the Orient,
no Chinese coolie or San Domingo negro, in that fever-infested
gehenna of disease and death yonder in Panama, not on God's
footstool anywhere was there a living slave to penury or power so
wretched or so poor as the Kentuckian on his native heath. Still
blessed by fertile soil, the sunshine, and the dew, but robbed of
nature's abundance and God's goodness by the merciless machi-
nations of this trust."

I sent that to press and was presently to learn what I have so
frequently observed since that I present it here as a guide to all
journalists. The trouble you get into, the rows you provoke,
the hard feelings you stir up, and especially the libel suits, come
most often when you are not looking. They come not from the
person who is in your mind when you are writing. About him
you know what you want to say, and you say it. If the matter
contains the potentiality of trouble you are careful. What most
often brings trouble is the incidental part of your article, upon
which your mind is not so directly concentrated.

It was so with my first attempt to introduce humor in a
Collier's editorial. I had set out to write about Congressman
Stanley; if there was to be protest it would be from him I should
expect it. My allusion to Colonel Watterson had been incidental, merely by way of facetious introduction to what I wanted
to say about Stanley. From Stanley I heard nothing; so far as
I know he may have been pleased with my paragraphs. But
from Watterson, to my astonishment and serious dismay, came
a retort which made me understand that I had involved myself

in literary duello with the most redoubtably pugnacious journal-ist of the time. Not merely had I given offense to Watterson as an editor and public character. I had committed an outrage upon a personal relationship, for, as I had not known when I wrote my paragraphs, Watterson was on terms of special friendship with both Robert and Peter Collier.

"*Collier's Weekly*," wrote Watterson in the Louisville *Courier Journal*, "goes out of its way to single Kentucky out for ridicule." Dissecting my editorial, Watterson hurled back at me his most Wattersonian epithets. I was guilty of "purest malevolence"; my editorial pencil was "an irresponsible bit of wood with a bit of lead at one end and a fool at the other." Alluding to his personal relationship with the Colliers, father and son, Watter-son felt sure that "neither can approve so sweeping and ill-natured a criticism." His exoneration of the two Colliers, and also of Hapgood, was ingeniously made to give added force to his contempt for the hireling who had betrayed them:

Obviously, some wharf-rat has crept into the *Collier* sanctum dur-ing the absence of Mr Norman Hapgood, who, though sometimes in error, is always a gentleman.

When I hastened to express my contrition to Hapgood and Robert Collier they, with characteristic generosity, merely smiled. I think the fun-loving quality in Collier got some amuse-ment from the incident. But the courteous gentleman in him led him to write a hearty letter of regret to Watterson.

A mistake of naïveté is often less serious in the eyes of the victims, if they are men of urbanity—as Collier and Hapgood were—than in the guilty conscience of the offender. The awk-wardness of my use of the first responsibility they gave me pro-moted rather than impeded my way into their confidence. The period during which they treated me as a neophyte was so brief as to be almost unnoticeable. With a rapidity that occa-sionally embarrassed me they were treating me as one of themselves, not only in responsibilities at the office, but in the intimacy of personal relations. Most of my leisure was spent with one or the other or both. They took me into their circles, which so overlapped as to be almost one—though Hapgood's included some heavy thinkers whom Collier found a little too heavy, and Collier's included some lively young polo players and fox hunters whom Hapgood found a little too lively for his not very large store of physical vitality.

II

If, any time during my association with Collier and Hapgood, it had occurred to me that I should someday have occasion to write intimately about the relation the three of us had to each other, and if I had supposed they would read what I had written, I would have been embarrassed to the point of panic. I would have dreaded being in the same room with them afterward. The encounter would have taken, from the first instant, one of two colors. Either it would have been sentimental —there would have been tears first in Collier's eyes, and then in mine, and Hapgood would have succumbed. That would have been trying, until we got through with it.

But it might have taken the other turn. It would have been certain to if Peter Dunne had been with us, as he often was. Either Dunne would have set the key with ferocious impugnations of my sincerity and truthfulness, in a manner of humorously growling truculence; or Collier would have made the same accusations with a shade of gay jeering, carefully watchful not to go so far as to hurt my feelings. Humor might have got us over a bad spot, as it often did. However, I have no need to speculate or apprehend; the time is gone when I could be in the same room with them.

Once Hapgood went to Europe, leaving me to take care of the editorial pages. While he was away news came out that Dunne, who had not been writing for several years, would resume his "Mr Dooleys" in the Sunday newspapers. From Europe Hapgood wrote me a letter. He said he had written an editorial about Dunne, which he enclosed; would I print it "when you can conveniently make it the leader—I am anxious to give Dunne as good a send-off in his new venture as possible."

The editorial was a touching appreciation, the finer because it did not at all conform to what is commonly described as a tribute. Hapgood just wrote a few simple sentences of truthful insight about Dunne's quality, picking out, with the penetration Hapgood had, the traits of Dunne that not everybody recognized, and that Dunne in his heart was most proud of. It was intellectual appreciation just faintly suffused with emotion—the sort of thing Hapgood could do superbly when his admiration for a writer's work went hand in hand with affection for the man himself.

While proofs of the editorial pages were passing about the office Collier came to my room, flustered. He asked could he see that editorial about Dunne. I gave him a proof, and he read. "Mark," he said, "Peter's just been in my room. He was all upset. He came in practically crying. I thought something serious had happened and let him talk. It was all about this editorial. He thought I'd written it. He said it was the most beautiful thing that had ever happened to him. I didn't interrupt him because at first I supposed he was in some kind of trouble and I wanted to give him a chance to spill it. Afterwards I couldn't tell him I didn't know anything about it—he'd have felt ridiculous; he'd have felt like the devil. I let him go away thinking I wrote it. I suppose I could wait awhile and tell him I didn't write it. But that would throw him off too. He'd be embarrassed. He'd think I didn't really feel about him the way he gave me credit for feeling. And I do."

Collier walked about the room, disturbed. Though he was athletic and utterly graceful, he had, when upset, an odd way of walking with one long step and one short step. Finally he turned to me, a little sheepishly, yet with humor that took the edge off his embarrassment. "Can't we," he said, "just let Peter think I wrote it for a while? Someday when I get him in the right humor I'll tell him and kid him about it."

Several weeks later Hapgood was returning from Europe. Collier, Dunne and I went to Jersey City to meet him. On the ferry Collier and I were conscious of our secret. Drawing apart from Dunne, we consulted about it. We decided that I should tell Hapgood. Hapgood listened soberly until he grasped it, and then grinned and joined us in the sort of conspiracy for consideration of each other's feelings that we were always practicing.

Collier built a new house in the country and gave a party. Though I was seeing him every day and practically every evening, and he had told me vivaciously of the preparations, he had to give himself the fun of writing an invitation to me, and of recounting the delights there would be. There would be fox hunting—"the hounds will meet at noon"; there would be polo; there would be flying—this word Collier underscored, as if to say, "Think of that, now!" In parenthesis he added, with a sly dig at the lack of venturesomeness about which he used to tease me, "for those who want it." To that, in turn, he added, as if to convey assurance, "with two experienced aviators."

One of the aviators was Tom Sopwith, later very well known in aviation, later still well known as the English challenger in Anglo-American yacht races. But Sopwith's skill in the air was not as well known then as it later became. Even had we had the prescience to know Sopwith had it in him to be one of the world's great aviators, we would have known also, not as a matter of prescience but of fact, that the art of aviation was, on that day of Collier's housewarming, slightly less than ten years old; indeed, it was only about three years since anybody much except the Wright brothers had flown.

Many of the guests went up, in a spirit of boys who want to show they won't take a dare. In resisting the boisterous urging Peter Dunne and I gravitated into a kind of defensive alliance, the strength of which lay in Peter's humor. We had children, we said. Many of the others, like Collier and Richard Harding Davis, we pointed out, had no children. In the lack of that attribute of manhood it was not surprising they should court death; they might just as well be dead. And as to those who had children, most of them were rich, and that fact was more important to their children than their other qualifications for fatherhood; on the whole, suicide would be a service to their children. On the other hand, Peter and I were important to our children, not only because they would have no support if we were killed, but because our singular and incomparable virtues made us a priceless example to them. Besides, we were valuable to the world.

By dint of superiority in such argument Peter and I managed to stay on the ground. And by pleading children as an excuse I continued to stay on the ground until after aviation had long been familiar; it was 1932 before I left the solid earth.

At Collier's party there was all he had promised in his invitation, and more, much more. Though the guests included many men of great and varied talents, by midnight their way of expressing the spirit of celebration did not vary materially from that of any party of males, of any endowment or condition, in any place. And the only feature that marked it in time, dated it, was the popular song of the day—the year was 1911— which everybody sang, until the singing became automatic; we were singing it with our eyes closed:

> When I talk, I talk with Billy;
> When I walk, I walk with Billy

—and one line, an interpolation which we thought very funny, and which would only be sung at a stag party, and which still seemed to us funny when we were singing it for the fiftieth time:

> When I sleep, I sleep with Billy.

The next morning I had to leave, to go to Manhattan Transfer and take a train to the West. While it was still half dark I was called up out of distant deeps of sleep by someone who stood in the middle of my room. When I could open my eyes for a sufficiently long period I saw that he was dressed in black and was clean-shaven and austere-looking. And when my ears were able to take in the question he was repeating, I took it to be, "Shall I shrive you?" The question seemed not surprising, considering what I could remember of the night before. Nor was it unwelcome, considering the way I felt. But if I were in extremis, there were some decencies and proprieties which should attend such a condition. Because of the lack of them now I began to generate inner resentment. A man's wife should be present; if she were not informed she ought to be told. My brother ought to be there—where was he? But as I struggled upward from coma, and my senses began feebly to function, I realized that the repeated question which I was hearing was not, "Shall I shrive you?" but "Shall I shive you?" and that the black-coated figure was not a priest, but Collier's English valet.

Between Collier and Hapgood (and including me after they took me into intimacy) was immense affection, accompanied by deep difference of personality. Of all the men I have known Hapgood had the best mental machine. But of all the men I have known Collier had the least need of a mental machine. Hapgood could take any problem, pass it with slow deliberation through his mechanism of thought, and arrive at the infallible answer. But Collier would have known the answer before Hapgood's mind even began to work. On occasions Collier would know what Hapgood never could—Collier would know a better answer than any that logic could arrive at, would know that as to many questions and situations, the answer lies not in logic but in instinct and emotion, sometimes in the arbitrary decrees of fate and circumstance. As to some questions, about which Hapgood cerebrated ponderously, Collier sometimes felt the answers to be not terribly important, nor worth striving to arrive at. This trait of nonchalance about what he deemed unimportant made Collier both more charming and more effective, added to his buoyant enthusiasm. With the passage of the years buoyant enthusiasm was interrupted by increasingly frequent moods of disillusionment. But that change did not set in until later years. The Collier I knew was buoyant, high-spirited, gallant; extremely able, with an ability that included quick grasp of overt circumstance, quick insight into conditions beneath the surface, and a deep inner wisdom which his quickness and gayety often hid.

Sometimes the answer that Collier leaped to by instinct did

not coincide with the answer Hapgood arrived at by logic. That would lead to a fleeting tension. Sometimes Hapgood had moments when he thought Collier's flair for the striking effect was a little garish—and sometimes Collier had moments when he felt that Hapgood's refinement of thought went so far as to be preciosity. Because they cared for each other so much, their moments of difference were painful to them. Even though the difference was only for an instant, and even though it expressed itself in a competition in deference, each trying to excel in accommodating himself to the other, nevertheless the moments were interruptions to affectionate camaraderie.

On such occasions I was useful; I was an emollient and buffer. With visible relief they would say, "Let's see what Mark thinks," and whatever I thought—whether it was with one or the other or somewhere between—it was hailed by both as high wisdom, not because it was wisdom at all, but because it brought an end to difference of opinion between two sensitive men. The end of the episode was a hurrying of the three of us out to lunch, a quick forgetting of the point at issue, a gay turning to something different and amusing.

On the whole I thought that, on many matters, Collier's instinct was better than Hapgood's judgment—and I knew that in matters having to do with journalistic effectiveness Collier was always right. Collier was a true journalist, of the highest order; Hapgood was not a journalist at all, he was an essayist. But I knew the enormous value of having Hapgood's scholarship and talent for exact thought brought to bear on current public questions. It was Collier who made the *Weekly* the most effective journalism of the time, but it was Hapgood who gave it the highly civilized touch that distinguished it.

I could sometimes get impatient at Hapgood's love of refined disquisition and his what seemed to me almost perverse pleasure in arriving at hairline distinctions, in politics, religion, morals and what not. On such occasions I felt that to Hapgood the most tragic accident in the world would be to fall off a hairline. I would reflect that Hapgood's only passion was to be dispassionate, and I would find relief for my exasperation in

[*229*]

thinking to myself that Hapgood, when engaged in his slow, sure progress toward a hairline, suggested a ruminating camel. But I never said that to Hapgood, nor any other word of irritation. My permanent feeling for him was affection, my permanent attitude exalted regard. Always I felt I was not doing enough for him—always he said I was doing too much. His letters, to me and to my wife, contain repeated urgings to rest—"I thought you looked tired yesterday; I hope it was an illusion, or temporary"; to my wife, "Tell Mark to go off and take a long idleness." The closest to any expression of irritation I ever heard from him was when, having gone to Europe for recreation, I returned sooner than Hapgood thought I should.

The two, Collier and Hapgood, differed in possession of humor. Collier had unlimited stores of it, he was a flowing well of it. Hapgood, though he richly appreciated humor in others, had to arrive at his own by way of cerebration—it was a little mechanical. Once when a lapse in the proofreading caused *Collier's* to commit a really classic "boner," printing a couplet from Browning as

> *. . . never could recapture*
> *That first fine, careless rupture,*

Collier was uproariously amused, Hapgood upset. Once Hapgood, consciously descending into lightness, and writing in the manner of the "Essays of Elia," discoursed about pie and the respective virtues of its varieties. When he adorned his disquisition with a pun contained in a quoted couplet

> *Currant pie, alternating current pie,*
> *First a currant, then a fly*

he plumed himself on his wit, yet felt some disquiet lest he had gone too far into levity. He would not print it until he consulted me as an authority on the permissible latitudes of ribaldry, and was assured it was quite all right.

Of Hapgood's lack of humor, certainly of the spirit of fun, there is illustration in his own account of his relations with Mark Twain. Hapgood knew Mark well; as a youth he had been an intimate of the Clemens family, had visited Clemens' home in Hartford, had acted in private theatricals that Mark wrote and staged, Hapgood playing the part of lover to a sweetheart that was played by Clemens' daughter Susie. During Hapgood's early years in New York he saw much of Mark, used to call at Mark's Fifth Avenue house noontimes, finding the humorist still in bed, with a pipe in his mouth, a writing pad in his hand.

There was close friendship between Mark and three of the Colliers' coterie, Hapgood, Robert Collier and Peter Dunne. Dunne was the only person I ever heard call Clemens "Mark" to his face, though all of us, a generation younger, spoke of him among ourselves as "Old Mark." Hapgood, Mark had taken into his circle as a family friend; Dunne he had taken in as a fellow humorist, one whom Mark respected; Collier he took in as a young man he liked. Collier told me that after some early contacts Mark had said to him: "You look to me like a promising young fellow; if you continue to improve on acquaintance I'll invite you to become a member of my club." To Collier's questions, Mark said the name of it was the G.D.H.R. Club, but the meaning of the initials Mark said he would not tell until he was satisfied that Collier was qualified to be a satisfactory member. The full name of the club, it turned out, was the God Damned Human Race; and revelation of the name was occasion for Mark to blow off to a friend a bitterness which an honored author must not reveal to the public. "The God damned human race," he would say, "look at them! Watch a crowd of them coming out of a subway station, potbellied, snaggle-toothed; compare them to horses; compare them to collie dogs."

Out of the long contact he had had with Mark Twain, Hapgood, when he came to write his autobiography, could recall only two jokes that he was moved to write down. One was Mark's bitterly cynical response to an inquiry about the health of himself and his family—"We have been doing so well lately that I sometimes fear Providence has forgotten the Clemens family." The other was Mark's drawling comment when Hapgood deplored the emphasis on wealth in New York: "In Hannibal, Missouri, where I was brought up, we never talked about money—in fact, there wasn't money enough in the place to form a topic of conversation."

Those faint bits of irony and hyperbole are all that Hapgood gleaned from a long association with one of the world's great humorists. Yet Hapgood knew, indeed participated in, an experience that was by its circumstances striking—a joke, not by Mark Twain, but on him.

Mark, to escape the admiring who in too generous numbers called at his home on Fifth Avenue, built a house in Connecticut, Stormfield, some fifty miles from New York. But once there, Mark found he had removed himself too far; he regretted the separation from his intimates in New York. To Collier, Hapgood and Dunne he complained that he was lonely. Humorously yet genuinely he said he had gone away to escape what bored him terribly, hearing the talk of persons he did not care to listen to; but he was also away from those he wanted to listen to; besides, he said, he liked to talk himself, and now had no one to talk to.

Instantly Collier took for himself a role of deeply moved gravity, which assumed that the loneliness of Mark Twain was the most serious matter in the contemporary world. It must be remedied at once, in whatever way possible. To Mark he said there was one thing that could be done promptly. "You ought to have a friendly animal in the house. It would be company for you in the long winter evenings—something you could talk to, but that won't talk to you. Not a dog, a dog wouldn't be it. It must be the most intelligent animal in the world. Ah, I know —I'll get you a baby elephant. It'll be a Christmas present to you. I'll fix it all up; it won't be any trouble at all."

The sweep of Collier's enthusiasm was such that Mark felt obliged to seem appreciative. Later, to Hapgood and Dunne, he expressed, profanely, his dismay: "I can't have a damn baby elephant up there. The thing would grow up. The ceilings of the house are low. You fellows have got to head Collier off." But Dunne and Hapgood told Mark they could not head Collier off: "You know how he is when he gets going; there's nothing we can do about it; you'll just have to take the elephant, for a while anyhow."

Collier busied himself with details. To Stormfield he sent a load of hay, with a letter to Mark saying the hay would last awhile and he would see it was renewed. He was, he told Mark, making further inquiry about the diet of young elephants and about their ways. It might be necessary to have a man to take care of the animal. But Collier would look after that too—everything would be arranged, Mark need not give it a thought.

At the office Collier twinkled into my room. We must pretend to send Mark a mahout—the very sound of the word delighted him. He called Mark on the telephone and told him the mahout would arrive a day or so before Christmas. For the role of mahout Collier considered one of the printers, whose stout figure would carry well the drapery of an oriental costume, and whose ruddy countenance would look impressive beneath a turban. We must get some books about elephants and their keepers, so that our mahout could instruct himself in the technical talk of that calling, and be able to convince Mark of his authenticity.

Presently Collier sent the mahout. And he sent the elephant. It arrived at Stormfield on Christmas morning. It would not, however, inconvenience Mark by growing up. It was of cotton.

A nephew of Mark Twain, Samuel E. Moffett, was one of *Collier's* staff. He did not have Mark's humor. His office function was to write the summaries of the news, "What the World Is Doing", and besides that, generously and usefully, to act as the office encyclopedia. Whatever you wanted, whether railroad statistics or a point in international law, to ask Sam Moffett was quicker and more agreeable than to turn the pages of a reference book.

Moffett, carrying in his head all the doings of the world, kept for himself a private dream. He was saving his money to buy a turkey ranch in California. When he talked to me about his anticipated combination of idyl and livelihood, his round face used to take on a touch of exalted longing. A friend of his, he said, had had such a ranch and fortuitously done well with it. One summer there came to that section a plague of grasshoppers. That, of course, troubled the turkey-ranch owner not at all; on the contrary, it brought feed without cost for his several hundred birds. There were in the same neighborhood, however, ranch owners who raised grain and alfalfa and fruit, but had no turkeys. To these the grasshopper plague brought menace of ruin. To them, in their perturbation, the turkey-ranch owner made a proposition. For adequate consideration he would hire out his flock of turkeys. To the owners of the turkeyless ranches the offer came as heaven-sent succor. They bid against each other for priority of opportunity for the turkeys' services; the successful bidder, as I recall Sam's account, was one who offered twenty cents per turkey per day. Meanwhile the owner of the turkeys rocked upon the porch of his ranch house in beatific content, reflecting upon that admirable equilibrium of nature which makes one man's ill wind another's good.

I remember Sam Moffett for another association. I was with Rob Collier at his camp in the Adirondacks. It was a gorgeous summer Sunday. Late in the afternoon, with the sun low upon the lake, Collier and I went in his motorboat over to the railroad station to get the Sunday papers. When we opened them the news that pealed in big headlines was about a sensational advance in flying—a French aviator, Bleriot, had flown across the English Channel. We were deeply impressed, as was all the world. We reflected upon the past, the crossings and attempted crossings of the Channel, from Caesar's legions on; and we reflected upon the future—England was no longer so secure, history would take a new turn. Collier and I gave thought to how *Collier's* should treat so sensational an event. We must, we said, see Moffett at the office the first thing next morning. When we arrived in New York we learned that Moffett was dead.

In an obscure way that increased my affection for him I felt sorry for Hapgood. There was a better way of life for him, I thought, than the one he was following, and a better use for the particular talent he had, a talent that was very precious, but, like any gift that is precious or rare, adapted to a limited scope. Someone else, many others, could write as forcibly as Hapgood in favor of the causes *Collier's* fought for, the income tax, the direct election of senators, votes for women, railroad rate regulation, pure food laws. Many others could as eloquently advocate child labor laws, workmen's compensation laws, limited hours for women in industry, the promotion of settlement houses, the abolition of slums. All that, I felt, was for blunter pens than Hapgood's.

What Hapgood could do that few could equal him in I can illustrate by a paragraph he wrote. It was in a field he knew well; one time or another I was with Hapgood when he talked or dined with many of the leading actors and actresses and playwrights of the time; always their attitude was that of affectionate regard and deference for one who, though outside their art, knew it as a master. With theatrical producers it was not wholly the same; the independent producers were Hapgood's strong friends, but the "theatrical trust" hated him; Hapgood had fought them. He felt the multiple ownership of theaters was bad, that the "trust" commercialized the art.

One day Hapgood saw in a newspaper a despatch that recalled his days as a dramatic critic. Moved by memory, partly in a spirit of nostalgia, of escape from his present immersion in hectic journalism, he wrote an editorial paragraph. As it appeared in print, part of its charm lay in its setting. Preceding it on *Collier's* editorial page was a paragraph of political denunciation, an attack upon William R. Hearst, then running for governor of New York against Charles E. Hughes; following it was an attack upon the evils of patent medicines, beside it a high-pitched exhortation to political reform in Philadelphia. Within that austere and commonplace frame Hapgood wrote:

Pause a moment, reader—gentle reader; turn from the sound and fury of politics and battle; remember a woman whose five and eighty years were given to inspiration and ideals. You shall have enough, and for several weeks perhaps more than enough, of the heat of struggle; give a moment to recalling one of the highest and loveliest talents of the passing day. Ristori is dead. After her brief and fitful fever on this earth nothing remains to us but her name and that small and evanescent shadow which is memory. Rising before man's gaze when Rachel had started downward from the zenith, she proved a not unworthy rival of the inspired French Jewess, and never once, through her years of passion and of thought, did she fail to keep before her eyes the uttermost reaches of her art. The drama to her was the material in which she molded into beauty the bravest, tenderest, warmest, most loving materials of our many-colored human soul. A noble woman, nobly dowered, she spent her talents as the Master would have her spend them. Of five she made ten, or a thousand, and all her being was kept afire in the service of the best. Remembering her, and beacons bright as she, we may now pass on, fellow citizens of the Republic, to investigate the business of our day.

A writer whose nature expressed itself in that was hardly at home in the hurly-burly of the causes and contests that *Collier's* was always deep in. Once, visiting him at a lovely place he had at Windsor, Vermont, I found him one afternoon with writing pad on his knee, sitting in a garden that lay in westward slopes and terraces below the house. It occurred to me that if I could order the universe and have each man where he ought to be, I would keep Hapgood in that country garden, writing just as much and no more than he was moved to write, on topics inspired by the blue delphiniums around him.

Like many men whose talent is fine and precious, Hapgood was not physically robust. The stream of his genius was pure and clear but not great in volume. Since his store of nervous force was not abundant, it was a pity any of it should have been given to the New York social life—dinners, the opera, country house parties—which Hapgood did not really care for but was drawn into by his association with the Colliers and their circle, especially the circle of the elder Collier. Young Rob understood Hapgood too well to drag him to parties of the social type; indeed, Rob cared little for them himself, and went to few, though his wife was a granddaughter of the then authentic social queen, Mrs William Astor. Old P. F., however, took social life seriously, perhaps more seriously than discriminatingly. P. F. admired Hapgood extravagantly, without knowing quite why he admired. How little P. F. understood what he was paying twenty-five thousand dollars a year for was illustrated by the remark attributed to him when he gave Hapgood an imported Dutch automobile. He wanted Hapgood to spend his salary. He feared that if Hapgood saved, he might retire. "A fat horse," said P. F. from his hunting lore, "a fat horse won't pull." P. F., proud of Hapgood, took him to a good many dinner parties at which, as Hapgood gently repined, "quoting Matthew Arnold's poems was a simple-minded breach of tact." One kindly and good-intentioned dowager, conscious of the burden of her social obligations, and making conversation with Hapgood as if tactfully groping her way into the other person's field of interest, said: "Don't you think it pleasant sometimes to spend one night at home and just read?"

Hapgood's life could have been better managed than it was, his talent more fruitful. I like to think that when we were together he did his best work; I was able to give something to him, as he gave much to me. My association with him carried me into fields of interest which my formal education had not included, gave me points of view that had not previously occurred to me but which I saw were sound. It is a fine experience to have a superior for whom one has both admiration and affection.

CHAPTER 25

Goethe, rejoicing over his career and explaining it, said that "When I was eighteen, Germany was also eighteen." Every career, proud or humble, has some such relation to the time when the career begins; everyone has a relation to, and is conditioned by, the world into which he emerges as adult. The degree to which he is adapted to it, his luck in making contact with the forces that are dominant, may determine the difference between a fortunate life and a frustrated one.

In several respects the America of about 1900 was a happy one for a person of journalistic taste and aptitude. Both the spirit of the time and the material cricumstances were favorable. The business of circulating printed words was flourishing as it had never flourished before. The manufacture of print paper out of wood pulp, much less costly than rag, had been perfected recently. The art of photography, invented not many decades before, had reached a point where the camera was becoming universal; the art of printing photographs on paper, less than ten or fifteen years old, had reached a point where periodicals and even newspapers could be rich in illustrations.

To support the expansion thus made possible, to serve as the economic foundation of newspapers and magazines, advertising was growing to the proportions of a major industry. Periodicals of the 1880s had had little or no advertising. By the early 1900s periodicals looked to advertising as their major source of revenue. Existing periodicals expanded in bulk; new ones were started. Demand for mediums in which to advertise led to increase of periodicals and newspapers; increase of periodicals and newspapers led to demand for writers to fill them.

I am not sure that a young man beginning journalism in 1938 would find opportunity in as great a mood of welcome as one who began about the turn of the century. About 1925 and after, advertising, which once fed the printed word alone, began to divide with the spoken word, the radio. The number of periodicals and newspapers began to contract. The little town of West Chester, when I started there in 1892, had three daily papers; by the 1920s it had but one. Philadelphia, when I spent a while on a paper there in 1900, had five important morning papers, four evening ones; by 1938 the numbers were two and two respectively. In every city similar contraction took place.

Not only did the market for writing shrink. New means of expression, of conveying thought and facts and description and narrative, came into the world.

Once during the 1930s, at a party in Washington, I talked with Noel Coward about his play, *Cavalcade*, and the motion picture that had been made of it. Coward, then on tour with another play, had never seen *Cavalcade* as a motion picture— he as author of the play had sold the rights to a motion picture firm and let them make a film of it. The picture was being shown in New York, but Coward, because he was on tour, could not go to see it. He asked me if I were going to be in New York soon, and if so, would I go to see *Cavalcade* and let him know what I thought of it. Because of this request I went alone and in a mood to observe the picture with especial concentration. As the film unfolded, and I realized its extraordinary beauty and distinction, and observed the art by which its remarkable effects were achieved, I experienced a dismaying reflection. Here am I, I thought, a writer, engaged in the business of conveying ideas to the public. And here, while I have been laboriously pushing pen across paper, here has arisen a new method of conveying ideas, a method in many respects more flexible, more direct and more effective than mine. I felt as if I were like one of those old monks, the scriveners, who continued to copy manuscript by hand long after printing had been invented. To young writers looking forward the lesson is as plain, and even more important, than to old writers looking backward. Learn the art of writing, of course, but learn also the art of the motion picture, and of the radio.

Not only were the material circumstances, the expansion of the printed word in periodical form, favorable to a young journalist who started about the turn of the century. The public mood was receptive to the kind of writing to which I was adapted. It was a time of intellectual insurgency. Ever since the Civil War in America the Republican party, and for more than sixty years in England Queen Victoria, had preserved a status quo. Beneath that status ideas had germinated, pushed upward and demanded expression. The condition existed in every field. In drama George Bernard Shaw was crying out against the conventional; in letters H. G. Wells; in English politics Lloyd George.

In politics in America the movement expressed itself, as respects writing, in a vogue of exposure, "muckraking." The best-known practitioner of it, Lincoln Steffens, put into his autobiography a photographic reproduction of the heading of his exposure of St Louis in *McClure's Magazine*. He captioned it "The First Muckraking Article." That St Louis exposure was printed in October 1902. But actually the first article of political muckraking was the one I wrote, "The Ills of Pennsylvania," for the *Atlantic Monthly* just a year before, in October 1901. The priority in time is not material. What is material is the fact that a muckraking of the politics of a state, written anonymously, by an obscure young law student, could attract national attention. It was not the writers who made the muckraking era. It was the public mood of the time.

That public mood was justified by the conditions. Not only in politics but in business—and especially where politics and business met—there were conditions and practices that invited exposure.

II

In the winter of 1905, in the legislature of Indiana, occurred a small drama in which the characters were two men named Baker. The two were not related, excepting the very strange relation they now came to have. One was a good Baker, the other a bad Baker.

The story began with the good Baker. He had the biblical mien that goes with goodness, and his biblical appearance was borne out by an Old Testament name, though, most paradoxically, the name was Ananias, Ananias Baker. He was a member of the legislature.

On the morning of February 22—appropriate date!—Ananias Baker rose from his seat. An anti-cigarette bill was under discussion. Baker the Good said he had "received a letter from the cigarette trust itself." The letter was still sealed. Baker the Good would open it. He did so—the contents were five twenty-dollar bills.

There was outcry, commotion, hurry and scurry. The greatest hurry of all was that which immediately animated the other Baker, Baker the Bad—his formal name was O. A. Baker. O. A. Baker was a former state senator of Indiana who spent much time around the state capital. Now he did so no more. He departed hastily and for several years the grand jury was unable to find him. So impetuous was O. A. Baker's departure from Indiana that he took nothing with him, did not even close his desk, which was in a small factory he owned. A little later the factory was bought by a man named Hughes. He, rummaging through O. A. Baker's desk, found forty-seven letters. Reading the letters, Hughes was stirred by civic virtue. He wanted those letters published. He offered them to me. I bought them for *Collier's Weekly*, paid fifteen hundred dollars for them.

They were worth the money. Even as entertainment they were worth it. They were addressed to O. A. Baker, who was the lobbyist for the American Tobacco Company at Indianapolis, and they came from the chief lobbyist of the company at New York, apparently a kind of general manager of the local state lobbyists everywhere. The public importance of the letters lay in the amounts of money named as having been paid to stop anti-cigarette legislation. The amusement of them came from the droll, picaresque camaraderie that existed between the head lobbyist in New York and his assistant in Indianapolis:

There seems to be quite an epidemic of cigarette agitations these days. Let us hope for the best, however, and keep in shape so that when the time comes we can meet the enemy and do him before he does us. . . . Better get those checks cashed at once and have the money in currency in case of necessity. Be a good boy and God will make you a good man.

P.S. Don't give up a dollar to those fellows until the gavel has gone down at the end of the session.

Some telegrams were in a code, of which the translations were entrancing: "dormant" meant "a hundred dollars"; "drollish" meant "two thousand dollars"; "Do you want hawthorn blossoms?" meant "Do you want help?" "Whistle" meant "Let me know the worst at once."

In buying the letters I had in mind to use them as the basis of exposure articles, which should be a history of the American Tobacco Company in the manner of Ida M. Tarbell's story of the Standard Oil Company. I sent copies of them to Booth Tarkington. Tarkington had been in the Indiana Legislature, had seen Ananias Baker's dramatic exposure of the attempt upon his virtue, and knew all the politicians mentioned in the letters. I thought that, with those vivid and bizarre letters as a backbone and skeleton, Tarkington, with his gift for narrative, could make an absorbing article.

Tarkington, at the time he got my letter, was in France. He wrote me a long reply, full of the hilarious amusement he had got out of the revelations about his former fellow members of the legislature. As to making an article out of the material, he wrote:

I could not write an article about all that without going home, but I have had it in mind for a long time to write a political story embodying that pathetic farce. If I ever do, it will (out of my own experience) show a strong sympathy with the tobacco trust. Because every Assembly for years, in Indiana, had an anti-cigarette bill, regarded by nine-tenths of the members as a "freak bill," a joke. The man who introduced it in my term did so in complete good faith, at the request of sincere anti-cigarette zealots, but he laughed and blushed as he did so. . . . It is mainly a joke, and for the rest, considerable of a "hold up." Many legislators support the measures sincerely, of course, but many another who isn't "there for his health" is joyously alive to the fact that he can get something out of the tobacco people. And he goes after it.

Tarkington, out of greater experience than I had had, and more innate understanding of men than I would ever have, knew that in bribery, the initiative, the solicitation, does not always come from the briber. I had naïvely supposed that support of anti-cigarette measures came always and only from well-meaning persons, and that injection of evil into the situation, the solicitation to bribery, came always from the corporate end of the transaction. I learned that some of the support came sometimes from persons who united with the honest zealots for the purpose of being bought off.

CHAPTER 26

ONE DAY Collier came to me with a suggestion which, when carried out, led to my getting an individual identity before the public, made my name a familiar brand, gave me the status that became my lifetime capital.

Collier proposed that I write, as a standing feature, a page to be called "Comment on Congress"—the title, like the idea, was fruit of his sure journalistic instinct. The page would be printed in editorial-size type, larger than the regular body type, and would otherwise be set off in a way that elevated it above the rest of the paper, except the editorial pages, and made it equal to them. Indeed, the fact that my page was signed, while the editorial pages were not, added the factor of personality, and made my contribution rather the most conspicuous feature of the paper.

With my weapon in my hand, a weekly page in *Collier's*, I set myself to a pretentious enterprise. With appalling casualness—as I see it now—I went about unhorsing two out of the three most powerful political figures in the United States—no less than that! One was Joseph G. Cannon, Republican Speaker of the House; the other, Nelson W. Aldrich, Republican leader of the Senate.

The objection to Cannon was not lack of integrity—he was honest. And while objection to him lay in his espousal of the great corporate interests, that espousal had no touch of corruption; it was honest espousal, not prostitution. And it was a union of equals: Cannon's role was not subservience or deference. Actually Cannon was the stronger partner. When he thought corporations should be denied, denied they were. By no means did Cannon grant all that the corporations wanted. But the corporations had come to have, in American life, politically and economically, a power that was intolerable, that hampered the freedom of individuals to engage in their own enterprises. This power was expressed through the Republican party; within the Republican party it was expressed in Congress; and, in effect, Congress consisted of Cannon and Aldrich.

I have spoken of Cannon's relation to the corporations as an espousal. It was not that. It was rather that Cannon, when he came into power, found the corporations occupying a certain status. That status Cannon preserved. He preserved it, not because it favored the corporations—but just because it was the status. Had the status favored labor unions or farmers, he would have preserved it the same. The key to Cannon's character lay in the epithet that was most often applied to him, and which fitted him better than it fitted any other political leader of the time; he was universally called a standpatter, and rarely has epithet so aptly fitted the man. If any precision in words could have found a more suitable term, it might have been "stand-stiller." To Cannon, said William Hard, in an article I got him to write for *Collier's*, "the present moment is always surpassingly the finest and noblest moment that was ever allowed to occur; all future moments should be postponed." What is, is good; what is new is bad, ipso facto bad. What is accepted is sound, what is proposed is wrong. "Had Cannon been present at the creation, he would have fought for the preservation of chaos." Once in Congress there was a bill to add a new function to the United States Commission of Fish and Fisheries, making it the United States Commission of Fish, Fisheries and Birds. Cannon strenuously resisted the "and Birds." "Fish and Fisheries" was long established, and was therefore good; "and Birds" was new, and therefore must be resisted.

It was this trait in Cannon that served the corporations. It was not at all that he gave them new privileges. What the corporations asked for that was new Cannon resisted as strenuously as he resisted proposals for something new from any other source. He would, and did, bully and defy the National Association of Manufacturers as readily as the American Federation of Labor. Cannon's service to the corporations was that he stood as a stone wall against change, and thereby protected the corporations in the advantages they had built up for themselves during the forty years since the Civil War and the Fourteenth Amendment to the Constitution. It was against these entrenched privileges that most of the reforms of the early 1900s were directed, and Cannon stood in the way. The spirit that Theodore Roosevelt crystallized, Cannon resisted.

There were minor objections to Cannon. He was vulgar. Once, years before, his third of a century in Congress had been interrupted by a defeat administered to him because of a coarse joke he had uttered in the House. Cannon's jest had been to the effect that an opponent in debate was blowing hot and cold at the same time. To say that was no harm; it had been said often before; it was a classic cliché of disputation. But Cannon said it in a different way, in terms of a frontier Illinois figure of speech, too earthy for the Victorian standards of the America of the 1890s. The old New York *Morning Sun* had pursued Cannon with cartoons showing just his mouth, and the slogan, "This foul mouth must not be returned to Congress." Cannon was rusticated to his Illinois home for a term.

One use of a bucolic figure of speech does not make a man vulgar; and a mere superficial vulgarity of language, even if habitual, would not necessarily make a man undesirable in high office. In fact, Cannon was habitually vulgar in speech; in private conversation he had metaphors compared with which his coarse utterance on the floor of the House was the chatter of a pink tea. Cannon's vulgarity was of the spirit; it was innate; it was of the essence of him. It was at once the unconscious and the deliberate expression of his personality; he was "positively fanatical in his vulgarity," said William Hard. He was in an office so high as to call for not only the substance but the manner of statesmanship—and to compare Cannon with men of corresponding rank in England, or with his own predecessors in the office he occupied, was to feel a little ashamed for America.

In his speeches he did not faintly approach statesmanship; he did not pretend to; he used the locutions and adopted the postures of a stump speaker before a frontier audience. On the platform he would caper and prance. Once he walked up the four steps to a platform as any person would. Then, turning to the audience, he said, "That is how a young man mounts a platform; now I'll show you how an old man does it." Thereupon he descended the steps, walked a few yards out in front of the stage, did a caper or two, and then, taking a running start, leaped upon the platform without aid of the steps.

No one ever heard of Cannon reading a book. His diversion was poker, in which he had a special vocabulary that became the language of Washington poker players. Three queens were "Minnie, Maude and Kate"; three tens, "thirty miles of railroad." When he was playing poker his habitual tobacco chewing was accelerated. If he was playing at a private home whose furniture did not include a spittoon he asked for one. Once one of his hostesses gave him the umbrella stand—it proved to be not wide enough in the mouth.

With Cannon's vulgarity, went, naturally, unenlightenment. Not only was he unsympathetic to the fine impulses that were pushing forward in every area of American life, he did not know such impulses existed; if one of them were explained to him carefully he would probably think it was a sissy thing, faintly decadent, effete, a little indecent. Movements for great national parks and for conservation, then getting under way, were to Cannon preposterous nonsense. When a proposal was pending to provide senators and representatives with individual private offices Cannon suggested the offices be provided by superimposing on the two ends of the Capitol Building two skyscrapers. The outraged protest, not merely from architects, but from everyone sensitive to the Capitol's beauty and dignity, Cannon could not understand. Such a point of view as his, held by a man as high in public office as he, had an effect of sodden repression on everything that was fine and forward-looking in the whole of national life.

Cannon's illiteracy in architecture and art and everything

that was fine would not necessarily have made him an undesirable Speaker, and attack on him on that point would not have made headway. The real objection to him was that the power he had as Speaker was used in such a way as to preserve the privileges of the corporations, safeguard them against reform. It was on this ground that I attacked him.

Cannon's power as Speaker, abundantly justifying the epithet "Czar," lay in the rules of the House. Under them Cannon appointed every member of every committee; consequently every member who wanted to be on a desirable committee was careful to act on bills the way Cannon wished them acted upon —to report out for action those that Cannon wanted out, to keep in committee those that Cannon wanted repressed.

To complete the power inherent in the rules the Committee on Rules, which alone could alter the rules or make exceptions to them, was made up of Cannon himself, with two Republican cronies, these composing a majority, and two Democrats who as a minority had no voice.

To explain these rules to the public and to make clear how they worked was the first step in my campaign against Cannon. I must make the explanation so simple that the average man could understand it. I could, of course, just rail at Cannon, throw bricks at him, and that was the method of some of his adversaries. I did some of that, too, but only after I had carefully explained that Cannon was a symbol, and just what he was the symbol of, and made clear the mechanism through which he exerted his power.

To explain the rules and how Cannon operated them was difficult—parliamentary rules are not appetizing to readers; they do not readily lend themselves to drama, nor even to exposition. In attempting explanation and in all my writing in my "Comment on Congress," I had a device which I habitually practiced. I used to imagine myself leaning across the counter of a druggist—for some obscure reason I located my imaginary druggist in Oklahoma—and explaining the thing in such a way that a man of a small-town druggist's background and experience could understand it. First and last that imaginary Oklahoma druggist listened to a good deal from me. I never mentioned him in print, until this moment. He was a wholly imaginary character; he existed only in my mind, but he was an important figure in my campaign against Cannon and in my subsequent writings.

One of my early talks to my imaginary druggist, as printed in my page in *Collier's*, began: "If you are a citizen of the United States, if you take an interest in the government at Washington, if you, or your family, or your business is affected by a tariff, by the Pure Food law, by any of the laws that Congress passes or declines to pass—then this article is of great importance to *you*. Please read it."

Having thus commanded my fictitious druggist's attention in a way that he could hardly refuse, I proceeded:

You sent John Smith to Congress from your district. You sent him, let us say, because you believe in an income tax and John Smith believes in an income tax. So John Smith introduces an income tax bill. Introducing it is the simplest thing in the world. He takes a sheet of paper, writes at the top, "Sixtieth Congress, Second Session." Below he writes out the bill. Then he folds the paper, walks up the aisle, and places it in a small square basket on a desk close by the right hand of J. Cannon, Speaker. That is all. The bill is introduced. Now what next? In a moment of leisure, Cannon takes that basket full of new bills and runs through them hastily. Each one he sends to a committee. What thoughts Cannon may think, what smiles he may smile, when he runs across John Smith's income tax bill, are matters of speculation, which belong in the uncertain field of other men's motives. But any Member of Congress will tell you that John Smith's income tax bill will be sent to the Judiciary Committee—the safest of all Cannon's safe committees. Cannon appointed that committee, and he made it iron-bound, bomb-proof, and water-tight. It is called "Cannon's morgue." Not a Republican on that committee but has an understanding with Cannon, express or implied, that the committee will report favorably only such bills as Cannon desires.

Congressman Smith's bill is now in the Committee on Judiciary. What, now, can Congressman Smith do? Smith can do, literally, nothing whatever. . . . John Smith is the choice of 200,000 people;

the income tax bill may be earnestly desired by 300 out of the 391 members of Congress, each in turn representing 200,000 people, every one of whom wants an income tax law—all told, they are as impotent as an ant in the Capitol basement.

That, I explained, is how Cannon prevented bills from getting on the floor of the House, kept them in those lethal chambers, the committee rooms. With similar concreteness I illustrated another phase of the rules. I showed how Cannon could stop a bill even if by any remote chance it got out of the committee.

In thus explaining the rules and making them concrete, my object was simplicity, clarity. I took careful pains to be accurate —in writing the explanation I went over it again and again with a friend of mine in the House, Victor Murdock, of Kansas, who was a parliamentary expert in a little group of rebel Republicans who were demanding change in the rules. While my object was accuracy and clarity, I had also the objective of provoking public indignation against the rules and the power of Cannon that was based on the rules. After explaining the impotence of the supposititious Congressman Smith, I wrote:

What, now, can Congressman Smith do? Smith can do literally nothing whatever except whine to his friends in the cloak-room, and in most cases, being a prudent man, he won't do that, lest the Speaker or the Speaker's half-score intimates hear about it, in which case he will be "in bad," an outcast, deprived of the only present avenue to power in Congress—which is to play the sycophant to Cannon, show a willingness to swallow orders, and, finally, worm a way into the little freemasonry of Cannon's intimates.

That explanation of the rules, buttressed by proof, was the basis of my fight against Cannon; without making the public understand the rules and how they worked I could have made no headway.

Having explained the rules and how Cannon operated them, and having often repeated the explanation—iteration was one of the arts of my strategy—I set out on my crusade. The objective was double: to change the rules and, as lawyers would put it, *and/or* prevent Cannon's re-election as Speaker. Of the two,

I knew that change in the rules was so technical that it would be difficult to get and hold the interest of readers; people do not readily become emotionally indignant about anything so abstruse as parliamentary procedure. I focused on Cannon.

On Cannon officially, not Cannon personally. Of Cannon as a man I never wrote a detracting word. On occasion I was explicit in paying tribute to his personal qualities. "I have nothing against Cannon," I said in an address to the Young Republican Club of Brooklyn—as an incident of my writing "Comment on Congress" I was invited to make speeches; "he is a sturdy gentleman who has faced the attacks upon him with resolute face and undaunted courage; in the thick of it he has shown no weakness."

This personal amenity Cannon returned. I never heard of his saying anything seriously harsh about me. Occasionally I heard that he had an esoteric remark which he used to make about me at small private gatherings. So far as I could understand it at all I took no offense at it. It struck me as cryptic, though analysis of it might reveal some hideous intensity of insult that I happily was unable to comprehend. Cannon used to say, "If I owed the devil a forfeit, I'd tender him Mark Sullivan on a gridiron, and cite him into court to make him accept."

Against Cannon as Speaker, Cannon as the agency which reduced Congress from a free deliberative body to the minionry of a dictator—against Cannon in that role I launched every missile in the armory of journalism, and devised some which were then new, though they have since become common, including the device of direct, organized pressure by constituents on congressmen.

I have said that the material objection to Cannon was his resistance to putting checks upon the power of corporations. The corporations, by their power, frustrated the economic liberty of individuals; there was a popular outcry on behalf of the common man, and Cannon prevented it from coming to fruit in legislation. That was the familiar public objection to Cannon. I felt another. I felt indignation at the repression which

[251]

Cannon and his system practiced against individual congress-men, his practice of reward for complaisance, punishment for independence. Of this I gave an example.

In the House was an able member from New York, William S. Bennet. He was a regular Republican, a thoroughgoing party man, an active party worker—he had served as director of the Speakers' Bureau for the Republican National Committee. He was regular also in the sense of supporting Cannon in the House, had voted regular on the tariff and on nearly all other issues. By ability he had come to have fairly important committee assignments and had made himself an authority on the subjects his committees dealt with. He was a member of the Committee on Immigration and ranking member of Private Land Claims. But there arose an issue on which Bennet departed from regu-larity. President Theodore Roosevelt had sent a message to Congress which gave offense to the party leaders, including Cannon, and they introduced a resolution of rebuke to the President. Bennet opposed it, argued and voted in behalf of the President. A few months later Cannon, rearranging his committees for the next session, removed Bennet from his com-mittees, demoted him to the demeaning foot of the obscure Committee on Elections No. 2.

That, and other incidents like it, and countless cases in which nothing overt occurred, but in which members, through in-timidation, quietly suffered sacrifice of their independence— that stirred me. There were scores of fine men in the House who, by Cannon's power, were frustrated from functioning as their ability and character entitled them to. I sympathized with them, was indignant on behalf of them. As I wished the individual to have his place in the economic sun, as against repression by organized wealth, so did I wish him to have his place in the political sun as against repression by Cannon and the system Cannon acted for.

A little group of Republican congressmen had rebelled. There were twelve who had voted against re-election of Cannon as Speaker, nineteen who had voted against readoption of

Cannon's rules. That was few, in a total Republican membership of 218 and a total House membership of 391. They thought of themselves as a group, even though a feeble one, and of their cause as a movement, even though a hopeless one. They spoke of themselves as "Progressives."

This group I espoused for my journalistic attack on Cannon— one of them described me as the "official journalist of the Progressive movement." I changed the name of the group, or added a new name. I called them "Insurgents." I think I invented the term, or was the first to use it in print; I am certain I popularized it. I felt that the rebellious, fighting quality of the word made it more effective than "Progressives," and more appealing to the spirit of the times.

On my page I printed the photographs of the Insurgents conspicuously, labeling them "Twelve Men of Courage." In connection with each of the twelve I printed the names of the counties that composed his district, thus:

Charles A. Lindbergh[1] of Little Falls, member for the 6th district of Minnesota, made up of the counties of Benton, Cass, Crow Wing, Douglas, Hubbard, Meeker, Morrison, Sherburne, Stearns, Todd, Wadena and Wright.

I explained that I printed the names of the counties the Insurgents represented "because the loyal backing of their constituents is as much entitled to recognition as the personal courage of the members; the counties named in this list have better reason to be proud of their representatives than any other constituencies." By this tribute to the counties I felt I would stir local pride in behalf of each Insurgent, and thus help them against reprisal by the regular Republicans. I felt also that publicity given certain counties for the merit of possessing an Insurgent congressman might stir other counties to try to achieve the same publicity by achieving the same merit.

[1]This name of an Insurgent congressman, eighteen years later, achieved greater fame, through the feat of a son who bore it, and who in a field that he made his own was an outstanding example of the same individualism that his father practiced in politics.

Over and over I implied that communities represented by Insurgents were superior. I printed a map showing the states from which most of the Insurgents came—Kansas, Nebraska, Minnesota, Iowa, Wisconsin. I presented argument—too long to reproduce here and perhaps not as convincing to me now as it seemed then—to prove that these states were a superior section of the nation, their population a chosen people. "They are States of small cities and towns, of rich farms, where economic and political independence is man's highest prize." To other states that remained in standpat benightedness I made an appeal that was at once reproach and ingratiation. "Is there no political vitality in Michigan?" I asked. "Surely the people of that State are of the same stock, the same ways of thinking, and the same interests as their neighbors in Wisconsin, Iowa, Minnesota and Kansas. Why have they not the same capacity for making themselves heard in the nation?"

The problem was to bring about, in the approaching Republican primaries, the nomination of candidates who, if elected, would be Insurgents, or at least would vote against Cannon for Speaker. To this end I printed on my page, in large type and often repeated, an appeal to readers, with a blank form for reply:

Any voter who is willing to aid in the election of anti-Cannon members of the next Congress is invited to send us his name and address. The time required of anyone who helps will be only so long as it takes to write three or four letters; the money outlay will be only the cost of the stamps. Fill out the blank below.

To the readers who replied I sent a form letter. This I asked them to copy and to send to the candidate for the Republican nomination for Congress in their district. The form letter read:

DEAR SIR:
I understand that you are a candidate for the Republican nomination for Congress in this district. As a voter in the district I wish to ask you these questions:
1. If elected to Congress will you vote *for* or *against* Cannon for Speaker in the Republican caucus?

[*254*]

2. If the Republican caucus should nominate Cannon for Speaker, will you then vote *for* or *against* Cannon in the regular session of Congress?

If you will be good enough to let me know your position on these questions, I shall feel that I can cast my ballot more intelligently.

Quickly, in the congressional districts throughout the country, hundreds of these letters were darting in upon the candidates. To the candidates they were stinging hornets.

As the candidates replied to the constituents who sent the letters, the constituents sent the replies to me, and I printed them on my page, with comment. All the candidates who pledged themselves to vote against Cannon were by that fact laudable men, worthy to be elevated to Congress. The ideal, the perfect perfection, was Congressman Hubbard, of Iowa, who replied to the questions with the brevity of two numerals and one word, repeated:

1. Against
2. Against

Any candidate who did not say forthrightly that he would vote against Cannon—him I excoriated. When Congressman Julius Kahn, of San Francisco, wrote that he "would discuss all such matters during the next campaign," I observed that Congressman Kahn "is an evader and procrastinator." When a distinguished Massachusetts congressman, George Edmund Foss, replied with a long letter ending, "on this matter as on all others I desire to represent the wishes of my constituents," I printed his prudent aspiration and wrote "Congressman Foss is extremely cordial, very willing, but undecided. We hope some thousands of his constituents will give him help toward making up his mind."

When Congressman McLachlen, of California, wrote: "I am sure Mr Cannon will not be a candidate for Speaker again," I said, "Yes, but Mr Cannon says he *will* be a candidate," and added, "There are yet ten days in which the Republicans of Los Angeles can put Mr McLachlen formally and positively on record." When Congressman Keifer, of Ohio, replied that the "inquiries involve matters that would be quite unwise for me to now express an opinion upon," I observed, "Of course! But isn't it quite unwise for Mr Keifer's constituents to wait until he is nominated before finding out how he will vote?" Menacingly I added, "The primaries which will either renominate or reject Mr Keifer will be held the third Tuesday in May."

One candidate there was who defied the demand for an anti-Cannon pledge, and for his refusal gave a sound reason. Had more congressmen made the same answer, I suspect my campaign might have blown up. The candidate who had the courage to refuse to pledge himself, and the penetration to base his refusal on a convincing reason, was Samuel W. McCall. McCall had served in Congress a long time; he was a man of high type, a gentleman and scholar, an author of worthy books; he was later governor of Massachusetts. His reply to one of my form letters was:

In the ordinary course of things it will be about two years before the next Congress is organized, and I should certainly regard it as some evidence of my unfitness for membership in the House if I should pledge myself for or against any man for Speaker so long in advance of the time when I should exercise my judgment upon the exact conditions existing at that time.

McCall was so right that I could only fan the air with a retort that was beside the point:

Congressman McCall's district [I wrote] includes Harvard University. Lately Mr McCall was invited, and declined, to be president of Dartmouth College. We suggest that he would be an admirable incumbent for the chair of Equivocation and Evasion in any college whatever.

I was blatantly partisan. Whatever Cannon and the Standpatters did was evil; whatever the Insurgents did was good. Whatever the Democrats did was good too. But my chief concern was to support the Insurgents, build them up in the esteem of the public, increase their numbers. If the word "Comment" in the title of my page, or the whole phrase "Comment on

Congress" implied a discursive mood, or leisurely pace, and a detached, impersonal point of view, any such implication was shockingly belied by the contents of the page. In mood I was impassioned; in manner I was high-pitched, even strident; in pace I was breathless—Arthur Ruhl said I made the impression of a runner in a hurdle race in which the jumps stretched out in an endless series, each higher than the last.

Sometimes I changed my tempo; slowing down my mood, I would write in the spirit of appeal to Cannon to resign. That he would take no notice of the appeal I knew well. Nor did I expect him to—what I was after was not the effect on Cannon, but the effect on the country and on other congressmen:

They say that Uncle Joe is a man of pride. Those who like him say, too, that loyalty to his friends in Congress and devotion to his party are chief among the qualities that have made him powerful in the Republican organization. All these traits, if he really does possess them, call him to an act of self-sacrifice.

Occasionally I would change my mood completely, or pretend to. I would write about Cannon in a vein which feigned to depart completely from politics and strife, a mood of gracious benevolence toward an elderly man whose age and public service entitled him to repose:

Whose is the pen that can paint the delights of a trip to Japan and a long, long rest among the flowers and lovely gardens of those gentle islands? From San Francisco to Tokyo is twelve slow settings of the sun, twelve days of quiet peace upon the long Pacific swell, each carrying a harassed man so much farther away from tumult and unlovely contention. How tired old eyes would freshen and brighten with long contemplation of the restful ocean! And, then, to see the soft colors of those islands rising from the sea! Weeks and weeks and weeks of rest among the cherry blossoms and the roses. Long afternoons on an easy chair, Ruskin or Wordsworth at hand to read, and, when reading tires, a lovely vista of soft green hills for the quickening eye to rest upon. The air is shot through and through with perfume; the very pores drink it hungrily in, and a cracked and grizzled old skin would assume again the soft pliancy of youth. In quiet lakes behind the hills, the swans float double, swan and shadow. In such a scene and such an air, anger, resentment, strife, all unlovely moods and malevolent impulses would fall away from the spirit like unlovely patches of old fleece from a sheep in spring. How a man would renew his youth! How long-forgotten aspirations for beauty, sweetness and serenity would lift their trampled heads and swell again with life. How far away and how humorously unworthy of effort, how like a half-forgotten nightmare would seem that huge room in Washington filled with three hundred and ninety-one turbulent men. For a man of seventy-four, at the end of a long life filled with fighting and scheming, whose age now calls him to physical repose and spiritual contemplation, how infinitely more desirable the climate of Japan, the scenery and the air of those gentle islands, than the harsh winters and the unlovely surroundings of Washington, District of Columbia.

Of another paragraph in a similarly feigned mood, the irony lay in public knowledge that Uncle Joe was notoriously a man lacking cultivation, lacking interest in books:

BOOKS FOR AN OLD MAN

We have assumed a task which we conceive to be not only a private kindness, but also not without dignity as a public service—the pointing out of those quiet pleasures which would make—we use the potential mood with care—which would make a serene old age in a substantial home on the outskirts of Danville, Illinois, preferable to the tumult and hurly-burly which are inevitable in an assemblage of three hundred and ninety-one boisterous men in a single room on Pennsylvania Avenue, Washington, District of Columbia. President Eliot of Harvard University is at the present time engaged in compiling a set which he aptly calls "five feet of books," a compilation of those one hundred volumes which, among all printed books, are of most worth. The idea is full of subtle appeal. We wish Dr Eliot would now address himself to a more limited task. We would like to have from him a list of, say, fifty books best adapted to a man of seventy-four who has passed his years in arduous political life, but now sees an opportunity for escape to quiet retirement and indulgence in those pleasures of taste to which he has long denied himself. We should like a list which would appeal powerfully to such a man, which would cause him to recall long-forgotten aspirations for the charm of cultivation and learning, a list the contemplation of which would help such a man to make decision between the clamor and strife of politics on the one hand, and, on the other, the fender and the book—a list so alluring that it would brace him to resist the demand of the public that he continue to serve them. As a start toward such a list, we suggest these (the titles of acceptable additions to the list will be welcomed):

> Cicero: "*De Senectute*" (*in the original*)
> Emerson: "*The Over-Soul*"
> Wordsworth: "*An Evening Walk*"

These books and slippered immunity from the exactions of public life, long days of quiet in Danville, Illinois—these would appeal to us; we wish they would appeal to him.

From irony I would swing back into driving assault and organized attack. If there was any possible device of polemic journalism that escaped my diligent ingenuity I did not know then what it could have been, and cannot think now. To enable readers to know whether their congressman was Standpat or Insurgent, I set up at Washington an office with a small staff which "will forward to any person a complete record of the votes of any Senator or Congressman on all the important roll calls." These records I called "Collier's Congressional Record." They enabled voters to check on how their congressmen voted —to the acute embarrassment, occasionally, of congressmen who felt that distant constituencies would not follow roll calls meticulously. I followed not only the public roll calls but the unrecorded actions of congressmen on committees. My mechanism had a consequence which the Richmond, Indiana, *Palladium* exaltedly put in words: "To the man in Congress who has violated his promises we can easily imagine that Mark Sullivan seems an angel with a fiery sword, by whose light all the excrescences of his twisted soul are exposed." I invented new methods and adapted old ones—one that I used was as old as "delenda est Carthago."

340 DAYS

It is 340 days from the date of this paper until any American citizen will have the opportunity to vote for a candidate for Congress pledged to vote against Cannon for Speaker.

When I gave the dates of the primaries in the various states I captioned the list menacingly, "The Deciding Days"—"The

[259]

People's One Chance in Two Years." This I followed with a solicitation, designed to stir ambitious young men to enter the primaries and take the congressional nomination away from the Standpat Republicans:

Who is the man, in each of these Congressional districts, responsible in character, intelligent, of Insurgent convictions, and willing to pledge himself against Cannon, who is ambitious to sit in Congress?

And again:

304 DAYS

It is 304 days from the date of this paper until any member of the present Congress comes up for re-election. The chief issue in the election of the next Congress will be Cannon.

I did not need to wait as long as Cato—Cannon did not last as long as Carthage. The outcome did not await the primaries and elections. The mounting excitement against Cannon brought explosion in the midst of the life of the existing Congress, when it still had a year to go. It was on March 16, 1910. One of the Insurgents, George W. Norris, of Nebraska (later senator), had for several weeks carried in his pocket a resolution for a change in the rules. Norris was skilled in parliamentary procedure; he knew there was no reason to expect confidently that he would ever have a chance to get his resolution before the House. But he waited and watched. The opportunity came when Cannon's own Standpatters brought up the subject of rules, in the form of a proposal to extend them. With the subject of rules on the floor, Norris leaped forward.

For two days the House was in uproar, there were twenty-nine hours of debate. All the Democrats would vote for the change as a matter of course. The Insurgents, now materially increased in number, would vote for it. The question was whether enough Standpatters had been scared by the campaign against Cannon to desert him and, added to the Insurgents and Democrats, make a majority. It turned out there were enough. By adoption of Norris' resolution, the appointment of committees was taken out of Cannon's hands.

After the battle I cheered of course. As a called-for celebration of the victory I printed as a border around my page the photographs of the forty-two Republicans who, by voting with the Democrats, had deprived Cannon of his power. In my text I wrote that the Insurgents had "won substantially all that they in the beginning expected to fight for." But, I added: "The Insurgent movement has come to mean much more than a change in parliamentary procedure, or the wresting of power from one arrogant man in a high place; it is the crystallization of the people's demand for progress and for relief from control of the United States government by and for organized wealth."

Then, having completed my ululation over victory, I concluded with a gesture toward the enemy which, I think, did me as much credit as the fight I had waged.

We would not [I wrote] willingly let the defeat of Cannon pass into history without rescuing from the official record one brief speech worthy of the best traditions of Congress, of a character extremely rare in recent generations.

The speech I thus elevated was not one of the Insurgents'. It was from a partisan of Cannon, one whom I had previously picked out for attack, the one who had most openly and courageously defied me:

Samuel W. McCall's face [I wrote] is at many critical points set against progress. But one is occasionally tempted to see a large compensation in high scholarship. Mr McCall made the last speech in behalf of Cannon. It was at the end of forty-eight hours of struggle; Cannon was beaten and McCall knew it; his little speech had both courage and eloquence.

Then I printed McCall's speech, not omitting the part that made indirect but unmistakable, and decidedly unflattering, allusion to *Collier's* and myself:

Mr Speaker, I desire to say a few words. This proceeding is aimed at the Speaker of the House of Representatives. I do not propose to vote for it. I do not propose to vote to deliver the Speaker bound hand and foot over to the minority—although I know that if you do he will go with head unbowed and erect. . . . This movement does not originate in the House of Representatives. You are about to do the behest of a gang of literary highwaymen who are entirely willing to assassinate a character in order to sell a magazine. I believe the Speaker of the House, by his conduct during the last three days, if the country had been permitted to know it, has shattered many of the criticisms that have been made against him; and as I see him there, his spirit reminds me of the old Ulysses starting off on his last voyage:

> Push off, and, sitting well in order smite
> The sounding furrows; for my purpose holds
> To sail beyond the sunset, and the paths
> Of all the Western stars, until I die.

Of that tribute to Cannon by McCall I wrote:

The capacity to make a speech so touched with genuine eloquence, at so dramatic a moment; the scholarship to draw on Tennyson and the Odyssey so aptly at a moment's notice, is worthy the Representative of a district which includes Harvard College.

I felt that McCall scored on me two ways. While he acknowledged the defeat of Cannon, he pictured the victim as a hero and the victor as a "literary highwayman"; and he surpassed me in technique of literary battle. Today I incline to think my final gesture of deference was as creditable to me as the acerbity of my two years of fighting.

But at the time my spirit was one of "up and at 'em." My next installment of "Comment on Congress," the following week, I headed:

NEXT, ALDRICH!

And I proceeded to lambaste Aldrich with a page of separate paragraphs, to which I gave emphasis by putting above each paragraph the same caption, "The Boss of the Senate."

CHAPTER 27

THE FIGHT against Aldrich in *Collier's* paralleled a fight waged against him in the Senate by a group of some dozen Insurgent Republican senators. It went on through 1910 and 1911. It merged into the fight against Taft for renomination by the Republicans for a second term in the presidency. That in turn merged into the starting of a new party, the Progressive, by Theodore Roosevelt, and that into the fight between Roosevelt and Wilson for the presidency.

In the Senate fight between Aldrich and the Insurgents Aldrich did not wait for decision. Giving up, he announced that when the end of his term arrived he would not seek re-election. Among other reasons he could see that the movement for direct election of senators by the people, instead of by state legislatures, was going to succeed. That surrender by Aldrich was a landmark, recognition by one of the most poised and intelligent men in public life, that the old order had come to an end, that the new forces could not be denied.

II

In the fight against Aldrich I came into association with most of the Insurgent Republican senators. The one who most appealed to me was Dolliver, of Iowa—he died soon after and is now forgot. Dolliver had force, momentum, and had it without effort. He was of large frame, well fleshed; seeing him at ease in his Senate seat, one might have thought of him as indolent. But within that easygoing body, back of those rounded cheeks, was a spirit that did not sleep, a mind that missed nothing, a mind which, when it got going, functioned as smoothly—and as powerfully—as a great dynamo.

He would take his Senate seat, he would dispose of himself comfortably, and for hours or days he would seem inert, not speaking, not even rising, hardly even stirring, while the more nervous Insurgents buzzed and darted like wasps against Aldrich and the Standpatters who controlled the body. One observed, however, that Dolliver's eyes moved about from desk to desk where the clashes took place. Presently one would see those brown eyes begin to glow, very faintly; a slow, very slow smile, hardly more than an expression of amiability, an appreciation of humor, would become perceptible on the curves of his broad features. Slowly he would rise from his seat—and one felt that Aldrich cringed, for Aldrich, wholly a man of action and arrangements, was quite without arms or armor against such a foe as Dolliver.

Dolliver might begin the fray—and conclude it—with one devastating epigram, and sit down. He it was who disposed of a Standpat senator, Warren, who owned great ranches and many sheep and took an interest in the tariff on wool, by saying genially that "the gentleman from Wyoming is the greatest shepherd since Abraham." In another epigram Dolliver described with complete accuracy and insight the whole heart of the controversy about grants of public lands to corporations by President Taft's secretary of the interior. Dolliver epitomized the controversy with utter exactness and also, or perhaps therefore, demolished Taft's side of it by saying, to a world familiar with Taft's physical bulk and temperamental easygoingness, "President Taft is a large body closely surrounded by men who know exactly what they want."

Epigrams were not all that Dolliver had in his arsenal. If a speech were called for he could talk with a force of thought and grace of phrasing that no opponent undertook to match. He was one of the rare men who can be sonorous to the ear, yet at the same time convincing to the mind and apt to the situation. The first words he ever directed to me personally remain in my mind to this day. I had been writing for some weeks about the Insurgents, including Dolliver. A situation arose about which I wished to talk with him. I called him on the telephone and explained to him who I was. Like a low-pitched, deep-toned bell Dolliver's voice came over the wire: "So great, Mr Sullivan, is my appreciation of your writing, and so complete my sympathy

[264]

with your position, that I am at your service at any time, for any purpose."

The one I saw most of was Beveridge. Our acquaintance began in a spirit of challenge. On my page I had quoted a charge by Aldrich that the Insurgents were not Republicans, that they were a "heterogeneous combination." And when Beveridge replied to him less belligerently than I thought he should, I wrote that "Beveridge, who is among the less courageous of the Insurgents, began to search his soul for sounds to tell how good a party man he is."

On the same page, against another charge by Aldrich, I came to Beveridge's defense. Aldrich had said "there are some Senators who are without imagination at all; I do not think the Senator from Indiana belongs to that class, because I think he has an inflated imagination." In defense of Beveridge, and in defiance of Aldrich, I wrote:

This is characteristic of the vulgar bullying with which Senator Aldrich intimidates some of the younger Senators who oppose him. Senator Beveridge has faults of boyish zeal and self-consciousness, and even of taste which, quite fairly, make older Senators smile at him; but there is not a more conscientious man in the Senate. Senator Aldrich's mis-statements of fact have no relation to an excited imagination—they are entirely cold-blooded, intended to deceive, and part of his general determination to achieve the purposes of organized wealth.

As between my tribute to Beveridge's conscience and my impugnment of his courage, it was—quite in accord with human nature—the latter that Beveridge took notice of. He wrote Hapgood in protest, and sought me out in a spirit compounded of protest and placation. We became close and lifelong associates. When, on a wintry afternoon in 1927, I read that he had died suddenly while talking with friends in his Indianapolis home, I had as acute a sense of dismay over the inexorable as any death of a friend has ever brought to me.

No one who had been in Beveridge's circle could have failed to feel that his going was a perceptible diminution of the vitality and stimulation that had once been available to them. When, in the later years of his life, he used to come to my home in Washington, I noticed that my children acted toward him as toward no other visitor. They would not leave the room while he was in it. Of his talk they knew nothing, for it was above their heads. His distinction meant nothing to them—one ex-senator and author was nothing in their young lives. Indeed, I doubt if distinction, place in the world, often counts with children. In the case of Beveridge it was the sheer vitality of the man that held them rapt.

Beveridge was aware of his vitality, knew its value. While he did not conserve it, on the contrary threw it out prodigally in the crises he was always involved in, yet he knew that vitality is a physical thing and took pains to keep his batteries charged. He told me that when he was still a struggling young lawyer in Indianapolis, at a time when long vacations were only for a few of the rich, he used to spend summers in Maine, feeling that the new health he stored up was more valuable than any professional advancement he might achieve by remaining in his office. He regarded his vitality as a political asset, felt it gave him advantage over associates and rivals, made him more formidable to his enemies. In an old letter I find him writing:

I have been thinking a great deal why it is that the financial powers are so bent on destroying me, more even than on destroying dear old Bob La Follette. I think I know the reason. Bob is supposed to be in bad health and badly broken, while I am reported to them to be in fine physical condition.

If Beveridge gave out vitality to others, so also did he absorb it from others. At the Progressive National Convention in 1912, when he made the keynote speech, I sat some fifteen or twenty yards away, facing him. He used me—entirely to my satisfaction, for I both liked him and wished his speech and the occasion to have éclat—as a kind of spiritual "stooge." Almost with every third or fourth sentence he would fix demanding eyes on mine, and I would feel his unspoken question, "Am I all right? Is it good?" to which my eyes signaled reply, "It's wonderful;

MARK SULLIVAN ABOUT 1913.

Photograph by F. de Gueldre.

go on." At the end—the speech was some two hours long—I was limp. If I did not pour out as much vitality as Beveridge, it was because his store of it was immense; I had poured out all I had.

Always Beveridge had to look straight in the eyes of any, individual or crowd, whom he addressed. We used to walk, after the day's work in the Senate was over, down Pennsylvania Avenue. That afternoon ambulation was commoner then than after Washington's streets lost their leisurely pace and acquired "Stop" and "Go" signs. Half of Congress used to walk to their homes and hotels, usually in twos or threes; a couple, striking in appearance and most strangely assorted in temperament and background, were the austere New England scholar, Senator Lodge, of Massachusetts, and the fire-eating Southerner, Senator Tillman, of South Carolina. As Beveridge and I walked together, he, two or three times in every block, would step in front of me, stop and hold me with his eye until he had impressed his point, while passers-by felt, I uncomfortably imagined, that I must have been guilty of some serious dereliction and was being sternly admonished.

Once, dining in the Willard Hotel, we were at a table so located that we had to sit side by side. Beveridge would eat a few bites, turn sideways toward me, pull my eyes to his and emit vehemence. During the dinner an old lady who had been my teacher when I was a boy happened to pass through the dining room. I rose and stepped aside to speak with her. She told me she felt reflected glory that a pupil of hers should be the confidant of so eminent and earnest a statesman; she said she had noticed, as she approached our table, the seriousness with which Beveridge turned and addressed me. Of course, she said, she would not ask me what he had said—it was obviously important and presumably confidential; but she had been thrilled to be an eyewitness of a brief part of the conversation of a great senator. Impressed by the way she had been impressed, I put my mind on recalling the particular remark Beveridge had made as she approached. He had been eating lima beans, I recalled finally, and one of them had dropped from his fork; he had looked for it in his crumpled napkin but it had eluded him, and he had turned to me and said, "What became of that damned bean?" I did not feel called upon to disabuse my old teacher's mind of an illusion that gave her pleasure.

Beveridge was egotistical, habitually dramatized himself. Once Theodore Roosevelt told me that when he was about to be nominated by the Republican National Convention of 1904, Beveridge came to the White House to say he would like to make the nominating speech. Tactfully Roosevelt explained that the honor had already been assigned; Roosevelt's lifelong friend, Senator Henry Cabot Lodge, was to make the speech. Beveridge took it in, rested his arms on Roosevelt's desk, leaned his head on his arms and in a voice leaden with woe said, "Alone on the farm; alone at college; alone in the Senate; always alone."

Once Beveridge came to New York to be at the bedside of his friend, David Graham Phillips, the author, who had been shot by a maniac. It happened that at the same time my wife and I were looking after Mrs Francis J. Heney, who, visiting in New York, had been taken ill. From time to time Beveridge and I called each other up, he to inquire about Mrs Heney, I to ask about Phillips. The time came when both of us had to say that the two sick persons must die. Beveridge talked of Phillips' achievement—at the age of forty-three he was a success-ful author and, even though dying relatively young, he could feel he had had a full life We went on to speak of death coming to all of us, and I remarked that Beveridge could feel, if death came to him, that he, too, had had a full life. "No, Mark," said Beveridge, "you're wrong; I'm forty-nine, and Alexander had conquered the world before he was thirty-three."

Beveridge at forty-nine, as it turned out, had ended his political career; after serving two terms in the Senate he had been beaten in 1910, and he did not succeed in future attempts to return. With his senatorial career behind him he did a thing that few have equaled, and which I would have said no one could accomplish after being fifty years old. After a career that had been wholly in the public eye, wholly in the forum and on the stump, his functioning dependent on the stimulus of an audience before him—following that, Beveridge made for himself a new career of a sort as distant as possible from his public one. Shutting himself in his closet, leaving it only to bury himself in the cloisters of libraries, he made the tedious and painstaking researches, and did the laborious writing, that resulted in the best biography ever written about John Marshall.

What I, and many others, viewed as faults of taste in Beveridge were, in some cases, not a low sense of taste but a high sense of obligation to what he deemed the requirements of his office of senator. Always as he emerged from the Senate cloakroom through green swinging doors onto the Senate floor, every detail of his erect bearing expressed self-consciousness. But it was a self-consciousness that did him credit, added something to the Senate's dignity and the country's good. One felt that, just before he opened the door, there had passed through his mind a realization of the office he held, an awareness of its power and dignity; a recollection of the long tradition, running back through the British Parliament to the Roman Senate, of which the American Senate was the latest embodiment. One felt he had thought for a second of Burke and Pitt, of Cato and Cicero, and said to himself, "I am a senator of the United States," and dedicated himself to living up to the office.

At all times, in every circumstance, Beveridge had sense of responsibility for the United States, concern that it should be well managed, care that no ill should befall it. He, like many other public men of that time—more at that time than now, I think—felt as much responsibility for the daily well-being of America as for any private concern of their own. To apprehend that America might be about to make a mistake, that it might suffer disadvantage or loss of prestige, was to endure acute personal anxiety.

What I wrote of, thoughtlessly, as lack of courage in Beveridge, was not that at all. What Beveridge had was caution before commitment. Once commitment was made, Beveridge was brave without limit. But he shrank from recklessness; he did not, as some of the other Insurgents did, prize daring for the mere sake of daring; he was not willing to offer irreconcilability as a price for conspicuousness. Never did he like to be merely eruptive. Always he liked to be sure of his footing.

After the Republican National Convention in 1912, when Theodore Roosevelt had broken with his party and made the decision to start a dissenting one, the leaders who had been on his side in the fight within the party were gathered in his headquarters at the Congress Hotel. There I saw how men of high spirit act under strain of a novel kind. Roosevelt, as he passed among his leaders, speaking to each quietly for a few minutes, was more subdued than I ever saw him at any other time. He had reason to be. He was asking men who had high place in a great political party to sacrifice their place and their membership, and to embark on a venture which, if it did not succeed, would leave them outlaws from their party and without public position. Roosevelt's manner, appropriate to his position, was like that which a general of high sensibility, Robert E. Lee, must have had when he asked officers of the United States army to go with him into secession.

One of those whom Roosevelt asked, or rather was not given the opportunity to ask, Senator Joseph M. Dixon, of Montana, practiced the high consideration that General Ulysses S. Grant did when, accepting Lee's surrender, and seeing Lee reaching for his sword, hastened to add to his stipulations for surrender: "Officers will retain their arms; soldiers will retain their horses." Dixon would not let Roosevelt ask whether he wished to go along into the new party. Quietly Dixon said a few words which took the question, and the answer, for granted, "I think we ought to hold the convention of our party as early as possible."

When Roosevelt came to Beveridge to say that he hoped Beveridge would come with him, but of course Beveridge like the others must take account of his circumstances and consider before deciding, Beveridge, uncomfortable, preserving punctiliously his freedom to make his decision later on, said he must consult his friends and lieutenants in Indiana. But when, after a few days, Beveridge made the decision, he gave service and gallantry without stint.

Of the Insurgents, La Follette was the most forthright. But neither pre-eminence in forthrightness nor in any other quality, could ever make La Follette a leader, in the true sense, of any group of men who were of his own caliber and in close association with him. His forthrightness was too much, he was too demanding; without being arrogant in the sense of assuming superiority of himself, he was intolerant in the sense of suspicion against any who in views or actions did not coincide with him completely.

Once Beveridge and I were lunching with La Follette in the cold, dark, cluttered office La Follette had beneath a flight of steps in the Capitol, an office that had been assigned to him in derogation and discipline when he first came to the Senate in the role of what the Republican Senate leaders regarded as troublemaker. La Follette held on to his obscure and inconvenient little cubicle when time and promotion to important committee memberships entitled him to any of the better committee rooms. La Follette had, as a streak of his strong instinct for self-dramatization, a bent for regarding immolation as a luxury; to him a hair shirt was preferable to silk underwear; he felt that if he was not being persecuted he must be guilty of some lapse from worthiness.

La Follette, Beveridge and I were discussing a question about to come to debate in the Senate, a question on which the Insurgents had decided to take a dissident position. This position they were in process of reducing to writing for public proclamation. About the phraseology there was difference of view, La Follette, of course, insisting on the most outright and far-reaching declaration of dissent, while Beveridge and some others favored a phrasing less provocative, one which would leave the way open for reasonable compromise and save the Insurgents from appearing before the public as irreconcilable extremists. La Follette's version of the document had been handed to Beveridge. This La Follette now asked him to let me see. Beveridge said he did not have it with him and that it was not in his office. He had given it to one of the others, one of the milder Insurgents, and he thought this depository had given it to another. As Beveridge explained, La Follette's figure grew erect in his chair, his face became stern, his eyes accusatory. "Albert," he said with a rigor which expressed suspicion, though suspicion was not at all called for, "Albert, where is that paper?"

I never saw La Follette abashed but once. It was on a Sunday afternoon at Robert Collier's country place in New Jersey, where I was spending the week end. Collier said he wanted exercise. The place provided every form of exercise imaginable and equipment for every game. Yet the one kind of exercise Collier must have at that moment was the one for which the equipment is the most elaborate and for which the means were there least available. He must play polo. There were polo ponies and mallets and balls in abundance. But there was no one who could play, except Collier. Upon Collier's urging I got on a pony, he on another, and we began to knock a ball about the lawn. Dashing down to the end of the lawn to recover a drive of Collier's, I saw the village hack approaching; it contained two men whom I recognized as La Follette and Lincoln Steffens. They had come to ask Collier for help; La Follette was publishing a paper which he called *La Follette's Weekly*, and Steffens had suggested to him that Collier might either take over the publication or contribute funds to keep it going. Collier took the suggestion seriously, considered merging La Follette's paper with *Collier's Weekly* or having La Follette write a weekly page. As the talk went on I could see in La Follette's face his sense of a certain mild bizarrerie in the situation—two men whose place in the world depended on appeal to the common man, asking a man of wealth, engaged at the moment in a wealthy man's diversion, to help promote La Follette's hold on his following. La Follette looked down, uncomfortable, as if he felt that Steffens had let him in for something not suitable to his role.

III

Of all the men with whom the Insurgent and Progressive fight brought me in contact, the outstanding one was—need I name him? To Theodore Roosevelt many superlatives have been applied, most of them justified. The superlativeness that most affected me—and stirred practically every man who was young in that time—was his capacity for stimulation, the dynamic quality of his personality, the sheer quantity of it. Having occasion, about the time Roosevelt left the White House, to write about him, and being hard pressed for words to express my own rather tumultuous thoughts, I borrowed some skilled sentences from a popular English novelist of the early part of the century, Mrs Humphry Ward:

Washington, at this time of the world's history, was the scene of one of those episodes—those brisker moments in the human comedy—which every now and then revive among us an almost forgotten belief in personality, an almost forgotten respect for the mysteries behind it. The guests streaming through the White House filed past a man who, in a level and docketed world, appeared to his generation as the reincarnation of forces primitive, overmastering, and heroic. An honest Odysseus—toil-worn and storm-beaten, yet still with the spirit and strength, the many devices, of a boy; capable, like his prototype, in one short day of crushing his enemies, upholding his friends, purifying his house; and then, with the heat of righteous battle still upon him, with its gore, so to speak, still upon his hands, of turning his mind, without a pause and without hypocrisy, to things intimate and soft and pure—the domestic sweetness of Penelope, the young promise of Telemachus. The President stood, a rugged figure, amid the cosmopolitan crowd, breasting the modern world, like some ocean headland, yet not truly of it, one of the great fighters and workers of mankind. . . . This one man's will had now, for some years, made the pivot on which vast issues turned—issues of peace and war, of policy embracing the civilized world.

To that skillfully drawn characterization I added a few sentences of my own:

The huge personality that crowds the room and dominates the very horizon may charm and grip you as it does most; or it may rub you on the raw as it did President Harrison. (Roosevelt himself has told how Harrison used to drum the table nervously with his fingers when Roosevelt, as a member of his Administration, was having conferences with him.) But whether you like Roosevelt or whether you don't, the bigness of his personality is the one undisputed thing.

The bigness of Theodore Roosevelt's personality, the out-giving fire of it, the stimulus he imparted to others, was phrased in hundreds of epigrams. To attempt epigrams about Roosevelt was a literary and political diversion as common as it was vain— as if that immense and varied Titan could be compressed into the small smooth mold of any epigram. Two characterizations that most aptly brought out the quantity and force of Roose-velt's personality were phrased by Richard Washburn Child, a young author of the time. "His personality," Child said, "so crowds the room that the walls are worn thin and threaten to burst outward." On another occasion Child wrote: "You go to the White House, you shake hands with Roosevelt and hear him talk—and then you go home to wring the personality out of your clothes."

The quantity of Roosevelt's personality, the dynamism of it, the stimulus it imparted, was the quality easiest to see, and therefore was most talked and written about. Equally attractive was the side that Mrs Ward described as "intimate, soft, and pure." Of that side of Roosevelt's nature the best account is in Owen Wister's *My Forty Years Friendship with Theodore Roosevelt*. Wister knew more of the subtleties of Roosevelt's soul than any other man, more than Roosevelt himself. To read Wister's chronicle of their friendship is to hear the most delicate over-tones of Roosevelt's voice.

I was attracted to Roosevelt, enormously. In my writings, my attitudes about public matters, I took inspiration from him with a literalness which I might not have practiced after I became more mature. Young though I was, there were occasions when I had a feeling of faint alarm about his impetuousness. One is mentioned in a letter I wrote to Hapgood, October 12, 1906— the letter is a record of my first visit to the White House:

"I spent two or three hours with the President last night. He asks me to see a good deal more of him the early part of next week, and in particular to take lunch with him, Secretary Taft, Secretary Root, and one or two others on Wednesday week. . . . The name of Harriman came up in the talk, and I suggested to him, purely in the way of allusion, that he ought to go after

Harriman, the Union Pacific, and the Southern Pacific. He at once sent for his secretary to notify three members of the Interstate Commerce Commission to call on him the next day."

That episode comes back to me. I recall feeling agreeably excited about being close to the springs of the machinery of government—but being also a little appalled by the spectacle of important action taken on a suggestion that had been, on my part, casual, and not meant to start so abruptly the turning of mighty wheels.

About some of my associations with Roosevelt, I have written in the volumes of *Our Times*. One, not heretofore told, comes back to me now with a flavor of humor, a kind of gargoyle fresco on the edifice of history, in the form of the aspect of Roosevelt that most impressed a Virginia countryman.

Roosevelt, while President, had bought a few acres of land in a remote part of Virginia, some sixty miles from Washington, and had built a little two-room house, to which he could retire over week ends for rest and hunting; he called the place Pine Knot. Once, a little while after he had left the presidency, he loaned Pine Knot to me and my wife for a week's vacation. Staying there, I met a man living near by who, on Roosevelt's visits to the place, had been his guide in wild-turkey hunting. The guide admired Roosevelt extravagantly, felt exalted by his association with him, enjoyed telling about their experiences together. One day, as I walked with the guide along the road, we came to a little run and a bridge, about two hundred yards from Pine Knot. The guide paused to recite a memory of Roosevelt associated with the spot, the most vivid memory he retained. With gusto, and also with earnest impressiveness, savoring his association with one of the world's most mighty, he said: "I used to come for him at three o'clock in the morning. Right at this spot, when I reached it, I would begin to hear him snoring. Gosh, but he could snore!"

IV

The nature of my writing attracted to me the favoring attention of Socialists. Many of them assumed I was one of them, or, if they learned I was not, urged me to unite with them. I attended meetings of groups of them and was treated as one of the fraternity. I think I never formally joined any Socialist organization, though I may have. I was invited into, and joined, many of the organized liberal groups occupying various positions in the gamut of progressive thought which were springing up all about. I find among my old letters a notice of a meeting of the February Club, which seems to imply I may have been a member—the meeting was to be held in the "barn room" of Mouquin's Restaurant and was to be addressed by a Socialist leader of the time, Morris Hilquit, on "Socialism as a Practical Program."

I find other old letters which suggest that a group of the young Socialists, friends of mine, delegated certain ones of them to "gang up" on me, to press me to unite formally with their cause. I shied from them. In a correspondence with one of them, a young writer, George Allan England, I wrote with humorous directness that I was not a Socialist, and that my philosophy, so far as I could identify any definite philosophy in myself, did not carry me toward the cult. England's response was that of one of the faithful who knows it is only a matter of time until the doubter will get the true religion and come to the mourners' bench.

If anyone could have got me to unite with the Socialists, England might have, for while he was earnest he had that in his make-up which saved him from being fanatic. He had humor, which not all Socialists have, and gusto, whimsicality, wide-ranging interests, including a flair for the picaresque. The letter of his that I have before me was in answer to one in which apparently I had strongly disavowed Socialism, but had tempered my disavowal with humorous overstatement. In his reply England said:

Yes, I always knew you were a reactionary; but that doesn't worry me any.

The statement that you don't take any stock in social reform is all pure buncombe, Sullivan. You can't cram that down my throat. A man that has rooted out as much fraud and graft and nastiness as you have, and done as much good in the world, can't come any misanthropic game on me. It very probably is true that you and I don't agree as to just what's best for the world; but I do know (from your work) that you take a lively interest in old Mother Earth, and are trying just the same as all the rest of us to cure up some of her ills. Aind't it?

The flavor of England's letter cannot readily be reproduced in type. It lay in his deliberate misspelling and intentionally grotesque use of capital letters, and in the bizarre footnotes and P.S.'s which he ingeniously and amusingly injected, and in the phrases he scrawled along the margins:

It's up 2 U 2 choose.

Sorry you don't think much of our propaganda. I have subscribed for *The Worker* for you.

I can't see any flaw in our aims—to abolish abuses and improve the condition of the masses. Another thing—the abolition of wars, armies and navies. O.K. eh?

Why don't you get after the fat and propertied church graft, 2? Holding stocks and bonds, etc., while the workers sweat? That beats all Hell for iniquity.

Sullivan, it's no use this muck-raking and trying to reform the various hydra heads of Graft in all its heejus guises until you kill the beast itself.

Why not get wise and kill the Root (not Elihu, tho he's pretty dam near it) which we call P R O F I T, i.e., Graft under another name? By profit I mean unearned increment, dividends &c. These are the main-spring which buzz the clock-work of wickedness roundy round.

Oh thou, Infinitely Wise, answer, We beseach Thee, Mark, We B-seech Thee!

A——men.
Yours faithfully,
England

For months England plied me with his mock-serious formula for reforming the unregenerate:

Look here, Sullivan, you are in a position of immense public responsibility. This new philosophy is dawning rapidly on the world, no doubt of *that*. What are you going to do with it? Going to blind-fold yourself and claim there's no horizon? Or light a tallow dip and chase the sun back over the horizon? Or get out your spectroscope and see what the light is made of? Well, I leave that for *you* to say. With which, benediction &c.

Platitudes,
ENGLAND

England's personality entertained me more than his cause attracted me. From Socialism I held off. Indeed, I moved faintly away from the radicalism that had been my own in my earlier period. One night, dining at the Lafayette with William Travers Jerome and Charles R. Crane and some others, something I said, or something I had recently written, led Jerome to remark, humorously, that I was getting less intolerant of capitalism. "Yes," said Crane with a humor that was his own, "Mark made a mistake—he saved two dollars from his pay envelope one Saturday night—it's ruined his career."

Jerome said, "Yes, Mark's had the same experience as that other Irishman," and he told the ancient story of the Irishman —Pat, of course, was his name—who was solicited to join the Socialists. Pat expressed favor for anything new and exciting, but before committing himself wished to have Socialism explained to him. Told that it meant dividing up, he said that it appealed to him, but he asked for a concrete illustration. When he was told that if anyone had two pigs, he would be obliged to give up one to the state, the question was settled for him, in the negative. Sententiously he said, "I have two pigs."

I had my two pigs. I had acquired both without gift from the state, and I had no notion of donating one to the state, or letting the state take it from me. Besides, I was fairly confident that someday I would have three pigs, perhaps four. I did not wish to give the state either my second pig, nor my third, nor my fourth.

Yet I was at that time ardently supporting a measure, the graduated income tax, which, after it was adopted in 1913, rather frequently took my tenth pig from me each year, occasionally more.

I was a sheer individualist, perhaps a naïve one. I believed in self-help, believed that America continued to offer oppor-

[*278*]

tunity as abundantly as ever, and took no stock in the theory that the ending of free land in the United States brought the end of man's chance to own his own home. Once on a *Collier's* editorial page I printed a photograph of a rude, small frontier house and wrote:

The picture on this page shows the house near St Louis which General Grant, a graduate of West Point, built with his own hands and lived in for a brief period in his early middle life. . . . The house, in which Grant, with the tastes of an educated man, lived several years of his mature life, could be built by any man, as Grant built it, with his own hands, in four weeks. The cry has become far too common that the time has passed when the poor man could hope to have a home of his own.

In the same spirit I returned to the theme, using again the same kind of illustration, a picture of a frontier log house:

The above picture is of the house J. Sterling Morton built with his own hands, when he began life on a Nebraska homestead. He was a college graduate, and the son and grandson of men with intellectual occupations. The young wife who did the cooking in this house had a similar cultivation and ancestry. In this home Morton had the career which ended in a Cabinet office, and raised a son who was also a Cabinet member. What young couple is so poor today that such a home is beyond them, granted the willingness to work with their hands, and granted that education and city life have not made them effeminate? . . . Much so-called social reform is governed by a spirit which puts the mark of intolerable burdens upon those conditions which call out initiative and hard work.

CHAPTER 28

ONE AFTERNOON while the Progressive movement was at its height a stranger came to my office at *Collier's*, introducing himself as Louis J. Alber of the Coit-Alber Lyceum Bureau. He was brisk. He said he had just called on the Rev. Hugh Black, then an outstanding Presbyterian clergyman in New York; that he had arranged with Dr Black to go on the lecture platform for four weeks at four hundred dollars a week, and that he would like to make the same proposal to me. I told him I had never done any lecturing, nor anything that could be even faintly regarded as public speaking; not more than twice or thrice in a lifetime had I talked to more than two or three listeners at a time, and no experience I had ever had would justify the supposition that a considerable number of people would listen to me for an hour. All that the lecture manager waved aside. With a technique of salesmanship which consisted of looking me up and down with visible approval he said that I had a good presence. Through my writings in *Collier's*, he said, I was widely and favorably known. Lecturing, he said, would make me known to yet more of the public, and in a way that writing could not. Besides, lecturing would help the Progressive movement and *Collier's*. His salesmanship beguiled me. I said I would try it, for two weeks anyhow.

In the routine of lecture management it was the custom of the bureau to engage what it called its "talent" many months ahead and arrange later the specific dates and places. In due course I received a list which informed me that I was dated to appear in the Methodist Church at Alliance, Ohio, on a Monday night some months ahead, and in other towns every weekday night for an aggregate of twelve.

Spurred by the necessity ahead of me, I took a few days off from my work on *Collier's*, immured myself in a hotel in New Jersey and wrote a lecture. It was, I think, a good composition;

at least I thought so as I wrote it, and had I ever had courage to look at it again after the experience I had with it, I think I should have found it a well-written, thoughtful exposition, worthy of delivery before the alumni of Harvard Law School as a discourse on the constitutional aspects of the reforms embodied in the Progressive movement.

With my manuscript in my pocket I entrained for Alliance, registered at a hotel and, in accordance with the usage prescribed by the lecture bureau, called on the man who was to introduce me, in order to confer peace of mind upon him by assurance of my presence in the town. He was a very nice man, the president of a local educational institution, and that night he performed his part of the ceremony to the satisfaction of all concerned, including myself. I could make no possible objection to his introduction of me, except, perhaps, that later I might have reflected that high expectations set up in the minds of an audience may emphasize disappointment when disappointment ensues.

I did not exactly read my manuscript; amateur as I was, I knew that to be contrary to the technique of popular lecturing. But I kept my manuscript on the lectern before me, and followed it with sufficient closeness to create on the audience the same psychological effect as literal reading. This form of delivery, coupled with the austerity of my subject and the seriousness of my treatment of it, was too much. It was a very nice audience, and it practiced a kindly courtesy in making its disappointment as little noticeable as possible. But not all its courtesy could steel it to enduring my lecture. Within five minutes after my opening words the audience began to tiptoe out. By the end of the hour not more than twenty were left; and it would have taken rare discernment to know whether that heroic little band was motivated by pity for me, by the fact that they were in the two front rows and could not escape with any pretense to inconspicuousness, or by the lack of any other place to go after eight o'clock at night in Alliance, Ohio.

It is said that the most associative of our senses, the most potent to conjure up memories, is that of smell. Commonly it is about pleasant scents that this generalization is made—roses recall young love, violets spring, lilacs an old-fashioned garden. Of such examples poetry and romance are full. But I know of no poet who has celebrated the associative power of unpleasant odors. I learned that the rule holds. The bed on which I tossed that night had a faint odor which may have been of some cleansing chemical, but which struck me as the odor of musty straw, and for the rest of my life any tragic experience has caused me to think of musty straw.

From the church in which I delivered the lecture I had gone directly to the telegraph office. There I wired the lecture manager to meet me the following morning at the Statler Hotel in Cleveland. He met me, his face grave. He foresaw gloom.

I told Alber it was a pity, we had both made a mistake, but of course I would take full responsibility; the remaining lectures, it was hardly necessary to say, must be canceled; I would meet any financial loss he might suffer. To this suggestion Alber did not respond with as much cheerfulness as I had expected should attend my willingness to bear all losses. On the contrary, he had a seriousness that could hardly be accounted for by any detriment accruing to him through a failure by one of his "talent." It might have been an infection from my own gloom. He said that of course if I would not deliver the remaining lectures, then I would not; he had no wish to insist against my will. But he would be obliged to tell the truth to the lecture committees who had been his clients for years and with whom he expected to continue to do business; he could not tell them any polite fibs about the lecturer being overtaken by illness— though in truth that would have been factual enough. And if he told them that I simply refused to go on, it would be a detriment to my public reputation.

Changing his manner and, as I reflected later, practicing a technique which suggested that he had probably had experience with temperamental "talent" before, he minimized my mood of disaster. He told me that even La Follette, the great La Follette of many hundreds of platform experiences, had had audiences walk out on him; that La Follette in his early days had had failures that were talked about for years. He suggested that I take a nap and think it over awhile; he would see me again in the afternoon.

After he left I realized that he had no intention of making it easy for me to cancel the engagements; indeed, I felt sure that he intended, by kindly persuasion but no less by firmness, to lead me to go on. With realization of this my gloom deepened. It was in that Cleveland hotel that I learned that "cold feet" is not a figure of speech, it is a literal, physical condition. I hugged the radiator. I wished that my wife were there; indeed, I felt it unreasonable that she was not there; no wife should be absent from her husband's side when he was enduring such tragedy.

When the manager returned that afternoon I realized that, for my own sake rather more than for his, he was going to press me to go on. He asked me if it would distress me more if he should go with me and sit in the audience at the lecture that night, which was to be in a suburb of Cleveland; from observing my delivery he might be able to give me some pointers. I told him that nothing conceivable could make my misery worse than I had endured the night before. He told me some tricks of the trade; at least once every fifteen minutes, he said, a lecturer should tell a funny story. He asked me if I knew any; but though I had a fairly plenteous repertoire for private conversations, none would come back to me at that moment. So he supplied me with four, talking over with me the substance of my lecture to find points at which the stories could be made to seem applicable. He told me I should give the audience a chance not only to laugh occasionally, but to applaud from time to time; thus the audience had an opportunity to feel they had a part in the entertainment, and that was not only the audience's right but the lecturer's advantage—for the lecturer to act as if he was giving a solo entertainment was egotistical and arrogant, and put a grossly unnecessary handicap upon himself. He told me how to take advantage of the few minutes during which I was being introduced; that I should survey the audience carefully, pick out two individuals, one on each side of the center and about the middle of the hall, ones with sympathetic faces, if possible ones that were stout and had humorous features, and that when I spoke I should look from one to the other of these, addressing them as if I were talking to them conversationally.

That night, while I did not quite have the courage to leave my manuscript at the hotel, I kept it in my pocket. In my mind I dismissed it. To that second audience I did not lecture, I talked. I picked out the two in the audience whom Alber had told me to seek; to them I owe not the least considerable of the debts of gratitude which, in a long life, I have incurred to persons to whom I was never able to give formal thanks. I talked to them, looked at them, found responsiveness in their faces and was put at ease. After ten minutes or so I told the first of my funny stories and got a laugh—and at that moment I swelled up with a feeling that lecturing was not difficult at all, that I was rather good at it. At the end of the lecture I had a sense of elated intoxication.

I completed the two weeks with varied degrees of fortune. On my return to New York I felt that whether or not I ever lectured again, I wanted to understand the art. With this purpose I consulted some friends. At the time William Gillette, the actor, famous as Sherlock Holmes, had been, like many other fine spirits of the time, infected by the fervor of the Progressive movement and the personality of Theodore Roosevelt. Gillette had volunteered to make speeches in the Progressive cause. Gillette knew the technique of public speaking, of course, but his devotion to his career had left him rather sketchily informed about public affairs. He was on fire with the fervor of the Progressive movement but knew little about its objectives, the direct primary, direct election of senators and the like. I was able to give him instruction about these, and he was kind enough to give me hints in the art of standing up before audiences.

I talked also with Augustus Thomas, who was not only an experienced playwright and producer of plays and trainer of actors, but also a finished speaker much sought on divers kinds of occasion, including Democratic National Conventions. Thomas gave me comfort about the dreadful sinking of heart I always felt just before I went on the stage, and the terrific perturbation as I faced the audience. That inner commotion, he said, was nature's indispensable preparation for an exertion of personality. If ever I failed to experience it I could know that something within me had dried up, that I was "through." And whenever an actor or speaker failed to have this inner commotion seethe spontaneously, and felt obliged to seek the equivalent in a pre-performance highball, something vital had gone out of him.

Thomas' notion was that a successful public performance, whether speech or theatrical performance, consists of waves of magnetism emanating from the person on the stage, passing out to the audience, and there starting responsive waves from the audience back to the person on the stage. He said that he did not pretend to understand the magic thing called personality, magnetism, but that he thought it was something physical, as directly so as electricity. If a person had it, he had it, and should thank God. As the old Scotch uncle put it in Barrie's *What Every Woman Knows*, when his niece Maggie was finding difficulty in holding her sweetheart, "Char'r'm's the thing, Maggie, if ye haven't it nothing else will do ye any good, and if ye have it ye need nothing else." In making a speech, Thomas' rule one was never to have a manuscript, never even write out a manuscript; if you do, when you go before the audience you are apt to try to remember the manuscript and recite it; in that case your mind—this was Thomas' theory—goes away, literally and physically, to the distant room in which you wrote the manuscript. And that will not do at all. The place for your mind is out in the audience. Thomas' vivid instruction was: "As you step on the stage take your mind into your hands and throw it out against the eyeballs of the audience."

For several years, some years for six or eight weeks, I talked on summer Chautauqua circuits and winter lecture courses.

It was hard work, yet the experience had the glamor of adventure. To lecture at one Chautauqua at three in the afternoon, take an automobile and at eight in the evening lecture a hundred miles away; to speak in the evening, hurry to the hotel and change clothes and pack a suitcase, take a midnight train, change to another at four in the morning at some lonely little junction in Illinois or Indiana, change again at ten in the morning and arrive at the next town three hundred miles away just in time to eat hastily and dress for another engagement, compels the lecturer to achieve a tempo of spirit which rises above the strain. As I look back on it some of the experiences that come back as agreeable memories include a sixty-mile automobile ride through a spring-scented night from a little town in Missouri to catch a Wabash train at Moberly; crossing the Ohio River at two in the morning in a skiff from Portsmouth, Ohio, to a station on the Chesapeake and Ohio Railroad in Kentucky; a three-hour automobile ride on a below-zero night from Watertown, New York, to catch a New York Central train at Syracuse.

Among my fellow performers on the Chautauqua I grew to have quite as much appreciation for the Swiss bell ringers and the operatic companies who unpretentiously carried *Patience* and *Erminie* to tents in country villages, as for the literary stars who undertook to instruct the public about Shakespeare, or the political ones who were dogmatically confident about the initiative and referendum, the tariff, and the improvement in human affairs that would be wrought by divers amendments to the Constitution. One time or another, many of the foremost writers in America and more of those in England appeared on the American Chautauqua. The motive of many of the literary lecturers, especially English ones, must have been in large part the financial remuneration. Hardly could persons of the literary temperament be imagined as doing it for pleasure, or because they preferred the hurried catching of trains and keeping onerous engagements above writing in the quiet of their studies. Yet some that I knew genuinely enjoyed it. Of the political lecturers, the motive, if not exclusively financial, certainly included that consideration, although a politician on the upward way could feel there was advantage in the acquaintances he made and the showing himself to large numbers of persons.

This generalization should not be made too broadly. Taft went into lecturing after he left the presidency and had no thought of running again. I think he enjoyed it quite as much as any other part of his career. He went into it with the wish to amass a modest competence. Edward Bok told me that just before Taft left the White House, Bok visited him to ask him to deliver some lectures at Hill School, for which Bok would pay a fee. Taft, with some feeling, turned to his wife and said: "You see, I told you there would be opportunities to make a living." With fine ethical taste Taft felt reluctant to practice law, because so many of the judges on the federal courts owed their appointments to him. He had some income from a professorship at Yale, and some from occasional appointments as arbitrator in legal disputes. On the Chautauqua he set one hundred thousand dollars as the amount he wished to accumulate. The lecture manager told me that Taft, as he went from city to city, would observe in the newspapers the price quotations of Liberty bonds; from time to time, as his accumulation of fees approximated a thousand dollars, he would telegraph his banker in New York to buy for him one more installment toward independence. Taft enjoyed the work; and audiences enjoyed him; he had a way of starting a laugh from a point far down below his diaphragm and letting the audience see it work its way upward in humorous wiggles of his immense torso. He had, too, the gift, always ingratiating to his audience, of laughing at himself. Irvin Cobb had the same gift; Cobb indeed encouraged audiences to laugh not only with him but at him. He had an art of just standing on the stage and luring the audience into a smiling mood from the mere sight of his misleadingly solemn countenance above the huge torso that seemed to shape itself into strange and incongruous protuberances. Having got the audience into the mood he wanted, Cobb would tell stories of his own invention. He originated some of the best ever told; as a teller of his own and others' creations, he was the best in his generation.

Lecturing led to agreeable contacts with fellow performers. During the season Chicago was a point of crossing for lecturers traveling back and forth from dates in Wisconsin and Michigan to others in Illinois and Indiana; any morning, eating in a station restaurant in Chicago, you would meet friends, compare experiences, exchange information about towns and audiences. Decatur, Illinois, was another crossing point of many railroads, upon which the trains seemed to have a way of arriving at about five in the morning; a lecturer dropping off a B. & O. train would give a passing hail to another arriving on the Wabash.

Once my schedule and William Jennings Bryan's brought us together for lunch in a hotel at Warsaw, Indiana—Bryan used to bring to his meals raw carrots and some strange kind of bread. We were due that night at points eastward, which we would reach by taking the same interurban electric. Bryan and I sat together, talking about politics. Bryan was usually looking forward to the next ensuing Democratic National Convention. On occasions when he was not an avowed candidate himself he usually had someone he was grooming. It was observed that Bryan's dark horse was sometimes so very dark that Bryan must have found him at some obscure state capital in his Chautauqua wanderings. Cynics sometimes said it was patent that a dark horse of such extreme inconspicuousness could not possibly win, and that Bryan was not unaware of the chance of himself becoming residuary legatee to the impossible one. On this occasion he dwelt upon the availability of a governor of a Southern state of whom I had never heard. But Bryan assured me he was "a coming man—keep your eye on him." Keeping my eye on emerging public men was part of my work on *Collier's*, but Bryan's dark horse never emerged far enough for me to hear of him again. As our interurban car stopped at a little Indiana town Bryan looked at the name of the station and was stirred to a pleasing memory. Putting his hand on my knee, he said,

"You know, Mark, when I ran in 1896, there was a man in this town who thought I was the second coming of Christ."

II

One of the values of lecturing was the knowledge it brought of America, present and past. Once, speaking during the forenoon at Charleston, Illinois, I was told that not far away was the churchyard in which Lincoln's father, Thomas Lincoln, was buried, and the farm on which the father had lived some years. After my lecture, procuring a car, I drove to the churchyard, saw the tombstone chipped by relic seekers, and inquired of the pastor of the church whether there was anyone still living thereabouts who remembered Lincoln. He told me there was a distant relative, the wife of a farmer near by. I drove to the farm, walked up a little pathway bordered by old-fashioned flowers, and found the old lady to be generously talkative. She told me that as a little girl she had been at the home of Lincoln's father when Lincoln came to visit him. Lincoln's visit, she said, was as much to see his stepmother as his father; he was fond of his stepmother and she of him. Lincoln had just been elected President and was about to go to Washington to be inaugurated. As he left, the stepmother put her arms around him and said: "Oh, Abe, I'll never see ye again." I asked where the Lincoln farm was and she directed me. It was in a section called Goose Prairie. The house had disappeared. The site of it was almost but not quite submerged in a field of corn, now August high. Two locust trees about thirty feet apart suggested where the ends of the house had been. A few yards away a huge lilac bush survived; a little farther off some tumbled stones were the remains of the well curb.

I am glad I had my Chautauqua experience. But glad also that I did not have it too continuously. Public men who make careers of Chautauqua work tend to lose capacity for other careers. To repeat substantially the same speech day after day, often twice the same day, for months at a time or even years;

to be conscious that applause is the sign of success and to reach for it, to have a stock of stories and striking phrases, and to repeat them the hundredth time as if it were the first, does not make for intellectual growth. I kept my Chautauqua journeyings brief; while I enjoyed them I was always a little anxious about my writing, and glad to get back to it.

CHAPTER 29

Hapgood had had grippe, and for recuperation was staying at P. F. Collier's country house. One night the two dined together, alone; later P. F. was to go in town to a horse show, to ride one of his jumpers, Greenfield. Throughout the dinner, from time to time, in a way that haunted Hapgood to the end of his life, a shade of concern passed over P. F.'s face. Once or twice he said, "I will stay here with you this evening if you don't feel well." Against that Hapgood of course protested. Later P. F. put it differently. "I would just as lief give up the jumping tonight if you are lonely." Again Hapgood protested. He felt it would be unforgivable for him to cause P. F. to miss an evening of the sort that all his life he had delighted in. Still later P. F. said, "I do not feel much like jumping tonight." By that time Hapgood's rather one-track mind was set in the thought that P. F. wanted to sacrifice his own pleasure out of consideration for his guest and friend. Hapgood dedicated himself to making P. F. go, made it appear that if P. F. did not go he would feel hurt. For that attitude, generously well meant, Hapgood reproached himself to his dying day; in his memoirs he wrote: "I might have saved him if my instinct had been surer; I knew later that the shades, at dinner, that came over him, were fears that his heart was not right and a wish for staying at home, if only I would furnish the excuse."

That night, late, I was wakened by the telephone. By the very first emanation from Robert Collier's voice I knew something tragic had happened. "Mark," he said very slowly—his voice ordinarily was brisk and joyous. "Yes, Rob?" I replied. "Father died tonight," he said.

The Colliers, father and son, had a thousand friends, could command a million services. The service that I and three or four others contributed had, I liked to think, a special sentiment. During the two nights that P. F. lay dead in his Fifth Avenue house, Frank Garvan and I and two or three others who were of Irish ancestry "sat up" with him. Though we made no self-conscious ceremony of it, though, indeed, none of us put it in words then or since, the spirit in which we did it was one of carrying out, even in a way so faint as to be only a recalling, the ritual of "wake" that for uninterrupted centuries had attended the deaths of Collier's forebears and ours.

At the head and foot of the coffin two nuns kneeled, heads bowed, their lips moving silently as the beads of their rosaries passed slowly through their fingers. Their presence was an attention paid by the church; it was not a necessary part of the Irish tradition. Quite likely the nuns had never been acquainted with P. F., and the emphasis of the Irish "wake" is on the presence of friends and neighbors. This our little group supplied.

We sat in another room. While we were grave and restrained and spoke in low voices, we conformed to the spirit of the Irish custom, in that we were not continuously silent, nor did we talk only of the dead. One of us was the young priest of P. F.'s parish in the country. He was perhaps a little nearer to Ireland than the rest of us, and aware of the custom which says that a too concentrated and uninterrupted lugubriousness is not the best tribute to the dead, nor the best service to the mourners. He told a story which contained a faint joke, of priestly and Irish flavor. I have remembered it while many jests of fuller flavor, and many more important experiences, at many times and places, have fled my memory. The story was about a priest in Ireland, conducting mass one Sunday in a hall that had a room above. In the midst of the mass there was a crash overhead and bits of plaster fell upon the congregation. The priest, looking up, beheld a woman's stockinged leg, which had come through the ceiling as far as the knee. The priest, horrified, wishing at once to protect a church service from unseemliness, and to guard the male portion of the congregation from sin, cried out, "Don't any man look up!" He added threat of divine punishment. "If any man looks up, God will strike him blind!" The sequel, of course, was what the sequel of an Irish story must be. One worshiper, with the daring of his race, said, "I'll take a chance with one eye," and satisfied his curiosity while avoiding fifty per cent of the danger.

II

P. F. living we had rather overlooked or at least taken for granted. But P. F. gone we became aware of.

Our contacts with him—mine and Hapgood's, that is—had been relatively rare, for he left the *Weekly* wholly to Rob and Rob's appointees; himself he devoted to the part of the business he knew, the part indeed that was himself, the bookselling. Whenever he talked to Hapgood or me about the *Weekly* it was usually after he had noticed an alarming rise in the *Weekly's* expenditures for writers and artists; he would ask us if it was all right. Would it come out all right? We would assure him that it would, that Rob knew what he was doing. He would sigh and say, "Darling Rob," meaning that if Rob wanted it, it must be done—and he would go back to put harder drive into the bookselling that produced the money we were spending. The bookselling, to us on the *Weekly*, was a thing remote, and a little below. We regarded the *Weekly*, and ourselves, as superior. P. F. and his book agents, we felt, ought to be grateful for the distinction we and the *Weekly* were giving to the Collier business.

On the rare occasions, once or twice a year, when P. F. came breezing through the editorial office, we sprang to our feet, partly in conscious deference to his greater years and his headship of the business, partly in instinctive reaction to the gale of vitality he brought with him.

Once when P. F. thus breezed into my office it happened that I was talking to Richard Washburn Child, a rising young writer of the time (later ambassador to Italy), about some short stories he was writing for us. I stood up to greet P. F. and remained standing while he was there—it was hardly more than a minute. I replied to his hearty "How ar're ye? How's everything?"—

[293]

always P. F.'s sentences seemed to bubble and tumble cheerily from his mouth, his lips moving humorously; and I received his farewell, a generously warming "Take good care of yourself." Then I turned again to Child, who had remained in his seat. Child broke out angrily: "See here, I want you to understand you can't treat me that way; I'm just as important as Pat Collier and you can't drop a conversation with me just because he comes into the room." I was astounded and I apologized. Later, reflecting on it, I continued to be astounded. I tried to put myself in Child's place and concluded that I would not have felt the faintest resentment. But if Child was hurt, he was hurt, and that night I supplemented my oral apology with a written one. Child replied:

I think our friendly understanding was already complete before you wrote. At any rate it is probably now even more complete than before the incident. I think my speaking to you has been justified by the fact that now appears—that I was mistaken.

Aside from P. F.'s infrequent appearances in the editorial department we had few contacts. He seemed distant from us, almost like a figure of the past, a legend. From office subordinates we heard that at his home in the country, and during his hunting seasons in Ireland, his custom was to rise at five or six in the morning, work for an hour or two, then ride two or three horses until the horses were tired, then return to a long day of dictation of letters to his branch managers and agents, analyzing their reports, pouring out stimulation upon them, pressing this one to put more drive into sales, that one to put more care into collections—drive, drive and still more drive. Once toward the end of his life one of his personal office force at his country house told me that P. F., always comparatively abstemious, had recently begun, rather shamefacedly, to put a pint of champagne beneath his bed at night, and drink a glass when he arose in the morning. The young man who told me was merely amused. But I knew that age was beginning to tell on P. F., that the fires of his blazing vitality were beginning to burn low, that he found it more difficult to get up steam for his five o'clock in the morning start. I knew this, and I knew that P. F. knew it. I felt sorry for him, though, in my young self-sufficiency, I wondered if all that lifelong fury of energy had been worth while, or necessary.

We found it was, after he was gone.

Installment bookselling is one of the most intricate of businesses —in my time I have known only two important firms that have been continuously successful. One of its arts lies in keeping a delicate balance between sales and collections, in the business as a whole and also in each branch office. On the ledgers a business may be sound, even rich, it may have assets enormously greater than liabilities. But the assets consist almost wholly of accounts due from individual book buyers, hundreds of thousands of them spread all over the country, accustomed to pay only as the collector calls on them. If the collectors do not call the assets shrivel up. Hence the collectors must be kept up to the mark. At the same time, in proportion as the collectors collect, new sales must be made in the same territory, so as to have always on every collector's route enough open accounts to keep the machine going and in balance. Always there must be strenuous selling; always there must be strenuous and careful collecting. Always the two must go hand in hand, always a delicate balance must be kept between the two. To keep an installment book business going successfully demands hard, exacting, unending work. A thousand men throughout the branches—phlegmatic, easygoing, indifferent or indolent—must constantly be stimulated to an activity beyond their normal by infusions of vitality from the supernormal man at the top.

That, after P. F.'s death, fell on R. J. He was not adapted to it. He had the vitality, an enormous abundance of it, but it was not the kind that was required, for it needed a touch of ruthlessness. Besides, R. J. had not had either the early poverty nor the lifelong experience of continuous hard work that was part of his father's equipment. The qualities P. F. had had were a most unusual combination, fury of energy in selling coupled with sure-footed care in collecting. That R. J. should have this pair of qualities, in addition to the editorial and artistic talent he had fully demonstrated, would have been a greater wealth of ability than the most fortunate of men could expect, even one so happily endowed as R. J. He became restless, sometimes tense, occasionally dispirited. To do the business function properly would have meant absence from the editorial function and from the agreeable associations that went with it. To keep up the editorial function, and the gayety that accompanied it, meant absence from the business grind. R. J. chose the absence that his nature dictated, he neglected the business end. Presently he was borrowing money, the first time in the firm's history.

The borrowing was from an intimate friend, immensely wealthy, Harry Payne Whitney. The money came freely. For Harry Payne Whitney to loan a hundred thousand dollars to Rob Collier was little more than for a clerk to loan five dollars to a friend on payday night. Probably the negotiation consisted of a casual sentence or two between billiard shots at the Meeting House, followed next morning by a telephone message from Whitney to one of the banking houses downtown that managed his affairs. But while Whitney would say yes quickly and heartily, as a matter of friendship, nevertheless the actual transaction, the delivery of the money and the taking of a promissory note—that was strictly business, that was done by the banking house. And the banking house was as vigilant about this personal loan as about any of Whitney's purely business investments. Strange auditors appeared in the Collier offices, a member of the banking firm took a kind of advisory authority in the Collier business.

The banker, looking after the safety of one of Whitney's loans, felt that *Collier's* as the beneficiary of the loan ought to so conduct itself as not to do injury to Whitney's other investments. Whitney himself, who carried his wealth lightly, would not have taken that position. Whitney, if he noticed *Collier's* attacking the tobacco trust or the New York traction company, would have been amused and laughed gaily and told Collier to "hit 'em again, Rob." At the same time Whitney's very competent understanding of business told him that he must give complete authority to the banking house that managed the loans he made. The banking house not only used its leverage with *Collier's* to protect Whitney's interests but thriftily extended its franchise to protect interests of its own. And the interests of Whitney and the banking house combined touched about every great industry in America. *Collier's*, for the first time, became aware of business interests outside its own. The condition distressed R. J., made him less and less himself. His carefree buoyancy fled him; trying to recapture it, he became reckless.

The condition gave concern to all of us; to Hapgood it caused distress, for he began to doubt whether the *Weekly* could now have the independence that had been its largest asset and greatest pride. Within a year or two after P. F.'s death care had a seat in our councils, and even intruded into our personal relations outside the office.

Worse than just care, it was a care that could not be shared nor lightened by talking freely about it. Into our camaraderie came restraint. For Hapgood and I knew, but could not say to Collier, that the intrusion of the banker and his tightening grip was due in part to R. J.'s scale of living. We felt the more strongly about this because, to Hapgood and me, lavishness of living was unattractive in any circumstances. We thought that the *Weekly* might escape from its thralldom to the banker if R. J. would drastically economize. Collier could not help sensing that we thought this, the fact was so patent. But he would no more open the subject to us than we to him. As for doing the thing he needed to do, his pride was the kind which, when it senses unspoken reproach, does more defiantly the thing which occasions the reproach.

Our concern was justified. As time went on the loan from Whitney was increased, it became half a million. The banker became more insistent. A business manager was given authority over all of us, including even R. J. He, his pride deeply wounded, stayed away from the office and from us. He became more reckless, poured his splendid vitality and charm into diversions of which not all were good for him. On the occasions when we saw him there was constraint between us. The days of our spontaneous camaraderie were over. The silver bowl was broken.

In the office the business manager declared there must be less muckraking, greater amiability toward business. Hapgood, with me seconding him, insisted the editorial department would continue to be free. Between banker and business manager on the one hand, and Hapgood and me on the other, there was sullen truce.

CHAPTER 30

Once, while at Harvard, a classmate asked me to do a personal service; he was obliged to be away, and would I help an old aunt of his, a widow without children near, move from a little apartment she had long occupied on Concord Square? Packing her books, I found one which had belonged to a German ancestor of hers, a gift he had received from a fellow student. On the flyleaf was written, "Amicitiae aeternite: Heidelberg, 1769."

I was moved. What had become of these two young Germans who pledged eternal friendship? How little could they have imagined the wanderings their token would follow until it landed in a dingy Boston boardinghouse a century and a third later—the token more long-lived than either the giver or the receiver, and longer-lived than the friendship that had been meant to be eternal. Had the friendship indeed been as eternal as the only eternity any friendship can have, the duration of the lives of the friends? Had they ever forgotten each other? Or worse, ever quarreled?

Of the three who composed a fellowship of friends on *Collier's*, two are now gone. Those two, until they died, felt that the sundering of that friendship was, of all the regrettable experiences they had ever had, the one they would most like to undo. The third, now writing these words, has the same feeling, and will have it until it comes to the same termination.

Tennyson says that "sorrow's crown of sorrow is remembering happier things." That is a foolish saying and reflects a selfish soul. To be sorry merely because happy experiences are gone and cannot be revived is not only a sentimentality but a repellent egoism. The truer crown of sorrow is to feel that the happy days might have continued, that the ending might have been averted. And the ultimate pang of poignancy is to feel that you were in part responsible—either that something you did helped to bring the end, or that something you failed to do might have averted it. That rue was felt by both Collier and Hapgood; on me, for a special reason, it weighed more than on them. For part of my place in the friendship was to hold the other two together, to act as a common denominator, to be a buffer and emollient between two men who loved each other greatly, respected each other enormously, but whose temperaments and ways of thinking were far apart and sometimes difficult to reconcile.

It is no surcease of sorrow to know that the sundering was part of a disruption that divided friends all over America, that divided a great political party, that indeed divided the nation. Maybe it is no wonder if the same cleavage that carried Theodore Roosevelt and William H. Taft from affectionate intimacy to violent animosity should have broken also the friendship of three private citizens. But there is no comfort in that reflection. Theodore Roosevelt and William H. Taft may have been important to the world—but Robert Collier, Norman Hapgood and Mark Sullivan were important to each other.

In the fight between Theodore Roosevelt and William H. Taft, all three of us, Collier, Hapgood and myself, were on one side; we all were with Roosevelt. Loyalty to Roosevelt in that fight was an addition to the many common points of view about public affairs and the many private ties that bound us.

But when another public figure, Woodrow Wilson, began to emerge, shadings of difference arose among us.

I can tell best, and it will be the clearest way to recite this narrative, if I tell first my own feeling about Wilson. Throughout the period of his emergence I was for him. Because my concentrated hostility was against the Old Guard Republicans, I welcomed Wilson. I took it for granted, during the early period, that in the 1912 campaign there would be only the usual two parties, and that the Republican candidate would be Taft running for a second term. Expecting that, I hoped that the Democratic candidate would be Wilson, and worked to bring it about that he should be.

When the man who was organizing to have Wilson nominated by the Democrats, William F. McCombs, came to the end of his slender personal resources, he confided his despair to me. I told the condition to Charles R. Crane; and Crane one day, asking me to come and see him off to Europe, told me to tell McCombs that Crane would be glad to contribute five thousand dollars— it was the first contribution McCombs received from any source, and he was enabled to keep the Wilson movement alive. McCombs was grateful to me, then and always, for that and other helps I gave toward promoting Wilson's rise. After Wilson was nominated and elected and in the White House, I, being asked by an organization, the Civic League, to use my influence with McCombs to persuade him to speak at their annual dinner, passed the request on, facetiously apologizing as I did so. McCombs replied:

After having "fit and bled" with you in the Wilson campaign, it is not at all unnatural that people should assume you have a pull with me. They are right. . . . I shall be most happy to attend the dinner.

I was sympathetic to Wilson's rise. I at no time worked against him. But my attitude about him changed with late developments in the campaign. After Roosevelt organized a third party, the Progressives, I was then for Roosevelt. I had been for Wilson against Taft, yes. But when it became Wilson against Roosevelt, no.

In the three-sided fight the campaign became, I supported Roosevelt and the Progressives, attacked Taft and the Republicans, said nothing about Wilson and the Democrats.

With this position of mine Collier agreed wholly, except that he was less willing than I to refrain from fighting Wilson. He liked and admired Roosevelt as I did; he opposed Taft and the Republicans as I did; but he affirmatively disliked Wilson, disliked what he called the "professorial" quality in him, and used to jeer at me mildly for not "pounding" him. But this was immaterial in what followed.

[301]

Hapgood, on the other hand, was strong for Wilson. He at that time, and indeed all his life, had great admiration for, and was much under the influence of, Louis D. Brandeis, later Justice of the Supreme Court—for some years Hapgood entertained a hope of seeing Brandeis President. And Brandeis believed strongly that Wilson was a better man than Roosevelt. He believed also that the Democrats had a better platform than the Progressive one.

So, during the early part of the campaign, I was strong for Roosevelt—but put my emphasis on supporting Roosevelt, not on attacking Wilson. Hapgood was strong for Wilson but did not confine himself to supporting Wilson—he sought to make his support of Wilson more effective by attacking Roosevelt.

In this rising rift between our political views Hapgood was the first to become restless, or at least the first to take action. He wrote me a note. Whenever, among the three of us, strain arose, we took to writing notes; it would have been funny to an outsider, had any outsider been close enough, to observe the irruption of note writing among three men whose habitual mutual attitude, ninety-nine days out of a hundred, was intimate, jocular familiarity, the essence of informality.

Hapgood in his note protested against the quantity of Progressive material that I was putting into the body of the paper, in the shape of articles, as distinguished from the editorials. He wrote that he felt himself

in a rather delicate position regarding the paper from the prospect that the general contents all through the summer are likely to be so energetically Bull Moose [pro-Roosevelt]. I cannot think it will be for the best good of the paper to reach our balance by having me forced to exaggerate one side of it in the editorials.

I did not reply for some three weeks. I should like to think that I would never have replied at all, except for a cause—my usual way with notes of irritation was to act as if they had never been received or sent. And I should like to think that the only cause of my replying was that Hapgood on his editorial pages became more strongly anti-Roosevelt, was beginning to treat Roosevelt, as I felt, with downright unfairness. But I suppose

Right to left: THEODORE ROOSEVELT,
ROBERT COLLIER, MARK SULLIVAN.

there was another cause: I suppose the increasing heat of the campaign carried me a little farther from urbanity—as it did practically everybody else in the United States. Anyhow, on September 6, 1912, I wrote Hapgood a note—unquestionably the first note containing irritation that I had ever written him. I quoted what he had written to me, and I said:

Did you apprehend that the general body of the paper could possibly have a character more energetically partisan than is given to it by the presence of the articles Brandeis has written in the current issues, coupled with the playing up of them by you in the editorial page?

And did you apprehend that the editorials could be more strongly partisan than they are in the same current issues?

These questions are rhetorical, of course. Two other questions, however, which are quite serious are these: Is it really your intention that the paper shall have balance? And are you willing that I shall be as unrestrained on my page as you on yours?

M. S.

Hapgood replied:

I have felt that you have done such good work that I have never felt like saying anything where we differed slightly. . . . I believe that if I were in your place and had been treated as considerately as I have at least *tried* to treat you, I should resign myself to the judgment of the person who holds the title of editor, on the rare occasions when he felt strongly enough to want his way.

This answers your last question as I see it. If you see it differently I shall scarcely contest your view.

N. H.

I think that my emotion, when I received that note, in spite of the heat of the campaign, was the same as my feeling now— that the note was touching, that it called on me for generosity. That, I am confident, was the way I felt. I warmed toward Hapgood. I did nothing about his note; and neither that, nor anything else that ever arose between Hapgood and me, would have caused what followed. Yet it is matter for a smile that Hapgood—so austerely impersonal about subjects that were impersonal, so strong a believer in reason, so superior to emotion—when he was himself involved in difference of opinion, relied, not upon reason but upon appeal to emotion. That was matter for a smile, but only for a smile. To me it was one of the traits that made Hapgood likable.

It was not between me and Hapgood that the trouble came. It was between Hapgood and Collier. And, while the materials for explosion existed, the detonation came, as often, from outside, and from accident.

On October 14, 1912, at Milwaukee, a madman shot Roosevelt. Roosevelt, with a bullet in his breast, went on the platform, declared that, "I have too many important things to think about to pay heed or to have any concern about my own death," and delivered the speech he had prepared. Afterward he went to the hospital. The wound turned out to be serious; Roosevelt went upon the operating table and was in the hospital for a considerable time; his dates for campaign addresses were canceled. Upon the country the emotional effect was tremendous. It was widely assumed the act of a madman would cause Roosevelt to win the election.

Hapgood, in his leading editorial the following week, wrote about the incident, as of course he must. His opening sentence was a cautious generalization: "Drama rules life." While he spoke of the "immense popularity of Colonel Roosevelt," he spoke also, and with apparent deprecation, of "the friendship that is universal toward a man of action appearing in a favorable position. . . . No amount of argument," Hapgood wrote, "no amount of reflection concentrated in many months, could have influenced as many Americans as were stirred by the shot of a madman." He seemed to wish to take away from Colonel Roosevelt the advantage that the shooting had been. Speaking with an air of apparent deploring, Hapgood wrote that "a pistol in the hand of a single heated and distorted person may count more than the suffrages of a million." In the body of the editorial he dwelt, not upon the shooting, but on collateral considerations. He made the incident an occasion for reproving violence of all kinds and seemed to imply that the violence of a madman with a pistol was not any more deplorable than the spectacle of "our leading Insurgent [Progressive party] orators declaring that, if they or their candidates are not elected to something, the French Revolution is here upon us."

Collier, reading the editorial in proof, found it enraging. He, nearer in instinct to the common man, shared the common man's emotion of outrage that Roosevelt should have been shot. That *Collier's Weekly* should treat the matter with Olympian detachment seemed to him monstrous.

So Collier himself wrote an editorial: "Theodore Roosevelt," Collier wrote, "is a fairly close presentment of what this nation likes to call *a man*. . . . No man could have used his power with a larger moral usefulness to his whole people, and we doubt whether any man in history has undertaken late in life as high and unselfish an adventure in the field of politics as the Bull Moose." With a manner of taking a slap at Hapgood, Collier concluded: "*Collier's* is not so hypercritical that it cannot recognize a man."

Collier wrote that and sent it to me, to insert on the editorial page. I realized that crisis was near, that my role of emollient and buffer between Collier and Hapgood now faced its moment of supreme need. I maneuvered to gain time, without seeming to want the delay for my own reason. I wrote Collier a note which, as I read it twenty-five years later, reflects how perturbed I was, how eager that we should somehow get past the incident without disruption. I wrote that "Mr Morrow [the foreman of the composing room] suggests of his own initiative that it will be better all around if this first editorial page is held over until tomorrow morning rather than close it up during overtime in the composing room this evening."

That part of my note to Collier I dictated to my stenographer. At the end I wrote in longhand: "In my judgment both your paragraph on the shooting, and Norman's, ought to be printed, because they do not overlap, Norman's devoting itself more to the question of free speech." Finally, to get rid of the sting against Hapgood that was in Collier's closing line, I said: "If I were you I should change the last line, it sounds a little more self-accusatory than is necessary."

Hapgood the next day learned that after he had closed the editorial pages and O.K.d them for the composing room, Collier, without speaking to him, had ordered the pages broken and an editorial written by himself inserted. Nothing like that had ever happened before.

Hapgood resigned. His letter to Collier began: "Dear Rob," and concluded, "Affectionately, Norman." He wrote:

I thought the situation could be bridged over, but I fear it can not, and I am extremely sorry. I have seen the Roosevelt editorial, although hearing nothing from you about it. Apart from the statements in it, which seem to me absurd, the fact that Sullivan could get you to take the most important issue of the moment out of my hands is conclusive. I had intended to wait until a time which might be more satisfactory to you, and which also might give a chance of a different outcome, but, with all due respect and with full appreciation and affection for you, I wish to make public my resignation before this issue appears. I am terribly sorry, Rob, but if I am no longer fit for the responsibility I have gained through the last ten years' work, I do not feel willing to admit it and remain. I have always boosted Sullivan as much as I could, knowing the danger to me, but also feeling that only in that way could I be just to his abilities.

While Collier and I were amazed by Hapgood's allusion to me, yet the inexactness of his charge against me was so patent that it robbed the mention of much of its sting. The idea that I had got Collier to write the editorial was so far from the facts as to mystify us. The notion that Hapgood, through the long years of comradeship, had ever thought of me as a "danger" to him was so preposterous that I was able to smile at it. I was able to smile, too, at the characteristic Hapgood turn—in one line he was accusing me of something monstrous, but in the next line he must be fair—"only in that way could I be just to his abilities." Even in excitement Hapgood could not be undiscriminating; even in anger he could not be unjust.

I knew the true reason for Hapgood's resignation was one which, out of affection for Collier, he could not say to him. It was hinted in the opening lines: "I thought the situation could be bridged over." By "the situation," Hapgood meant the intrusion of the banker into the management of *Collier's*, the pressure to make the editorial department subordinate to the business office.

When the newspapers made a sensation of Hapgood's resignation and asked for statements, Hapgood gave his real reason. He said he was resigning because the paper was being commercialized. "When I saw Mr Collier break the custom of years by seeking occasion to interfere with me, I knew its meaning and acted at once." Collier's action, Hapgood said, "was a way of clinching the authority of the business department over the editorial department."

Me, Hapgood not only exculpated, he put me in the role of dupe:

Mr Sullivan's discontent with my attitude toward Woodrow Wilson was seized upon by Mr Collier for his purpose. . . . His deep feeling about my support of Wilson gave Mr Collier his chance, and Mr Collier acted with shrewdness. At another time Mr Sullivan would probably have left the paper with me rather than stay after its freedom was ended. But now, by his cleverness in supporting Mr Sullivan in a political grievance, Mr Collier has tied him up and Mr Sullivan finds himself in the unenviable position of being a subordinate to two businessmen who have definitely undertaken to commercialize the paper. Mr Sullivan has been played upon shrewdly for the moment, but I do not believe he will remain on the paper a year. He has been outwitted by two shrewd men.

To Hapgood's public statement, Collier made public replies. There were statements and counter statements. Collier in one of his statements made an attribution of power to me that seemed to me as absurd as Hapgood's charge against me:

Mr Sullivan was the political writer. Most of the political inspiration of the paper for more than five years past has come from him. The great bulk of the political writing was done by him. Most of the decisive attitudes that have been taken by *Collier's* in the field of politics have been dictated by him or myself.

There were rebuttals and counter rebuttals. Old personal letters and incidents were dug up and published. Hapgood reiterated and re-reiterated that he was resigning because of the intrusion of banking and business influence into *Collier's*. Outrageously he intimated that the condition was due to Collier personally "degenerating from his former high ideals through influences which I do not care to discuss . . . a surrender which I believe to be the result entirely of undesirable modes of life." Of one of Collier's statements, Hapgood said, "the public must wonder just what state he was in when he wrote it"—an action which Hapgood was to atone twenty years later by writing in his autobiography: "In the quarrel that marred the end of our relations . . . I well know that I lacked gentlemanliness and due recognition for the years that were past, enriched by his magnanimity and power."

The public exchange between Collier and Hapgood was humiliating, awful. They had lost their heads utterly. If I seemed to keep mine, it was because I thrust it in the sand. To keep my tongue in leash while in the very center of a frenzy of flying brickbats and flailing pick handles, to become more silent as others become more belligerently vocal, was a trait which, with some effort over many years since my youth, I had incorporated into a personality which did not start out with great self-mastery. My sole contribution to the columns of newspaper acrimony was confined to five words in the New York *Times:*

"Mark Sullivan refused to comment."

CHAPTER 31

ONCE Owen Wister, in a letter urging me to do a book about my life, made the penetrating observation that "all we've been, known, and done remains in us."

Wister illustrated from his own experience. He had, in his youth, spent some years in the West, during the 1880s, when the West was still the "Far" West and lived up to what was then a common term for it, "the frontier"—the West of Indians still primitive, of cowboys still authentic, before they had become appurtenances of dude ranches. This experience Wister, while still a young man, embodied in an American classic, *The Virginian* (and another which, to my taste, equally deserves high standing, *Lin McLean*). Subsequently there ensued for Wister several years during which ill-health, a personal grief he suffered, other interests that absorbed him, and continued residence in the East drove the West from his mind and memory. Then, when upward of sixty, he was asked by a publisher to write again about the West of his early days. He did not think he could:

But I tried. I had a hard time writing the first two stories. Then they came easier and easier until the ninth, which would have been impossible to bring off at the beginning, was written in a very few days, and needed but trifling amendment.

I write my fiction in a condition of partial hypnosis. All we've been, known, and done remains in us; but most of it has to be evoked. As I had grown very distant from the West, the evoking of it took long. Once it had returned to me, hypnosis was easily induced by not more than thirty minutes concentration over my writing pad, making a few false strokes, and then getting speed. I guess all creative work happens in this state: you think and feel yourself out of your actual surroundings, and into whatever region your imagination is dealing with.

Wister's notion is held by other writer friends of mine. Garret Garet spent the first half of his mature life as a newspaper executive and as a reporter in Wall Street, where his writing was austerely factual. Then he wrote a novel. I asked him if the transition to creative writing had been difficult. He said it had; only by prolonged and patient concentration did he manage it. Morning after morning, in stern self-discipline, he sat down at his desk at the same hour, before him blank paper, in his hand a pencil. Morning after morning nothing happened. After several weeks a little trickle emerged. It grew. Presently it flowed freely. The materials for his story—experiences he had had, situations he had observed, conversations, sights and sounds and smells—all long forgotten, now crept up from the deeps of his subconscious mind, assembled themselves and marched out on paper.

This process of evocation, which Wister said "takes place in a condition of partial hypnosis," is more familiar to creative writers than understood by them. They merely know it takes place; they do not know how or why. One American author, whose stories I published when I was editor of *Collier's*, thought, quite seriously, that the evocative agency was not within herself but without. She told me that her writing was dependent upon a spirit, a "familiar," who, when he deemed proper, would come to her at her desk and stand behind her right shoulder. So real was he to her that she had a name for him; she referred to him as "Mr Summer." She never spoke to him, nor he to her. She never saw him and did not think of him as visible. She only knew that sometimes she could write, sometimes not. When she could write, it was because Mr Summer deemed it well that she should; he stood behind her, made it possible for her to write, provided what flowed out from her pen. On occasions when she was unable to write stories she had intended to produce she, with utterly naïve sincerity, explained by saying that Mr Summer, for some reason she did not know but for which she did not reproach him—she had the utmost confidence in his wisdom and benevolence—Mr Summer had been away.

I never wrote fiction. Though for years, as an editor, I read scores of fiction manuscripts every day, though I learned much about the technique and came to have a feeling for the art, though many plots and situations occurred to me, I never made use of one, except occasionally to suggest it to some author friend. The first occasion I had to do writing of the kind in which the materials are drawn mainly from within was this volume. Memoirs, as respects their content, are, of course, the opposite of fiction. Yet as art—form, structure, handling of materials, style—the best autobiographical writing is that which most closely parallels the method of fiction. I acquired no familiar. But I came to have some acquaintance with the mystery of evocation. I think—at least I think I think—it is true that all we have ever seen or heard or read or felt or reflected remains in us. Experiences that seemed as forgotten as if they had never happened, incidents as slight as the glance of an eye, all remain, and under favoring conditions grope upward through overlying strata of subsequent experiences.

But only under favoring conditions. The process of evocation, the "condition of partial hypnosis," can take place only in a special state of mind and spirit. The usual word for this mental state is concentration, but it is different from concentration, it is a kind of spiritual saturation, a deep immersion in the scene with which the writer is dealing. The first essential of it is that the present should be walled out. One must go, with his past, into a deep well. The condition has some characteristics of a trance. It is not so much an active focusing of the mind as, so to speak, a sustained receptivity, a receptivity that opens inward, a receptivity of one part of the mind to another part. The conscious part of the mind makes itself receptive to the subconscious, in which old experiences are stored. Presently, if the welcoming mood of the conscious is prolonged, memories begin to creep upward from the subconscious. They come, and they bring their associations with them, in the order and relation which they had when they were not memories but existing experiences. A detail of a scene emerges, a scent or a color, and crowding after it come the faces with which it was associated, the room in which the incident took place.

But they are shy, these visitors from the past. They come only when they are sure they are welcome. And they will not think they are welcome unless they know they will not be jostled by other visitors, strangers to them. The past will not sit in the same room with the present.

Essential to the mood that can accomplish evocation is immunity from interruption. The writer must be, spiritually, in a watertight compartment, with his ordinary preoccupations barred out. And the mood should be prolonged, not only for hours during a day but for days at a time, preferably for weeks.

I believe all this to be true. But, except very slightly, I do not know it from my own experience. It is not by that method that these memoirs were written. On a few occasions, when I was alone at the farm for a week end, the past would peer shyly out at me, invited by the surroundings in which I spent my childhood, evoked by the scent of St-John's-wort, the call of the knee-deeps in spring; the ticking, in a house otherwise silent, of the same clock that counted the minutes when I was a child; waking in the night and seeing the moon through the same pane of glass through which as a child I watched it and puzzled about it.

But always the stay of the timorous visitor from the past was cut short by some intrusion of my present work, a telegram or telephone call having to do with my current newspaper articles, an announcement coming over the radio about some development in public affairs which suggested the need of comment in a despatch. Rarely was I able to devote myself to the past for more than three days at a time. For during the years in which I was writing this volume about the past I was also obliged to keep my footing on the very top of the bubble of today. I was writing, four times each week, newspaper articles dealing with the latest news of a world which provided news as it rarely had before. This I had been doing, without interruption, for nearly twenty years—the period and the kind of work which composed the second half of my career.

II

After Hapgood resigned the editorship of *Collier's* the post was taken by Robert Collier. After about a year he transferred it to me. The work, broader than I had been doing before, required me to take responsibility not only for that part of the *Weekly* which dealt with public affairs but also for the part devoted to entertainment. In the evolution through which all popular periodicals were passing, to meet the need for greater circulation required by the great advertisers, entertainment became increasingly important, discussion of public affairs less so. I gave more and more of my time to contacts with writers of fiction, less to politics. For some years authors and their writings were my major interest.

I dropped my page of "Comment on Congress," but kept up, with the aid of my staff, the editorials. Whatever merit the editorials might have in the eyes of readers, they did not give pleasure to those who now controlled the paper. The banker representing the money the paper had borrowed became more important in the management. The banker was Fred W. Allen, partner in the house of Lee, Higginson & Co. I liked him, we were friends, we spent many hours of leisure together. He was a man of character, had fine ideals. But his background and present associations, and the temperament that had led him into those associations, deprived him of the endowment for understanding editorial needs. He could never see that a periodical needed to reflect the public, or share the public's moods, or even take much account of the public's tastes or desires or convictions. The function of a periodical, he thought, should be merely to instruct, and the kind of instruction he thought should be given was that which comported with the well-being of business. With the tenacity of a strong mind and a character of complete integrity, he held the view that was the prevailing view of business of the period.

During the Great War, Allen became one of the group of businessmen who went to Washington to help direct the material side of our participation. When issues arose within the group, or between the group and President Wilson, Allen took the strongly conservative side. He felt, for example, that there should be no limitation on prices; that prices and profits were, in wartime as in peace, the reward and incentive to initiative and accomplishment; that, therefore, by letting prices go where they would, the largest amount of war materials would be produced in the shortest time, the war would be best fought and quickest won.

On this and other matters we differed. I knew that many of my editorials grieved him, that he had to endure reproach from his business associates because of them. Yet he never let disagreement interrupt his friendliness with me. Finally, with the completest good feeling, acting honestly in my interest as much as in any other, he asked me if I would not be happier if I were relieved from responsibility for an organ of which the dominating financial interest had views differing from mine. I agreed; and it would have been better for me if the separation had taken place earlier. In the parting he was generous, financially and in other ways. He said that he, and those whom he represented, respected and valued my writing; that if I would write over my own signature and on my own responsibility, *Collier's* would print it, and pay for it at a rate that would equal the salary I had received as editor.

For some two years that arrangement went on. Then, one day in late 1919, I received a message from Edwin F. Gay, saying he was sending one of his associates to see me. Gay had been professor of economics at Harvard. During the war he had put his understanding of economics, and his extraordinary skill with statistics, at the service of the government. After the war he became publisher of the New York *Evening Post*. The paper, with a century of fine history behind it, had recently been bought by Thomas W. Lamont, who turned it over to Gay with a franchise, in freedom and funds, to make it the worthiest possible paper. Gay, assembling and enlarging his staff, looked about for a writer on national politics. He recalled the contact with that field I had had up to some five years before. He employed me. To papers throughout the country outside New York, he offered syndicate rights to print my articles; approximately a hundred took them.

My first work, beginning in December 1919, was to report the developments within the two political parties looking toward their respective nominations for the presidency in June 1920. I renewed my old contacts with political leaders, made acquaintance with new ones who had arisen, traveled up and down the country, carried on an enormous correspondence with local leaders and other sources of information. As my despatches, dealing with the issues that were arising, began to reflect my information that the League of Nations was not popular, and that America would not enter it, Gay was surprised and disappointed. Indeed, he was skeptical about my information and judgment, for he believed almost as strongly as Wilson in the value of the League, in the necessity of America's joining and in the likelihood that America would join. But Gay extended to me the freedom he received from the paper's owner; when despatches of mine ran contrary to the line of the paper's editorials he called attention to the difference, advertised it and exploited it; he regarded disinterestedness and accuracy of reporting as more important than the paper's policy, dear though that policy was to him.

After I had been some four years with the *Evening Post*, Gay was about to retire from it to return to the Harvard faculty. His going would end my personal obligation to him, which was great. I was free to accept an urging, agreeable professionally and personally, from Mrs Helen Rogers Reid, that I transfer my writing to the New York *Tribune* (later the *Herald-Tribune*). If any one should ever call on me to submit evidence of professional ability I would cite the fact that Helen Reid asked me to write for the *Herald-Tribune*. Her engaging me implied a broad vision on her part; she foresaw that column writing about public affairs from an independent standpoint, then new, was adapted to the times and would grow. Later she sought out and brought to the *Herald-Tribune* two commentators who were among the very ablest, Walter Lippmann and Dorothy Thompson.

Into her contract with me in 1923, Mrs Reid put something to the effect that "choice of topics and manner of treatment" was to be the commentator's. That assurance of freedom was not, from the *Herald-Tribune*, necessary. Though at times some of my writing has been not in agreement with the paper's policy, the *Herald-Tribune* has never failed to print an article I wrote. On occasions when articles of mine provoked irritated dissent from groups of readers, I never heard of it, except infrequently when, months afterward, someone on the staff told me, with humor, of the trouble I had brought upon them.

During the twenty years of newspaper syndicate writing that composed the latter half of my career, practically all my associations, both personal and those that went with my work, were with public men. I was drawn closer and closer into contact with the inner circles of politics and government. Especially was this so after Herbert Hoover became President.

I had become acquainted with Hoover in Europe during the early months of the Great War, and was as much attracted by his qualities of personality as impressed by his extraordinary ability. After he came to Washington to reside he lived in a house close to mine, and there arose between our families the informality of any two neighbors on the outskirts of a town. As I grew to know him well the quality in him that most impressed me was his kindness, the deep well of good will that his shyness and reticence hid from many who did not see him in intimacy. It was a good will not measured merely by the sum of the pains he took, and the pleasure also, in being helpful to individuals. It extended to all humanity; it was an attitude toward all life. If I were called upon to pick out, as most uniquely characteristic of him, one among a myriad associations I had with him, I would think of one Sunday afternoon when we sat together on the back porch of his house, he with his feet resting on a stool. I noticed him doing what I had recognized before as a sign of inner content: he was rubbing the toes of his slippers against each other. It was a mannerism that came to him when he was pleased and free from anxiety—the occasions were rarer and rarer as care descended upon him. On this Sunday afternoon I noticed that as he talked abstractedly with me, his eyes were on a point among the shrubbery some fifty feet away. Presently he said, "I knew they'd like it;

I've got a customer." Following his eyes, I saw they were on a bird which, with a combination of wariness about something new and pleasure about something it liked, was perched on the edge of a bird bath which Hoover the day before, with shovel and stone and mortar, had set up in the garden.

At first, during the early and middle 1920s, my column writing was not exacting. It was about American politics. I rather kept myself away from foreign affairs, for there were other commentators who knew it better, especially my Harvard classmate, Frank Simonds. The personnel and minutiae of politics, the leaders, their relative weight, their associations, the local party organizations throughout the country and the heads of them—all that I knew well and kept up with readily. The political issues in the country and in Congress during most of the 1920s, excepting the League of Nations, which Congress would have none of, were the familiar ones—the tariff, prohibition, allowances and bonus for veterans, aid for farmers. As the depression of 1929 began and grew, it was necessary for a commentator to become familiar with farther reaches of economics and finance. The course of the depression, the successive blows against our economic and social institutions I saw from where the blows struck hardest, within the White House, for the relation between Hoover and myself that had grown up during ten years went on as a matter of course after he was President.

As the early 1930s passed it became necessary for a commentator to learn issues that were new and very strange—issues symbolized by a pair of new terms that began to edge into the American political vocabulary, "left," "right." Writing about politics in the days of Franklin Roosevelt made my beginning in the days of Theodore seem long ago and faraway.

But all that—the experiences I had during the more recent years of my work—all that is, in Kipling's phrase, another story.

INDEX

INDEX